The Apostolic Fathers

The
APOSTOLIC
FATHERS

An American Translation

by

EDGAR J. GOODSPEED

HARPER & BROTHERS, PUBLISHERS

New York

To
Elfleda,
1880-1949
Our last book together

Contents

Introduction

The group of early Christian writings known as *The Apostolic Fathers* was first formed in the seventeenth century, when a series of short works came to light and were published, which seemed to that uncritical generation to be from the hands of men who were the disciples of the original apostles, or at least might have known them. The first of these were I and II Clement. It was the coming of the Codex Alexandrinus to London in 1628, as a gift from the Patriarch of Constantinople to the King of England, that first made I and II Clement known to Western learning, and Patrick Young, the King's librarian, lost no time in publishing them both, as the Letters of Clement, in 1633. In the same year, Halloix published the Greek text of Polycarp's Letter to the Philippians, chapters 1–9, all that has ever been found in Greek, except for the thirteenth chapter, so obligingly quoted by Eusebius.

In 1645 Ménard d'Achery published the Greek text of Barnabas (5.7–21.9), and the Greek text of the Letters of Ignatius made their appearance in Greek, edited by Voss, in 1646. The idea of assembling these subapostolic figures into a collection led Cotelier in 1672 to publish the works of the holy fathers "qui temporibus apostolicis floruerunt," and twenty-seven years later Ittig, in 1699, repeated the feat in his "Library of the Apostolic Fathers" (Bibliotheca Patrum Apostolicorum). In modern times Dressel published an edition of the collection in Leipzig in 1857; Gebhardt, Harnack, and Zahn issued one there in 1876–1877; while Funk brought out his first edition in 1881. The Lightfoot-Harmer

Apostolic Fathers, embodying the Greek texts Lightfoot had worked out for most of the documents, appeared in 1891, two years after his death. Hemmer, Oger, Laurent and others produced the Paris edition, *Les Pères Apostoliques*, in 1907–1910, and Lake's edition of texts and translations appeared in the Loeb Library in 1912–1913. These have generally sought to keep pace with the new discoveries of papyrus fragments and Oriental versions that have been made. Bihlmeyer in 1924 published the first volume of a text edition, revising the text of Funk; I cannot learn that his second volume has appeared. It was to comprise a new edition of Hermas, which Bihlmeyer postponed in order to take advantage of the anticipated publication of the important Michigan papyrus of Hermas, assigned to the third century, which had been announced in 1923, but was not fully published until 1934. It preserves an ancient text of Parables ii.8 to ix.5:1, with some fourteen gaps, and enables us to control the Athos Greek text for these portions. I have made constant use of its testimony, in Campbell Bonner's fine edition (1934), to correct and improve Lake's text in his Apostolic Fathers in the Loeb Classical Library.

The canon of the Apostolic Fathers has varied greatly in these various editions. Cotelier included Barnabas, Hermas, Clement, Ignatius, and Polycarp, both the Letter and the Martyrdom. But additions have been made with more or less reason, until the Didache, the fragments of Papias, the fragment of Quadratus and the so-called Letter to Diognetus have been included. I have ventured even further and propose the inclusion of the Doctrina, which can now be shown to be the source of the Greek Didache, and of the Greek Barnabas, as well as of most of the later documents that have long been regarded as reproducing material from the Greek Didache. To establish this position, a table exhibiting the parts of the leading documents involved has been presented as an appendix to this volume.

The various pieces have been variously arranged by recent

editors. A strictly chronological order would separate II Clement widely from I and be in other respects confusing. I have begun with Doctrina, as almost the oldest and certainly the most primitive document in the list, following it with the kindred pieces Didache and Barnabas. I Clement is doubtless the next oldest after Doctrina, and with it should go the so-called II Clement. Modern study has shown Hermas to belong at the very end of the first century, rather than toward the middle of the second, as the Muratorian Canon so misleadingly suggests. Ignatius and Polycarp fall about A.D. 107–117, and while the Martyrdom of Polycarp is forty or fifty years later, it is natural to append it to Polycarp's letter. Quadratus, A.D. 125–129, Papias, about 140, and the Address to Diognetus (third century?) form a miscellaneous group, chronologically arranged.

The Apostolic Fathers include some of the earliest Christian writings outside the New Testament that have come down to us, and for the study of early Christianity constitute a most important supplement to the New Testament itself.

Definite advances in textual materials for Hermas, and even at a few points in Greek lexicography, as well as the need of a franker, more modern and unflinching translation are reflected in the present version. And the literary relationships of the several writings to one another and to the books of the New Testament can now in some cases be more definitely determined.

This translation is based on the Funk-Bihlmeyer edition, vol. 1, published at Tübingen in 1924, except for the Shepherd of Hermas, which I have translated from Lake's edition in the Loeb Library, (1913), with occasional emendations derived from the papyri.

EDGAR J. GOODSPEED

Bel-Air, Los Angeles

The Apostolic Fathers

The Teaching of the Apostles

THE DOCTRINA

Over against Paul's bold doctrine of the all-sufficiency of faith, and probably at Antioch, about the end of the first century, Christians more in the Jewish tradition thought it necessary to draw up a set of rules of conduct, which would make the Christian's practical moral obligations more definite. For this leaflet they claimed the authority of the Twelve Apostles, naming it The Teaching of the Apostles. *It is predominantly negative, telling what sins to avoid. It depicts first the Way of Life in some seventy short commands, most of them prohibitions, in the style of the Ten Commandments, and then in a list of almost forty more the Way of Death, not neglecting the characteristic heathen practices of magic, astrology, and enchantment. But it is totally lacking in art or genius, and seems to attempt to foist the essence of the old legalism upon the new religion, reducing its living faith to the keeping of a set of rules.*

No Greek manuscript of this curious little work has yet come to light, and the two known Latin manuscripts of it or part of it, have been mistaken for translations of the Didache. One Latin fragment containing the first part of it was published more than two hundred years ago from a Melk manuscript of the tenth century, by Bernhard Pez, the Melk librarian. When in 1883 the Greek Didache was published, this Latin fragment of the Doctrina was generally accepted as a portion of a Latin transla-

1

tion of the Didache. But in 1899 in a Munich manuscript of the eleventh century a second Latin text was discovered, which went right on with about four times as much similar material, to a well-rounded liturgical conclusion. This too has been generally accepted as a Latin version of Didache 1-6a.

But as a translation of the Didache into Latin, the Doctrina, to call it by its Latin name, leaves much to be desired, for, in the first place, it covers less than the first half of Didache and, in the second, of this half it leaves out almost a fifth, and this fifth consists of enrichments of the text by appropriations from five different works, mostly from the Sermon on the Mount—just the sort of thing that would creep into the document when it was being expanded, but not at all the sort of thing that any translator worth the name would leave out of it. Further, the Doctrina is rounded off with a liturgical ending, much better than that of the Didache. These are not at all the traits we should expect in a translation.

So much for the internal evidence. But the external is even more convincing. It has been loosely claimed that the Didache, or most of it, was incorporated into a whole list of subsequent Christian writings, but a closer examination shows that it is the Greek original of the Doctrina, not the Didache, that was wrought into the Greek Barnabas, the Apostolic Church Ordinances, about A.D. 300, the Summary of Doctrine, A.D. 350-370, the Fides Nicaena, A.D. 375-381, and the Coptic Life of Schnudi; while it was the fuller Greek Didache that was worked into the Didascalia, A.D. 250-300, and the Apostolic Constitutions, about A.D. 380. Most of the literary influence, in fact, that has long been claimed for the Didache rightfully belongs to the Greek original of the Doctrina. More definite evidence for this view of the Doctrina will be found in the Appendix.

If, as I suppose, Paul's letters were first published not long *before* A.D. *95, such a counterblast as the Doctrina represents would probably be written not long after, perhaps toward the year 100.*

The Teaching of the Apostles
THE DOCTRINA

There are two ways in the world, that of life and that of death, **1** of light and of darkness. Over them are set two angels, one of right, the other of wrong. Moreover there is a great difference between the two ways. The way of life is this: first, you shall **2** love the eternal God who made you; second, your neighbor as yourself. Moreover, anything that you would not have done to you, you shall not do to anyone else.

Now the meaning of these words is this: **3**

You shall not commit adultery, you shall not commit murder, **2,2** you shall not bear false witness, you shall not corrupt a boy, you shall not commit fornication, you shall not practice magic, you shall not use enchanted potions, you shall not murder a child by abortion, nor kill one when it is born, you shall not desire any of your neighbor's goods, you shall not commit perjury, **3** you shall not speak evil, you shall not hold a grudge, or show **4** duplicity in giving advice, or be double-tongued, for the tongue is a deadly snare. Your speech shall not be vain or false. You **5,6** shall not be covetous or avaricious, or rapacious or an idolater, or contentious or ill-humored. You shall not entertain an evil **7** design against your neighbor. You shall hate nobody; some you shall love more than your own soul.

My son, flee from an evil man, and from everyone like him. **3** Do not be irascible, for anger leads to murder, nor shall you be **2,3** eager for malice, or proud, for all these things breed anger. Do **4**

5

not be an astrologer, or an enchanter, which things lead to
5 idolatry, and do not want to look at them or hear them. Do not
be a liar, since lying leads to theft, or a lover of money or vain.
6 For all these things breed thefts. Do not be a grumbler, for it
leads to cursing. Do not be self-willed, or evil-minded, for all
7 these things breed curses. But be meek, for the meek will possess
8 the holy land. Be long-suffering and upright in your business
9 and reverent of all the words that you hear. You shall not exalt
yourself or honor yourself among men, or admit arrogance to
your soul. You shall not join yourself in soul with higher men, but
10 you shall associate with upright and humble men. You shall
accept the adversities that befall you as good, knowing that
nothing happens without God.

4 Night and day you shall remember the one who speaks the
word of the Lord God to you; you shall honor him as the Lord.
2 For the Lord is in the place from which his words come. Moreover, you shall seek the faces of the saints, to refresh yourself
3 with their words. You shall not cause divisions. Reconcile those
who are quarreling. Judge justly, knowing that you will be
4 judged. You shall not discourage anyone in his misfortune, nor
5 shall you doubt whether it will be true or not. Do not keep
stretching out your hands to receive, and drawing them back
6 when it comes to returning. If through your hands you have
7 earned a ransom for your sins, you shall not hesitate to give it,
or grumble when you give, for you know who is the good payer
8 of such wages. You shall not turn away from the needy, but
shall share everything with your brethren, and you shall not say
it is your own. For if we are partners in what is immortal, how
much more ought we to consecrate from it! For the Lord wishes
9 to give of his gifts to all. You shall not withhold your hand from
your sons, but from their youth up you shall teach them the
10 fear of the Lord. You shall not give orders in your anger to your
man or woman slave, who hope in the same Lord; let him fear
both the Lord and you. For he came not to call men with

partiality, but those in whom he found the Spirit. You slaves, 11 moreover, be subject to your masters, as a symbol of God, with modesty and trembling. You shall hate all hypocrisy, and you 12 shall not do anything that is not pleasing to the Lord. Therefore, 13 my son, keep what you have heard, and do not add to them what is contrary to them, or take anything from them. Do not approach 14 prayer with an evil conscience. This is the way of life.

But the way of death is the opposite of it. First, it is bad and 5 full of curses,—adulteries, murders, false witness, fornications, base desires, magic arts, enchantments, thefts, idolatry, robberies, hypocrisies, pride, malice, willfulness, covetousness, foul speech, jealousy, insolence, boastfulness, exaltation, falsity. Not 2 fearing God, persecutors of good men, hating truth, loving falsehood, ignorant of the wages of truth, not adhering to the good, not giving just judgment, lying awake not for good but for evil; from whom gentleness is far away, and to whom boastfulness is close, seeking those who will reward them, without pity for the poor, not grieving for one who is grieved, not recognizing their creator, murderers of their sons, abortionists, turning away from good works, oppressing one who is afflicted, neglecting the appeals of the upright.

Abstain, my son, from all these things, and see that no one 6 leads you astray from this Teaching; otherwise, you will be taught outside the true instruction. If you do these things daily 2 with reflection, you will be near the Living God, but if you do not do them, you will be far from the truth. Lay up all these things in your mind, and you will not be disappointed in your hope, but through these sacred contests you will attain the crown, through our Lord Jesus Christ, who reigns and rules with God the Father and the holy Spirit for ever and ever. Amen.

The Teaching of the Twelve Apostles

THE DIDACHE

Before the churches had reached agreement as to what books should be read in church, and before Christian practices in prayer and worship had become fixed, Christian leaders felt the need of a brief handbook that would regulate church rites and practices. Country churches especially would need to know what to do about traveling missionaries and prophets, and what hospitality to extend to them. And toward the middle of the second century, such a little church manual was prepared, probably in the region of Antioch, and appended to the useful summary of Christian morals already widely used, known as The Teaching of the Apostles. *Indeed, it took over the name of this little code, and presented itself as an enlarged edition of that work, under the title "The Teaching of the Lord through the Twelve Apostles for the Heathen."*

The writer did not hesitate to enrich his inherited code of Christian morals with a block of sentences from Matthew, Luke-Acts, I Peter, Hermas, (Commands ii.4–6) and an unknown work (1.6) thus making up Didache 1.3–2.1—a clear indication that the Greek Didache is not a primary document but is built up out of earlier ones. This secondary character of the Didache is also plainly indicated by the abruptness with which it turns from its bare code of morals, "thou shalt" and "thou shalt not," to its new materials: "About food, bear what you can," 6.3.

9

This new part consists of simple authoritative directions about fasting, prayer, the Lord's Supper, the treatment of visiting Christians, especially prophets, (who seem to have become a problem in the churches), contributions, worship on the Lord's Day, and church officers. An apocalyptic cento made up of a score of echoes of Matthew, Paul's letters, Luke-Acts, Barnabas, and the Revelation, concludes the little pamphlet.

The writer's gospel is Matthew; he does not know the fourfold gospel, and his use of Luke is to be explained by his possession of Luke-Acts; in the Lord's Supper, he holds to the Lucan order, with the cup preceding the bread, against Paul, Mark, and Matthew. But on the welcome to be extended to itinerant missionaries ("apostles") and prophets, he virtually refers his readers to the Gospel of Matthew, (10:40-41), which he describes simply as "the Gospel," and goes on to repeat its injunction on the subject. His Lord's Prayer too is in Matthew's form: on the subject of prayer and charity he again refers them to "the Gospel of the Lord," evidently meaning Matthew 6:1-15. It is to guide them in all their acts. Like the writer of the Pastoral Epistles, he holds to the twofold ministry, bishops and deacons.

Most of the literary influence so long claimed for the Didache really belongs to the primitive form of it, the original Greek Doctrina, but the Didascalia, *late in the third century, and the* Apostolic Constitutions, *late in the fourth, clearly made use of the full form of the Greek Didache.*

Lost for centuries, the Didache was discovered in a Greek manuscript at Constantinople in 1873, and published by Bryennius ten years later. Two small Greek fragments have since been published from two leaves of a parchment manuscript found at Oxyrhynchus, and a longer Coptic fragment in the British Museum was published in 1924. Two extracts in Ethiopic also have come to light, and a Georgian version.

The Teaching of the Twelve Apostles

THE DIDACHE

The Teaching of the Lord to the Heathen by the Twelve Apostles.

There are two ways, one of life and one of death, and there 1 is a great difference between the two ways.

The way of life is this: first, you shall love God, who made you; 2 second, your neighbor as yourself; and everything that you would not have done to you, do not do to another.

Now the teaching of these words is this: Bless those that 3 curse you, and pray for your enemies, and fast for those that persecute you; for what merit is there if you love those that love you? Do not even the heathen do that? But love those that hate you, and you will have no enemy.

Abstain from physical and bodily cravings. If someone strikes 4 you on the right cheek, turn the other to him too, and you will be perfect. If anyone forces you to go one mile, go two miles with him. If anyone takes away your coat, give him your shirt too. If anyone takes from you what is yours, do not demand it back, for you cannot.

Give to everyone that asks of you, and do not demand it back. 5 For the Father wishes that from his own gifts it should be given to all. Blessed is he who gives according to the command, for he is innocent. Woe to him who receives; for if a man receives

11

because he is in need, he will be innocent; but he who receives when he is not in need will stand trial, as to why he received and for what, and being put in prison he will be examined about what he has done, and he will not come out of it until he pays

6 the last penny. But of this it was also said, "Let your charity sweat in your hands until you know to whom to give."

2,2   The second command of the Teaching is: You shall not murder, you shall not commit adultery, you shall not corrupt boys, you shall not commit fornication, you shall not steal, you shall not practice magic, you shall not use enchantments, you shall not

3 murder a child by abortion, or kill one when born. You shall not desire your neighbor's goods, you shall not commit perjury, you shall not bear false witness, you shall not speak evil, you shall

4 not hold a grudge. You shall not be double-minded, nor double-
5 tongued, for the double tongue is a deadly snare. Your speech
6 shall not be false or vain, but fulfilled in action. You shall not be covetous or rapacious, or a hypocrite or malicious or proud. You
7 shall not entertain an evil design against your neighbor. You shall not hate any man, but some you shall reprove, and for some you shall pray, and some you shall love more than your life.

3   My child, flee from everyone evil, and from everyone like him.
2 Do not be irascible, for anger leads to murder, or jealous, or contentious or passionate; for all these things breed murders.

3   My child, do not be lustful, for lust leads to fornication, or foul-spoken or one who lifts up his eyes; for all these things breed adulteries.

4   My child, do not be a dealer in omens, since it leads to idolatry, or an enchanter, or an astrologer, or a magician, and do not wish to see or hear them, for all these things breed idolatry.

5   My child, do not be a liar, since lying leads to theft, or avaricious, or vainglorious, for all these things breed thefts.

6   My child, do not be a grumbler, since it leads to blasphemy, or self-willed or evil-minded, for all these things breed blasphe-
7,8 mies; but be meek, since the meek will inherit the earth. Be long-

suffering and merciful and guileless, and quiet and good, and
always revere the words that you have heard. You shall not exalt 9
yourself, or admit arrogance to your soul. Your soul shall not
associate with lofty men, but you shall live with upright and
humble men. You shall accept the experiences that befall you as 10
good, knowing that nothing happens without God.

My child, night and day you shall remember him who speaks 4
the word of God to you, and you shall honor him as the Lord,
for where the Lord's nature is talked of, there the Lord is. And 2
you shall seek daily the faces of the saints, to find rest in their
words. You shall not cause division, but you shall reconcile 3
fighters. You shall judge uprightly, you shall not show partiality
in reproving transgressions. You shall not doubt whether it will 4
be or not.

Do not be stretching out your hands to take, and closing them 5
when it comes to giving. If you have earned it through your 6
hands, you shall give a ransom for your sins. You shall not 7
hesitate to give, nor grumble when you give, for you shall know
who is the good payer of wages. You shall not turn the needy 8
away, but you shall share everything with your brother, and
you shall not say it is your own. For if you share in what is immortal, how much more in mortal things!

You shall not withhold your hand from your son or from your 9
daughter, but from their youth up you shall teach them the
fear of God. You shall not give orders in bitterness to your man 10
or woman slave, who hope in the same God, lest they cease to
fear the God who is over you both; for he came not to call men
with partiality, but those whom the Spirit prepared. And you 11
slaves shall obey your masters, as a symbol of God, with modesty
and fear. You shall hate all hypocrisy, and everything that is 12
not pleasing to the Lord.

You must not forsake the commandments of the Lord, but you 13
shall keep the teachings you have received, neither adding to
them nor taking from them. In church you shall confess your 14

transgressions, and you shall not approach prayer with an evil conscience. This is the way of life.

5   But the way of death is this: First of all, it is wicked and full of cursing; murders, adulteries, lusts, fornications, thefts, idolatries, magic arts, enchantments, robberies, false witnessings, hypocrisies, duplicity, fraud, pride, malice, willfulness, covetousness, foul speech, jealousy, arrogance, exaltation, boastfulness.

2 Persecutors of good men, hating truth, loving falsehood, ignorant of the wages of uprightness, not adhering to what is good, nor to upright judgment, lying awake not for what is good but for what is evil, from whom gentleness and patience are far away, loving vanity, seeking reward, without pity for the poor, not toiling for the oppressed, ignoring their Maker, murderers of children, corrupters of God's creatures, turning away the needy, oppressing the afflicted, advocates of the rich, unjust judges of the poor, utterly sinful. May you be delivered, my children, from all these!

6   See that no one leads you astray from this way of the Teach-
2 ing, for he teaches you without God. For if you can bear the whole yoke of the Lord, you will be perfect; but if you cannot, do what you can.

3   About food, bear what you can, but abstain strictly from what is offered to idols, for it is a worship of dead gods.

7   About baptism, baptize in this way: After first repeating all these things, baptize in running water, in the name of the Father
2 and of the Son and of the holy Spirit. If you have no running water, baptize in other water, and if you cannot use cold water,
3 use warm. If you have neither, pour water on the head three
4 times, in the name of Father and Son and holy Spirit. And before the baptism let the baptizer and the one who is to be baptized and any others who can do so fast. And you must order the one who is to be baptized to fast one or two days beforehand.

8   Your fasts must not be on the same days with the hypocrites, for they fast on Monday and Thursday, but you must fast on

Wednesday and Friday. And do not pray like the hypocrites, 2
but pray thus as the Lord commanded in his gospel:

"Our Father in heaven, your name be revered, your kingdom
come, your will be done on earth as it is done in heaven. Give
us today our bread for the day, and forgive us our debt, as we
forgive our debtors; and do not subject us to temptation, but
save us from the Evil One; for yours is the power and the glory
forever!"

Three times a day pray thus. 3

Now about the Thanksgiving, give thanks thus: First about 9, 2
the cup, "We thank you, our Father, for the holy vine of your
servant David, which you have made known to us through your
servant Jesus. Glory to you forever." And about the piece of 3
bread, "We thank you, our Father, for the life and knowledge
you have made known to us through Jesus your servant. Glory
be yours forever. Just as this piece of bread was scattered over 4
the mountains, and then was gathered together and became one,
so let your church be gathered together from the ends of the
earth into your kingdom. For the glory and the power are yours
through Jesus Christ forever." But let no one eat or drink of your 5
Thanksgiving but those who have been baptized in the name
of the Lord. For it was of this that the Lord said, "Do not give
dogs what is sacred."

After you are satisfied, give thanks thus: "We give you thanks, 10, 2
Holy Father, for your holy name, which you have made dwell
in our hearts, and for knowledge and faith and immortality, which
you have made known to us through Jesus your servant; glory to
you forever. You, almighty Master, have created all things for 3
your name's sake, you have given men food and drink to enjoy,
that they may give you thanks, but you have granted us spiritual
food and drink and everlasting life through your servant. Above 4
all we thank you that you are mighty; glory to you forever.
Remember, Lord, your church, to save it from all evil and to 5
make it perfect in your love, and gather it together in its holiness

from the four winds, into your kingdom which you have prepared for it. For the power and the glory are yours forever.
6 Let your favor come and this world pass away. Hosanna to the God of David! If anyone is holy, let him come; if anyone is not,
7 let him repent. Lord, come quickly! Amen." But permit the prophets to give thanks as much as they please.

11 Whoever comes and teaches you all these things said above,
2 you must welcome. But if the teacher himself turns away and teaches another doctrine, to destroy them, do not listen to him. But if his teaching is for the promotion of uprightness and the knowledge of the Lord, welcome him as you would the Lord.
3 About apostles and prophets, follow the rule of the Gospel,
4 which is this: Let every apostle who comes to you be welcomed
5 as the Lord. But he shall not stay more than one day, and if it is necessary, the next day also. But if he stays three days, he is a
6 false prophet. And when an apostle leaves, let him take nothing except bread to last until he finds his next lodging. But if he asks for money, he is a false prophet.
7 You shall not test or examine any prophet who speaks in the spirit. For every sin will be forgiven, but this sin will not be for-
8 given. But not everyone who speaks in the spirit is a prophet, but only if he has the ways of the Lord. So the false prophet and
9 the prophet will be known by their ways. No prophet who orders a meal under the spirit's influence shall eat of it; if he does, he is
10 a false prophet. Every prophet who teaches the truth, if he
11 does not do what he teaches, is a false prophet. No prophet, tried and true, who does anything as an earthly symbol of the church, but does not teach others to do what he does, shall be judged among you, for he has his judgment with God, for the ancient
12 prophets also did this. But whoever says in the spirit, "Give me money," or something else, you shall not listen to him, but if he tells you to give for others who are in want, let no one judge him.
12 Let everyone who comes in the name of the Lord be welcomed,

and afterward when you have tested him you will know him, for you will have understanding of true and false. If the one who 2 comes is a traveler, help him all you can. But he must not stay with you more than two or if necessary three days. If he wants 3 to settle among you and has a trade, let him work for his living. But if he has no trade, see to it in your understanding that no 4 one lives among you in idleness because he is a Christian. If he 5 will not do this, he is trading on Christ. Beware of such men.

But every true prophet who wants to settle among you deserves 13 his food. In like manner, a true teacher, like the workman, de- 2 serves his food. So you shall take the first fruits of the produce 3 of the wine press and the threshing floor and give the first fruits to the prophets, for they are your high priests. But if you have 4 no prophet, give it to the poor. If you make bread, take the first 5 fruits and give them according to the command. In like manner, 6 when you open a jar of wine or oil, take the first fruits and give them to the prophets. And of money and clothing and everything 7 you get, take the first fruits, as you think best, and give, according to the command.

On the Lord's own day, gather together and break bread and 14 give thanks, after confessing your transgressions, so that your sacrifice may be pure. Let no one who has a quarrel with his 2 comrade meet with you until they are reconciled, so that your sacrifice may not be defiled. For this is what was said by the 3 Lord, "At every place and time offer me a clean sacrifice, for I am a great king, says the Lord, and my name is wonderful among the heathen."

So appoint for yourselves overseers and assistants worthy of 15 the Lord, men who are humble-minded and not avaricious, but are true and tried, for they themselves also render you the service of the prophets and teachers. So do not despise them, for they 2 are your honorable men along with the prophets and teachers.

Do not reprove one another in wrath, but in peace as you find 3 it in the gospel. If anyone wrongs his neighbor, let no one speak to him, and let him not hear a word from you until he repents.

4 And offer your prayers and do your alms and all your acts as you find it in the Gospel of our Lord.

16 Be watchful for your life; your lamps must not go out, and you must not be unprepared, but be ready, for you do not know
2 the hour when our Lord is coming. Gather together often to seek the things that benefit your souls, for the whole time of your faith will not profit you unless you are found perfect at the last
3 time. For the false prophets and the corrupters will be multiplied, and the sheep will be turned into wolves and love will be turned
4 into hate, for as lawlessness increases, they will hate and persecute and betray one another, and then the world-deceiver will appear as a son of God, and will do signs and wonders, and the earth will be delivered into his hands, and he will commit law-
5 less acts which have never been since the beginning. Then created mankind will pass into the fiery trial and many will fall away and perish, but those who endure in their faith will be saved by the
6 curse itself. Then will appear the signs of the truth, first, the sign of the opening in the heaven, then the sign of the sound of
7 the trumpet, and third, the resurrection of the dead, but not of all, but as it was said, "The Lord will come and all his saints
8 with him." Then the world will see the Lord coming on the clouds of the sky.

The Letter of Barnabas

From the beginning, the Old Testament was a problem for Christian believers. As early as A.D. *52 Paul had touched upon it in Galatians, and a hundred years later Marcion was rejecting the Old Testament, while Justin was accepting it. But even in the time of Paul one Jewish scholar, Philo, at Alexandria, had allegorized it, very much as the Stoics had so successfully allegorized Homer, until they had made it, as some say, the Bible of the Greeks. Before the end of the first century allegory had been adopted as a Christian approach to the Old Testament in the Letter to the Hebrews, and a generation later, about* A.D. *130, a Christian teacher, perhaps at Alexandria, and certainly in the Alexandrian tradition, applied it boldly to the Law, the Prophets, and the Psalms, in the earliest form of the Letter of Barnabas. He takes the position that the Jews' literal understanding of their Law was the work of a wicked angel, who deceived them. The six days of creation are really the six thousand years the earth is to endure before the return of the Messiah, and the food laws of Leviticus only mean that we are not to be like swine or birds of prey.*

The reference to the building of a temple in Jerusalem by the heathen seems to reflect Hadrian's building of a temple to Jupiter there in A.D. *130-131, and the mention of the ten kings, in chapter 4, would also bring us to the time of Hadrian, if the writer*

19

reckoned emperors as the Revelation did, omitting Galba, Otho, and Vitellius.

In its original form, the letter probably stopped with chapter 17, as the Latin manuscript found at St. Petersburg does, for at the end of it the form and interest change completely, and with the crudest possible transition: "So much for that. Now let us pass to another lesson and teaching" ("Gnosis and Didache"). The Greek form of the Letter then continues with more than fifty brief commands from the primitive form of The Teaching of the Apostles *(Doctrina), twenty-three positive and twenty-eight negative. Much of what Barnabas omits in its use of Doctrina is covered elsewhere in Barnabas, chapters 17-21, so that its use of Doctrina is not inferior to Didache's use of it; it is in fact superior to it. Moreover, Barnabas presents its moral code less as vices to be shunned than as virtues to be sought, a far superior method. This expansion was probably made between* A.D. *150 and 175.*

It is striking that the two component parts of Barnabas have come down to us in Latin versions, not in their Greek originals, though these may sometime be found. The manuscripts of the full Greek Barnabas have an interesting history. For a long time it was known to modern learning only in a group of eight manuscripts all derived from one which had lost several leaves, and so their contents skipped from Polycarp to the Philippians 9.2 to Barnabas 5.7. But when Tischendorf in 1859 found the Codex Sinaiticus in the convent of St. Catherine on Mount Sinai, he observed the full Greek text of Barnabas in it, immediately after the Revelation, and sat up all that night to copy what he knew would be a great treasure of early Christian literature. Later, in 1873, Bryennius found it again in the Constantinople manuscript of A.D. *1056, which contained the Didache. It is upon these two manuscripts that our knowledge of the Greek Barnabas principally rests.*

The appearance of Barnabas immediately following the Revelation and followed by Hermas in the oldest complete Greek manuscript of the New Testament shows the regard in which it was held in Christian Egypt in the middle of the fourth century. Clement of Alexandria, toward the end of the second century, accepted it as scripture, and commented on it in his lost Outlines. *Origen too included it among the disputed books that he accepted as scripture. Jerome speaks of it as read among the apocryphal writings. The list in the Codex Claromontanus, representing Christian usage in Egypt about* A.D. *300, has it at the end of the General Letters, between Jude and the Revelation of John. Eusebius classes it as disputed and rejected. The* List of the Sixty Canonical Books (*before* A.D. *800*) *puts it among the rejected books, and the* Stichometry of Nicephorus, *about* A.D. *850, classes it with the disputed books—the Revelation of John, the Revelation of Peter, and the Gospel of the Hebrews—but not among the rejected ones.*

The Letter of Barnabas

Greeting, sons and daughters, in the name of the Lord who 1
has loved us, in peace.

Great and rich as the ordinances of God are toward you, I 2
rejoice extremely and exceedingly over your blessed and glorious
spirits, so congenially have you received the favor of the gift of
the spirit. Therefore I congratulate myself the more in my hope 3
of being saved, because in you I really see that the spirit has
been poured out upon you from the rich Lord of the fountain.
So much has my longed-for sight of you amazed me about you.
So being convinced of this and conscious that since I spoke to 4
you I have come to know many things, because the Lord has
journeyed with me in the way of uprightness, I am absolutely
forced to this, to love you above my own soul, because great faith
and love dwell in you, in the hope of his life. So since I have 5
decided that if I am concerned about you to share with you some
part of what I have received, I will be rewarded for having been
of service to such spirits, I have been eager to send you a short
letter, so that you may have your knowledge keep pace with your
faith.

There are three rules of the Lord: the hope of life is the 6
beginning and end of our faith; uprightness is the beginning and
end of judgment; love of joy and gladness is the proof of acts
of uprightness. For the Master has made the past and present 7
known to us through the prophets, giving us also the first fruits of
the taste of the future. When we see these things coming to pass

one after another, as he said, we ought to make a richer and
8 loftier offering to his fear. And not as a teacher but as one of
you I will show you a few things over which you will rejoice
in the present time.

2   Since the days are evil, and the Worker himself is in power,
we ought to take heed to ourselves, and seek out the Lord's
2 ordinances. Fear and endurance therefore are the helpers of
3 our faith, and our allies are patience and self-control. So as long
as these abide in purity in relation to the Lord, wisdom, intel-
4 ligence, understanding, and knowledge rejoice with them. For
he has made it plain to us through all the prophets that he needs
neither sacrifices nor burnt offerings nor offerings, for he some-
5 where says, "What is the multitude of your sacrifices to me? says
the Lord. I am full of burnt offerings, and I do not want the fat
of lambs and the blood of bulls and goats, not even if you come
to be seen by me. For who has required this at your hands? You
shall not tread my courts again. If you bring fine flour, it is vain.
Incense is an abomination to me; your new moons and sabbaths
6 I cannot bear." So he abolished these things in order that the new
law of our Lord Jesus Christ, which is free from the yoke of
7 necessity, might have its offering not made by man. Again he
says to them, "Did I command your forefathers, when they came
out of the land of Egypt, to offer burnt offerings and sacrifices to
8 me? No, this is what I commanded them: "Let none of you bear
a grudge in his heart against his neighbor, and do not love a false
9 oath." So we ought to perceive, if we are not without understanding, the benevolent purpose of our Father, for he speaks
to us, because he does not wish us to go astray like them, but to
10 seek how to make our offering to him. This then is what he says
to us: "A broken heart is a sacrifice to the Lord; a heart that
glorifies its maker is a fragrant odor to the Lord." So, brethren,
we ought to inquire closely about our salvation, so that the Evil
One may not smuggle some error in among us and dislodge us
from our life.

So he says to them again about this, "Why do you fast to me, 3
says the Lord, so that your voice is raised in a cry to me? This
is not the fast that I have chosen, says the Lord, not a man
humbling his soul, not even if you bend your neck like a ring, 2
and put on sackcloth and lie in ashes, not even so can you call it
an acceptable fast." But to you he says, "Behold, this is the fast 3
I have chosen, says the Lord: Undo every unrighteous bond, untie
the knots of violent agreements, set the bruised at liberty, and
tear up every unfair contract. Break your bread to the hungry,
and if you see a man naked, clothe him. Take the homeless into
your house, and if you see a humble person, you shall not look
down on him, nor shall the members of your household. Then 4
your light will break forth early in the morning and your healing will rise quickly, and your uprightness will go before you and
the glory of the Lord will envelop you. Then you will cry out 5
and God will hear you; while you are still speaking, he will say,
Here I am! if you strip from you every fetter and lifting up of the
hand, and grumbling word, and give your bread to the hungry
from your heart, and show pity to the soul that is oppressed."
So, brethren, he that is long suffering, foreseeing that the people 6
he had prepared in his Beloved would believe in guilelessness,
made all plain to us beforehand, so that we might not suffer
shipwreck by being converted to their law.

We must therefore examine closely the things of the present 4
and seek out the things that can save us. So let us flee absolutely
from all lawless doings, so that lawless doings may not overtake
us, and let us hate the error of the present time, so that we may
be loved in the time that is to come. Let us give our souls no 2
liberty to have power to associate with sinners and evil men, so
that we may not become like them. The final stumbling block 3
is at hand, of which it is written, as Enoch says, "For this is why
the Lord has cut the times and the days short, in order that
his Beloved may make haste and come to his inheritance."
And thus says the prophet also: "Ten reigns shall reign over the 4

earth, and after them will rise a little king who will subdue three
5 of the kings under one." Similarly of the same one Daniel says,
"And I saw the fourth beast, which was evil and strong and
fiercer than all the beasts of the sea, and that ten horns sprang
from it, and out of them sprang a little horn, an excrescence, and
6 that it subdued three of the large horns under one." You ought
therefore to understand. And besides I ask this also of you, as
one of your own number, and especially as loving you all more
than my own life, that you now take heed to yourselves and be
not like some, piling up your sins and saying that the covenant
7 is theirs as well as ours. It is ours, but they lost it completely
just after Moses received it, in the following manner. For the
scripture says, "Now Moses was on the mountain fasting forty
days and forty nights, and he received the covenant from the
Lord, stone tablets written upon with the finger of the Lord's
8 hand." But they turned to idols and lost it, for thus says the
Lord: "Moses, Moses, go down quickly, for your people whom
you have led out of the land of Egypt have broken the Law."
And Moses understood and he threw the two tablets from his
hands and their covenant was broken in pieces, in order that the
covenant of the beloved Jesus might be sealed on our hearts in
the hope of his faith.
9   Though I would like to write, not as a teacher but as one
who loves to leave out nothing of what we have, I hasten to
write—I, your humble sacrifice. Therefore let us take heed in the
last days, for the whole time of our life and faith will do us no
good unless we now in this lawless time withstand also the
10 offenses that are to come, as befits sons of God. In order therefore that the Black One may have no chance to enter, let us
flee from all vanity, let us absolutely hate the doings of the evil
way. Do not withdraw by yourselves and live alone, as though
you had already become upright, but gather together, and
11 seek out the common advantage. For the scripture says, "Alas for
those that are wise in their own eyes, and understanding in

their own sight." Let us be spiritual, let us be a perfect temple
for God, as far as it is in our power. Let us practise the fear of
God and strive to keep his commandment, so that we may delight
in his ordinances. The Lord will judge the world impartially; each   12
one will receive according to what he has done. If he is good his
uprightness will precede him, if he is bad, the wages of evildoing
awaits him. Let us never, because we are called, rest in that,   13
and fall asleep over our sins, and so the evil ruler will get control of us and thrust us out of the kingdom of the Lord. Con-   14
sider this too besides, my brethren: when you see that after such
signs and wonders were done in Israel, even then they were
abandoned, let us take care that we are not found as it is
written, "many invited, but few chosen."

For it was for this that the Lord endured giving up his flesh to   5
corruption, that we might be purified by the forgiveness of our
sins, that is, through sprinkling with his blood. For what is writ-   2
ten about him has to do partly with Israel, partly with us. And
this is what it says: "He was wounded because of our transgressions, and bruised because of our sins. By his stripes we were
healed. He was led like a sheep to slaughter, and he was dumb
like a lamb before its shearer." We ought certainly to give thanks   3
exceedingly to the Lord because he has made known to us the
past, and made us wise about the present, and about the future
we are not without understanding. For the scripture says, "Not   4
unjustly are nets spread for birds." This means that a man will
justly perish who when he knows the way of uprightness keeps
to the way of darkness. There is this, too, my brethren. If the   5
Lord endured it to suffer for our life, though he was Lord of all
the world, to whom God said, at the foundation of the world,
"Let us make man in our image and our likeness," then how
did he endure it, to suffer at the hands of men? Learn then!
The prophets being favored by him prophesied about him, and   6
he, in order to bring death to naught, and show the resurrection
from the dead, because he had to be revealed in flesh, endured

7 it, so as to fulfill the promises made to the forefathers and himself prepare the new people for himself, and show while still on earth that he himself when he has effected the resurrection will be
8 judge. Finally, he preached, teaching Israel and doing such
9 signs and wonders, and loved them intensely. And when he chose his own apostles who were going to preach his gospel, though they were indescribably lawless, to show that he had not come to call the upright but the irreligious, he showed himself to be
10 the Son of God. For if he had not come in flesh, how could men have looked at him and been saved, when as they look at the sun, which is destined not to be, which is the work of his
11 hands, they cannot gaze at its rays? So the Son of God came in flesh for this purpose, that he might fill out the total of the sins
12 of those who had driven his prophets to death. So it was for that purpose that he endured. For God says that the wounding of his flesh was from them: "When they strike down their own
13 shepherd, the sheep of the flock will perish." And he himself chose to suffer thus, for it was necessary that he should suffer on a tree, for he that prophesied said of him, "Spare my soul from the sword," and "Nail my flesh, for assemblies of evildoers have
14 risen up against me." And again he says, "Behold, I have offered my back to scourges, and my cheeks to blows, and I have set my face like a solid rock."

6   When therefore he made the command, what did he say? "Who is he that goes to law with me? Let him oppose me. Or who is he that seeks vindication against me? Let him approach
2 the Lord's servant. Alas for him! For you will grow old like a cloak, and a moth will devour you." And again the prophet says, since he was put in place like a mighty stone to crush them, "Here I lay a choice stone in Zion, a costly, valued cornerstone."
3 What does he say next? "And whoever believes in it will live for ever." Does our hope then rest on a stone? Not at all, but because the Lord has set his flesh in strength. For he says, "and
4 he has set me like a solid rock." And again the prophet says,

"The stone that the builders refused has become the corner-stone." And again he says, "This is the great, wonderful day that the Lord made." I am writing to you very simply, so that 5 you can understand—I, a humble sacrifice of your love. Then 6 what does the prophet say again? "A gathering of evildoers has encircled me; they surrounded me like bees around the honey," and "for my clothing they cast lots." Then, since he was to appear 7 and suffer in flesh, his suffering was predicted. For the prophet says of Israel, "Alas for their soul, for they have formed an evil design against themselves, saying, 'Let us bind the upright man, for he inconveniences us.'" What does that other prophet 8 Moses say to them? "Behold thus says the Lord God: 'Go into the good land, which the Lord swore to Abraham, Isaac, and Jacob, and take possession of it, a land flowing with milk and honey.'" And learn what knowledge says. Hope, it says, in 9 Jesus, who is to be manifested to you in flesh. For man is earth capable of suffering, for the formation of Adam was from the face of the earth. What then does "into the good land, a land 10 flowing with milk and honey" mean? Blessed be our Lord, brethren, who put in us wisdom and understanding of his secrets. For the prophet is uttering a parable of the Lord; who can understand it but one that is wise and understanding and loves his Lord? So since he has renewed us by the forgiveness of sins, 11 he has made us another type, so that we should have the souls of children, as though he were creating us anew. For the scrip- 12 ture is speaking of us, when he says to the Son, "Let us make man in our image and likeness, and let them rule the wild animals of the earth, and the birds of the heaven and the fish of the sea." And when the Lord saw our goodly form, he said, "In-crease and multiply and fill the earth"—addressing the Son.

Again I will show you how he refers to us. At last he has 13 made a second creation. And the Lord says, "Behold, I am mak-ing the last things like the first." So it was with a view to this that the prophet declared, "Go into a land flowing with milk

14 and honey, and take possession of it." Notice then, we have been
created anew, as he says again in another prophet, "Behold,
says the Lord, I will take out of them," that is, of those whom
the spirit of the Lord foresaw, "their hearts of stone, and put in
them hearts of flesh," because he was going to be manifested in
15 flesh and to live among us. For the habitation of our hearts,
16 my brethren, is a temple, holy to the Lord. For the Lord says
again, "And with what shall I appear to the Lord my God, and
be glorified?" He says, "I will confess you in the assembly of
my brethren, and sing to you in the midst of the assembly of
17 saints." So it is we that he brought into the good land. Then why
the milk and the honey? Because a child is fed with honey first,
then with milk. So we too are fed with faith in the promise and
with the word and will live and take possession of the earth.
18 For he said before, "And let them increase and multiply and rule
the fish." Who, then, can rule wild beasts or fish or birds of the
heaven? For we ought to perceive that to rule implies authority,
19 so that one gives orders and is obeyed. So if this is not now the
case, then he has told us when it will be; when we ourselves are
perfected to become heirs of the Lord's covenant.

7   Observe, therefore, children of gladness, that the good Lord has
revealed all these things to us beforehand so that we may know
to whom we ought to give thanks and praise for everything.
2 So if the Son of God, though he was Lord, and was to judge the
living and the dead, suffered in order that his wounds might
bring us life, let us believe that the Son of God could not
3 suffer except for us. But when he was crucified he was given
vinegar and gall to drink. Hear how the priests in the temple
revealed this. When the command was written, "Whoever does
not keep the fast shall be put to death," the Lord commanded it
because he himself was going to offer the vessel of the spirit
as a sacrifice for our sins, in order that the pattern set up in the
case of Isaac, who was offered upon the altar, might be ful-
4 filled. What then does he say in the prophet? "And let them eat

of the goat that is offered at the fast for their sin." Give close
heed! "And let all the priests but no others eat the entrails
unwashed, but with vinegar." Why? Because you are going to 5
offer me gall with vinegar to drink when I am about to offer
my flesh for the sins of my new people, you alone must eat,
while the people fast and lament in sackcloth and ashes—to
show that he must suffer at their hands. Observe what he com- 6
manded: "Take two fine, well-matched goats, and offer them,
and let the priest take one for a burnt offering for sins." But 7
what shall they do with the other? The other, he says, is accursed.
Notice how the type of Jesus is revealed. "And spit upon it all of 8
you and prick it, and tie scarlet wool on its head, and in that
condition let it be thrown into the desert." And when this is done
the man that has charge of the goat leads it into the desert and
takes off the wool and puts it on the bush called rache, the
shoots of which we are accustomed to eat when we find them in
the country; only the fruit of the rache is sweet, in this way.
Then what does this mean? Notice, "one for the altar, and the 9
other accursed," and why the one that is accursed, crowned?
Because then, on that day, they will see him with the scarlet robe
about his body, reaching to his feet, and they will say, "Is
not this he whom we once crucified, setting him at naught and
piercing him and spitting upon him? It was certainly this man
who said then that he was Son of God." For how is he like it? 10
For this reason: "Two goats, alike, fine, well matched," in order
that when they see him come then, they may be amazed at the
likeness of the goat. Behold therefore the type of Jesus who was
to suffer. But what does it mean that they put the wool in the 11
midst of the thorns? It is a type of Jesus set before the church,
because whoever wishes to take away the scarlet wool must
suffer much, because the thorn is terrible, and he can only get
possession of it through pain. So, he says, "those who wish to
see and touch my kingdom must go through affliction and suffering to get me."

8   But what do you think it typifies, that Israel was commanded that the men whose sins were full grown should offer a heifer, and slaughter it and burn it, and then boys should take the ashes and put them into bowls, and tie scarlet wool on a stick of wood (notice again the type of the cross and the scarlet wool) and take hyssop, and then the boys should sprinkle the people

2   one by one, so that they may be purified from their sins? Notice how plainly he is speaking to you. The calf is Jesus, the sinful men who offer it are those who brought him to be slain. Then they are no longer mere men, the glory no longer belongs to

3   sinners. The boys who sprinkled are those who preached to us the forgiveness of sins and the purification of the heart. To them— they were twelve in number, as a testimony to the tribes, for there are twelve tribes of Israel—he gave authority to preach the

4   gospel. But why are there three boys that sprinkle? To testify to Abraham, Isaac, and Jacob, for they were great in the sight of

5   God. And why was the wool placed on the stick of wood? Because the reign of Jesus rests upon wood, and those who hope

6   in him will live forever. And why the wool and the hyssop together? Because in his reign there will be evil and corrupt days, in which we will be saved, because he who suffers in body

7   is cured through the juice of the hyssop. And that they happened for this reason is evident to us, but obscure to them, because they have not listened to the voice of the Lord.

9   For he speaks further about the ears, how he has circumcised our hearts. The Lord says in the prophet, "At the hearing of the ear, they obey me," and again he says, "Those who are far off will surely hear, they will know what I have done." And "Cir-

2   cumcise your hearts, says the Lord." And again he says, "Listen, Israel, for thus says the Lord your God." And again the spirit of the Lord prophesies, "Who is there that wishes to live forever?

3   Let him be sure to listen to the voice of my servant." And again he says, "Listen, heaven, and give ear, earth, for the Lord has spoken." These things are to prove it. And again he says,

"Hear the word of the Lord, you rulers of this people." And again he says, "Hear, children, the voice of one who is shouting in the desert." So he has circumcised our ears, so that we may hear the word and believe. Besides, the circumcision in which 4 they trusted has been abolished, for he has commanded that there should be a circumcision not of the flesh, but they disobeyed, for an evil angel deluded them. He says to them, "Thus 5 says the Lord your God" (here I find a command), "Do not sow among thorns, be circumcised to your Lord." And what does he say? "Circumcise your hardheartedness, and do not be stiff-necked." Take another: "Behold, says the Lord, all the heathen are uncircumcised in flesh, but this people is uncircumcised in heart." But, you will say, surely the people were circum- 6 cised for a seal. But so is every Syrian and Arab and all the priests of the idols. Do these also, then, share in their covenant? Why, even the Egyptians practice circumcision! Learn, there- 7 fore, dear children, richly about everything, for Abraham, who first imparted circumcision, did so looking forward in spirit to Jesus, for he received instruction in three letters. For it says, 8 "And of his household Abraham circumcised eighteen and three hundred men." What, then, was the knowledge given him? Notice that he mentions the eighteen first, and after a space the three hundred. The eighteen is I, ten, and H, eight; you have (the abbreviation for) Jesus! And because the cross was going to express God's favor in the T, he says also "three hundred." So he discloses Jesus by the two letters and the cross by the other. He who has planted the gift of his teaching in us knows this. 9 No one has ever learned from me a sounder lesson, but I know that you are worthy of it.

Now, because Moses said, "You shall not eat swine or eagle 10 or hawk or crow or any fish that does not have scales on it," he had three teachings in mind. Further, he says to them in 2 Deuteronomy, "And I will set forth my ordinances to this people." So, then, God's command is not that they should not eat, but

3 Moses spoke in the spirit. This, then, is why he mentioned the swine: "You shall not associate," he means, "with men who are like swine," that is, when they are in luxury, they forget the Lord, but when they are in want they acknowledge the Lord, just as the swine when it is feeding does not know its master, but when it is hungry it squeals, and when it has been fed,

4 it is quiet again. "Neither shall you eat the eagle or the hawk or the kite or the crow"; you shall not, he means, associate with or come to resemble such men as do not know how to provide their food by toil and sweat, but lawlessly seize what belongs to others, and while pretending to live in innocence, watch and look about to find whom they can plunder in their greed, just as these birds are the only ones that provide no food for themselves, but sit idle and seek ways to eat the meat of others, since they

5 are pests in wickedness. "And you shall not eat," he goes on, "sea eel or polyp or cuttlefish." You shall not, he means, associate with such men and come to resemble them, who are utterly ungodly and already condemned to death, just as these fish alone are accursed and swim in the depths, not swimming on the sur-

6 face like the rest, but living in the mud at the bottom. Moreover, you shall not eat the hare. Why? You shall not, he means, be a corrupter of boys or come to resemble such men, for the hare gains a passage in the body every year, for it has as many

7 openings as it is years old. But do not eat the hyena either; you shall not, he means, become an adulterer or a corrupter of boys or come to resemble such men. Why? Because this animal changes its nature from year to year and becomes now male, now

8 female. But he did well to abhor the weasel, too. You shall not, he means, be like those men who, we hear, commit iniquity with their mouths for the sake of uncleanness, and you shall not associate with unclean women who commit iniquity with their

9 mouths. For this animal conceives with its mouth. Moses received three decrees about food and uttered them in the spirit, but they in their fleshly desire received them as having to do

with eating. But David understands the meaning of these three 10
decrees, and says, "Blessed is the man who has not gone in the
counsel of the ungodly"—as the fish go in darkness to the bottom; "and has not stood in the pathway of sinners"—as those
who claim to fear the Lord but sin like the swine; "and has not
sat on the seat of the pestilent," like birds that sit and wait for
their prey. You have in full the lesson about eating. Again Moses 11
says, "Eat anything that has cloven hoofs and chews the cud."
What does he mean? That when it is fed it knows who feeds it
and, relying on him, seems to be glad. Well did he speak, re-
garding the command. What, then, does he mean? Associate with
those who fear the Lord, with those who meditate in their
hearts on the command they have received, with those who talk
of the things ordained by the Lord and observe them, with those
who know that meditation is a work of gladness and ruminate
on the word of the Lord. But why does he speak of the cloven
hoofed? The upright man both lives in this world and looks forward to the holy age. See how well Moses made laws. But 12
how could they understand or grasp these things? But we, having an upright understanding of his commands utter them as the
Lord intended. This is why he has circumcised our ears and
hearts so that we may grasp these things.

But let us inquire whether the Lord took care to foreshadow 11
the water and the cross. About the water it is written of Israel
how they would not accept the baptism that brings forgiveness of
sins, but would build for themselves. For the prophet says, "Be 2
astonished, heaven, and let the earth shudder the more at this,
because this people has done two evil things, they have forsaken
me, the spring of life, and have dug themselves a pit of death. Is 3
my holy mount Sinai a desert rock? For you will be like a bird's
nestlings, fluttering about when they are taken away from their
nest." And again the prophet says, "I will go before you and level 4
mountains and shatter gates of brass and break iron bars, and I
will give you treasures of darkness, hidden, unseen, so that they

5 may know that I am the Lord God." And "You will live in a lofty cave in a strong rock, and its water is unfailing. You will see the king in glory, and your soul will reflect on the fear of the

6 Lord." And again in another prophet he says, "And he that does these things will be like the tree that is planted by the streams of water, which will yield its fruit in its proper season, and its leaf

7 will not fall off, and all that he does will prosper. It is not so with the ungodly, it is not so! but they are like the chaff that the wind sweeps from the face of the earth. That is why the ungodly will not rise up in judgment, nor sinners in the counsel of the upright; for the Lord knows the way of the upright, and the way

8 of the ungodly will perish." Observe how he has defined the water and the cross together. For this is what he means: Blessed are those who have set their hope on the cross and gone down into the water, for he speaks of their wages when they are due: Then, he says, I will pay them. And when he now says, "His leaves will not fall off," he means this: that every word that goes out of your mouths in faith and love will bring conversion and

9 hope to many. And again another prophet says, "And the land of Jacob was praised above all the earth." He means this: he is

10 glorifying the instrument of the spirit. What does he say then? "And there was a river flowing from the right hand, and beautiful trees grew out of it, and whoever eats of them will live for

11 ever." This means that we go down into the water full of sins and pollution, and we come up bringing forth fear in our hearts and with hope in Jesus in our spirit. "And whoever eats of these will live forever" means this: whoever, he says, hears these things said and believes them will live forever.

12   Likewise he further ordains about the cross, in another prophet, who says, "When shall these things be accomplished? The Lord said, When a tree shall be bent down and rise up, and when blood shall drip from a tree." You have a fresh allusion to the

2 cross and to him who was to be crucified. And he said again to Moses when Israel was warred against by aliens, and so as to

remind them when they were being warred against that it was
because of their sins that they were delivered to death—the
spirit said to the heart of Moses, that he should make a symbol
of the cross and of him who was to suffer, because, he says,
unless they hope in him, they will be warred against forever. So
Moses piled one shield upon another in the midst of the fray, and
taking his stand high above them all he stretched out his hands,
and then Israel was victorious again; then when he let them fall,
they were slain again. Why? To show them that they cannot be 3
saved unless they hope in him. And again in another prophet he 4
says, "All day long I have stretched out my hands to a people
that disobeyed and disputed my upright way." Again Moses 5
gives a symbol of Jesus, showing that he must suffer and he whom
they will think they have destroyed will himself give life, in a
figure given when Israel was falling. For the Lord made every
serpent bite them, and they were dying (since transgression
arose in Eve through the serpent), in order to convince them
that because of their transgression they would be consigned
to the affliction of death. Finally Moses, though he commanded, 6
"You shall not have anything cast or carved for your God," made
one himself to show them a symbol of Jesus. So Moses made a
bronze serpent and set it up conspicuously and assembled the
people by a proclamation. So when they had come together, they 7
besought Moses to offer prayer for them, for their healing. But
Moses said to them, "Whenever," said he, "one of you is bitten,
let him come to the serpent that is placed upon the pole, and
hope and believe that though it is dead it can give him life, and
he will immediately be saved." And they did so. Here again you
have the glory of Jesus, because all things are in him and point
to him. Again, what did Moses say to Jesus (Joshua) the son of 8
Nun, when he gave him, as being a prophet, this name, solely in
order that all the people might hear that the Father was revealing
everything about his Son Jesus? So Moses said to Jesus the son 9
of Nun, after he had given him this name, when he sent him to

spy out the land, "Take a scroll in your hands and write what
the Lord says, that the Son of God will in the last days cut out
10 the whole house of Amalek by the roots." See, again it is Jesus, not
a son of man, but Son of God, and symbolically revealed in flesh.
Since therefore they were going to say that the Christ is the son
of David, David himself prophesied, fearing and understanding
the error of the sinners, "The Lord has said to my lord, Sit at my
11 right hand until I make your enemies your footstool." And again
Isaiah says, "The Lord said to my Lord Christ, whose right hand
I have laid hold of, that heathen would listen before him, and
I will shatter the might of kings." See how David calls him Lord,
and does not call him son.

13   Now let us see whether this people is the heir, or the former
people, and whether the agreement relates to us or to them.
2 Hear, then, what the scripture says about the people: "Isaac
prayed for his wife Rebecca, because she was barren; and she
conceived." Then "Rebecca went off to consult the Lord, and
the Lord said to her, Two nations are in your womb, and two
peoples in your body, and one people will master the other, and
3 the greater will serve the less." You must understand who Isaac
was, and who Rebecca was, and of whom he has shown that
4 this people would be greater than that. And in another prophecy
Jacob speaks more clearly to his son Joseph, saying, "Behold,
the Lord has not deprived me of your face; bring me your sons,
5 so that I may bless them." And he brought Ephraim and
Manasseh, wishing that Manasseh should be blessed, because
he was the elder; for Joseph led him to the right hand of his
father Jacob. But Jacob saw in the spirit a symbol of the future
people, and what does it say? "And Jacob crossed his hands, and
put his right hand on the head of Ephraim, the second and
younger son, and he blessed him. And Joseph said to Jacob,
Transfer your right hand to the head of Manasseh, for he is my
first born son. And Jacob said to Joseph, I know, my child, I
know, but the greater will serve the less, though he also will be

blessed." Observe on whom he laid hands, that this people should 6
be first and inherit the agreement. If, then, in addition he men- 7
tioned it also in speaking of Abraham, we reach the perfection
of our knowledge. What, then, does he say to Abraham, when he
alone had faith and was ordained to be upright? "Behold, I have
made you, Abraham, the father of the heathen who though uncircumcised will believe in God."

Yes, but let us see whether he has given the people the agree- 14
ment which he swore to their forefathers to give them. Let us
inquire. He has given it! But because of their sins they were not
worthy to receive it. For the prophet says, "And Moses was 2
fasting on Mount Sinai for forty days and forty nights, to receive
the agreement of the Lord for the people. And Moses received
from the Lord the two tablets written in the spirit by the finger of
the Lord's hand," And Moses took them, and was carrying them
down, to give them to the people. And the Lord said to Moses, 3
"Moses, Moses, go down quickly, for your people whom you have
led out of the land have broken the law." And Moses understood
that they had again cast images for themselves, and he flung
the tablets from his hands, and the tablets of the Lord's agreement were broken in pieces. Moses received it, but they them- 4
selves proved unworthy. But learn how we received it. Moses
was a servant when he received it, but the Lord himself gave
it to us, as the people entitled to the inheritance, after he had
suffered for us. And he was revealed in order that both they might 5
attain the fulness of their sins and we might receive the agreement through the Lord Jesus, the heir to it, who was prepared for
this purpose, to appear and redeem from darkness our hearts,
already destroyed by death, and given up to the iniquity of error,
and make an agreement with us by his word. For it is written how 6
the Father charged him to redeem us from darkness and prepare
a holy people for himself. So the prophet says, "I, the Lord your 7
God, have called you in uprightness, and I will grasp your hand
and strengthen you, and I have made you an agreement with

the people, a light of the heathen, to open the eyes of the blind, and to bring forth from their fetters those that are bound, and from the prison house those that sit in darkness." So we know
8 from what we have been redeemed. Again the prophet says, "Behold, I have made you a light for the heathen, to be a means of salvation to the ends of the earth, says the Lord God who has
9 redeemed you." And again the prophet says, "The spirit of the Lord is upon me, for he has consecrated me to preach the good news of his favor to the humble, he has sent me to heal the brokenhearted, to announce to prisoners their release, and to the blind the recovery of their sight, to proclaim the year of the Lord's favor and the day of recompense, to comfort all that mourn."

15   Further, then, it is written about the sabbath also in the Ten Words which God uttered to Moses face to face on Mount Sinai, "And treat the sabbath of the Lord as holy with clean
2 hands and a pure heart." And in another place he says, "If my
3 sons keep the sabbath, I will let my mercy rest upon them." He mentions the sabbath at the beginning of the creation: "And in six days God made the works of his hands, and ended on the
4 seventh day, and he rested on it and made it holy." Observe, children, what "he ended in six days" means. This is what it means, that in six thousand years the Lord will bring all things to an end, for a day with him means a thousand years. He himself bears me witness, for he says, "Behold, a day of the Lord will be like a thousand years." Therefore, children, in six days, that is, in six thousand years, all things will be brought to
5 an end. "And he rested the seventh day" means this: When his Son comes and destroys the time of the lawless one, and judges the ungodly and changes the sun and moon and stars, then he
6 will rest well on the seventh day. Further he says, "You shall treat it as holy, with clean hands and a pure heart." If, then, anyone can now, by being pure in heart, treat as holy the day God
7 declared holy, we are entirely deceived. Observe that we will

find true rest and treat it as holy only when we shall be able to do so having ourselves been made upright and had the promise fulfilled, when there is no more disobedience, but all things have been made new by the Lord. Then we shall be able to treat it as holy, after we have first been made holy ourselves. Further he says to them, "Your new moons and sabbaths I cannot 8 endure." You see what he means: it is not the present sabbaths that are acceptable to me, but the one that I have made, on which, having brought everything to rest, I will make the beginning of an eighth day, that is, the beginning of another world. This is why we also observe the eighth day with rejoicing, 9 on which Jesus also rose from the dead, and having shown himself ascended to heaven.

In addition, I will also tell you about the temple, how those 16 wretched men went astray and set their hope on a building, as being the house of God, instead of on God who made them. For they propitiated him in the temple almost like the heathen. 2 But learn how the Lord speaks, in abolishing it: "Who has measured the heaven with a span, or the earth with his hand? Have not I? says the Lord. The heaven is my throne, and the earth is my footstool! What kind of house can you build for me, or in what place can I rest?" You know that their hope was vain. Further, he says again, "Behold, those that tore down this temple 3 will build it up themselves." This is taking place. For because 4 they went to war, it was torn down by their enemies; now the very servants of their enemies will build it up again. Again, 5 it was revealed that the city and the temple and the people of Israel were to be delivered up. For the scripture says, "And it shall come to pass in the last days that the Lord will deliver up the sheep of the pasture and the sheepfold and the tower to destruction." And it took place as the Lord had said. But let us 6 inquire whether there is a temple of God. There is, where he himself said he would make it and finish it. For it is written, "And it

shall come to pass, when the week is ending, a temple of God
7 will be built in glory in the name of the Lord." I find, therefore,
that there is a temple. Learn, then, how it is to be built in the
name of the Lord. Before we believed in God, the dwelling of our
heart was perishable and weak, like a temple actually built with
hands, for it was full of idolatry and was the home of demons,
8 because we did what was opposed to God. "But it will be built
in the name of the Lord." But take heed that the temple of the
Lord may be built in glory. Learn how. When we received forgiveness of sins and set our hope on the name, we became new,
created again from the beginning, and therefore God really lives
9 in us, in the dwelling which we are. How? His word of faith,
the call of his promise, the wisdom of his decrees, the commands of his teaching, he himself prophesying within us, he himself dwelling in us, opening the temple door, that is, the mouth,
and giving us repentance, leads us, who were enslaved to death,
10 into the indestructible temple. For the man who longs to be
saved looks not at the speaker but at him who dwells in him
and speaks through him, amazed at him, and at never having
heard him utter such words with his mouth or having himself
ever wanted to hear them. This is the spiritual temple that is
being built for the Lord.

17 As far as it was possible to show them to you with simplicity,
my soul hopes that, as I have desired, I have not left out any of
2 the things that have to do with salvation. For if I write to you
about the present or the future, you will not understand because
they are put in figures.

18 So much for that. Now let us pass to another lesson and teaching. There are two ways of teaching and power, that of light
and that of darkness, and there is a great difference between
the two ways. For on one are stationed light-giving angels of
2 God, but on the other angels of Satan. And the one is Lord from
eternity to eternity, while the other is ruler of the present time
of iniquity.

This then is the way of light, if anyone wishing to make his **19**
way to his appointed place will be zealous in all his works. The
knowledge, then, that is given us so that we may walk in it is as
follows: You shall love your Maker, you shall fear your Creator, **2**
you shall glorify him who redeemed you from death; you shall
be simple in heart and rich in spirit. You shall not join those who
walk in the way of death. You shall hate everything that is not
pleasing to God, you shall hate all hypocrisy. You must not forsake the commands of the Lord. You shall not exalt yourself, **3**
but shall be humble-minded in all things. You shall not take
glory to yourself. You shall not form an evil design against your
neighbor, you shall not admit arrogance to your soul. You shall **4**
not commit fornication, you shall not commit adultery, you shall
not corrupt boys. The word of God shall not go forth from you
among the impure. You shall not show favoritism in rebuking
anyone for transgression. You shall be meek, you shall be quiet,
you shall stand in awe of the words that you have heard. You
shall not hold a grudge against your brother. You must not doubt **5**
whether a thing shall be or not. "You must not take the name of
the Lord in vain." You shall love your neighbor more than your
life. You shall not murder a child by abortion, or kill it when it
is born. You must not withhold your hand from your son or from
your daughter, but from their youth you shall teach them the fear
of God. You must not desire your neighbor's goods, you must **6**
not be covetous. You shall not join heartily with haughty people,
but shall associate with humble and upright men. You shall accept
the experiences that befall you as good, knowing that nothing
happens without God. You shall not be double-minded or double- **7**
tongued, for the double tongue is a deadly snare. You shall obey
your masters with modesty and fear, as a symbol of God. You
must not give orders in bitterness to your man or woman slave
who hopes in the same God, lest they cease to fear the God who
is over you both, for he came not to call men with partiality, but
those whom the spirit had prepared. You shall share everything **8**

with your neighbor, and shall not call things your own. For if you share what is imperishable, how much more the things that are perishable? You shall not be quick to speak, for the mouth is a deadly snare. As far as you can, you shall be pure for your

9 soul's sake. Do not be stretching out your hands to take, and closing them when it comes to giving. You shall love as the apple of your eye everyone who speaks the word of the Lord to you.

10 Night and day you shall remember the Day of Judgment, and every day you shall seek the company of the saints, either laboring by word of mouth, and going out to exhort, and busying yourself in saving souls by the word, or you shall work with

11 your hands for the ransom of your sins. You shall not hesitate to give, nor grumble when you give, but you shall know who is the good payer of wages. You shall keep the teachings you have received, neither adding to them nor taking from them. You

12 shall absolutely hate evil. You shall judge uprightly. You shall not cause division, but shall bring fighters together and reconcile them. You shall confess your sins. You shall not approach prayer with an evil conscience. This is the way of light.

20 But the way of the Black One is crooked and full of cursing. For it is a way of eternal death and punishment, and in it are the things that destroy men's souls—idolatry, arrogance, the exaltation of power, hypocrisy, duplicity, adultery, murder, robbery, pride, transgression, fraud, malice, willfulness, enchantment,

2 magic, covetousness, disregard of God; persecutors of good men, hating truth, loving falsehood, ignorant of the wages of uprightness, not adhering to what is good nor to upright judgment, paying no heed to the widow and orphan, lying awake not in the fear of God, but for what is evil, from whom gentleness and patience are far, far away, loving vanity, seeking reward, without pity for the poor, not toiling for the oppressed, ready with slander, ignoring their Maker, murderers of children, corrupters of God's creatures, turning away the needy, oppressing the afflicted, advocates of the rich, unjust judges of the poor, utterly sinful.

It is well, therefore, after learning the ordinances of the Lord **21** above written to live by them. For the man who does so will be glorified in the kingdom of God; the one that chooses their opposites will perish with his works. This is the reason for resurrection, this is the reason for recompense. I entreat those who are **2** in high position, if you will accept my well-meant advice, you have among you those whom you can benefit: do not fail them. The day is near when all things will perish with the Evil One. **3** The Lord is at hand, with his reward. Again and again I entreat **4** you; be good lawgivers to one another, remain faithful counselors of one another, put away from you all hypocrisy. May God, who **5** rules over the whole world, give you wisdom, intelligence, understanding, knowledge of his ordinances, and endurance. Be taught **6** of God, seeking to find what the Lord asks of you, and do it, so that you may be found on the day of judgment. And if there is **7** any remembrance of what is good, remember me as you meditate on these things, so that my desire and vigilance may lead to some good; I ask it of you as a favor. While you are still in this **8** fair vessel, do not fall short of any of them, but earnestly seek these things, and fulfill every command, for they deserve it. This **9** is why I have been the more eager to write to you as well as I could, to cheer you. Win salvation, children of love and peace. The Lord of glory and all grace be with your spirits.

The First Letter of Clement

TO THE CORINTHIANS

The earliest Christian document that has come down to us outside the New Testament is the letter written in the name of the church at Rome to the church at Corinth, probably about A.D. 95. The Corinthian church, which had from the beginning made so much of spiritual gifts and endowments, was showing marked hostility to the office of elder or presbyter in the church, and the Roman church, probably stirred by the charge made in Hebrews 5:12 that it was remiss in not teaching the other churches, undertook to correct this attitude. This explains the strangely awkward apology for not having written them before on the subject, with which I Clement begins. The Roman church was at the same time addressing what we know as I Peter to the churches of Asia Minor, doubtless in response to the same sense of responsibility awakened by Hebrews.

It was a decade of extraordinary literary activity on the part of the new religion.. The publication of Luke-Acts, a sketch of the beginnings of Christianity, in two volumes, had been followed by the publication of the collected letters of Paul, the Revelation of John, and, to offset its bitter attitude toward the empire and the emperor, I Peter. And at about the same time that the Roman church was seeking through that letter to save the churches of Asia Minor from the danger of hating their enemies, it sought with I Clement to correct what it considered the rebellious attitude of the Corinthians toward their church officers.

It does not name its writer, but from ancient times the letter has been ascribed to Clement, who was bishop of Rome from A.D. 88 to 97, and no serious objection to this authorship can be raised. The free use of the principal letters of Paul, the writer's familiarity with Hebrews, and the marked kinship of the letter with I Peter strongly favor a date about A.D. 95, and the writer's nonacquaintance with the fourfold gospel accords well with this date. Clement is spoken of by Hermas, about A.D. 100, as in charge of communications with the churches of other cities, Visions ii.4.3, which sounds like a reminiscence of the service of this kind he had performed in I Clement.

I Clement is a good example of the letter form of Christian instruction that had been standardized by the recent collection and publication of the Pauline letters, perhaps about A.D. 93. The writer condemns the Corinthians' insubordination, and urges them to follow the great Old Testament examples, showing great familiarity with the Greek version of the Old Testament. He points out the humility of Christ and the order that prevails in the world of nature, and counsels love, forgiveness, humility, and reconciliation.

I Clement has come down to us in Greek near the close of the Codex Alexandrinus, of the fifth century, and in the eleventh-century manuscript found by Bryennius in 1873. Syriac, Latin, and Coptic versions of it have also come to light.

The First Letter of Clement
TO THE CORINTHIANS

The church of God that is staying in Rome to the church of God that is staying in Corinth, to those who are called and consecrated by the will of God through our Lord Jesus Christ: may God Almighty bless you and give you peace abundantly through Jesus Christ.

Because of the sudden and repeated misfortunes and calamities that have befallen us, we think we have been very slow in giving attention to the matters that are being discussed among you and to the foul and impious uprising, so alien and foreign to God's chosen people, which a few headstrong and willful men have kindled to such a frenzy that your good name, respected and renowned and universally beloved, has come to be greatly reviled. For who that ever visited you did not approve the virtue and steadfastness of your faith? Who did not admire the seriousness and Christian gentleness of your piety? Who did not proclaim your magnificent disposition toward hospitality? Who did not congratulate you on your full, sound knowledge? You did everything without partiality, and lived in accordance with the laws of God, obeying your leaders and paying the older men among you the respect due them. Young people you instructed to think modestly and properly, and women you charged to do everything with a blameless, devout, and pure conscience, showing their husbands rightful affection; and you taught them to respect their sphere of subjection and to keep house with dignity and good sense.

2   You were all humble-minded and not at all arrogant, subordinating yourselves instead of subordinating others, giving more gladly than receiving. You were satisfied with what Christ supplies, and heeding his words you laid them up carefully in your **2** hearts and kept his sufferings before your eyes. So a deep, rich peace was granted to all of you, and an insatiable desire to do good, and the holy Spirit was poured out in abundance upon you **3** all. You were full of holy designs, and with pious confidence, in eager goodness you stretched out your hands to Almighty God, beseeching him to have mercy if you had involuntarily com- **4** mitted a sin. Day and night you engaged in a conflict for all the brotherhood, that through mercy and conscience the num- **5** ber of his chosen might be saved. You were sincere and without **6** guile, with no malice to one another. Any uprising or division was abominated by you. You mourned over the transgressions of your neighbors; you considered their shortcomings to be your **7** own. You had no regrets for any act of kindness, you were ready **8** for any good work. Adorned by your virtuous and august manner of life, you did everything in fear of him; the commands and decrees of the Lord were written on the tablets of your hearts.

3   All glory and expansion were given you, and the scripture was fulfilled: "My Beloved ate and drank, and he expanded and grew **2** fat and began to kick." So arose jealousy and envy, strife and **3** uprising, persecution and confusion, war and captivity. So the worthless were stirred up against the reputable, those of no repute against those of good repute, the foolish against the sensible, the **4** young against their elders. For this reason uprightness and peace are far off, while each one abandons the fear of God and faith in him grows dim, and men do not walk in the rules of his commandments or live as befits Christ, but each follows the desires of his wicked heart, adopting that unrighteous and ungodly jealousy through which death came into the world.

For thus it is written: "And it came to pass in the course of **4**
time that Cain brought some produce of the soil as an offering to
God, and Abel also brought some of the first born of his sheep
and some fat pieces of them. And God noticed Abel and his gifts, **2**
but he took no notice of Cain and his offerings. And Cain was **3**
very much hurt and downcast. And God said to Cain, 'Why are **4**
you hurt, and why are you downcast? If you offer rightly, but
do not decide rightly, do you not sin? Be silent. He shall turn **5**
to you, and you shall rule him.'

"And Cain said to his brother Abel, 'Let us go off into the coun- **6**
try.' And it came to pass while they were in the country, that
Cain attacked his brother Abel, and killed him." You see, **7**
brethren, jealousy and envy brought about a brother's murder.
Because of jealousy our father Jacob ran away from the presence **8**
of his brother Esau. Jealousy caused Joseph to be persecuted even **9**
to death and be reduced to slavery. Jealousy forced Moses to flee **10**
from the presence of Pharaoh, king of Egypt, when his own
countryman said to him, "Who made you a ruler or judge over
us? Do you mean to kill me, as you killed that Egyptian yester-
day?" Because of jealousy Aaron and Miriam were made to lodge **11**
outside the camp. Jealousy carried Dathan and Abiram alive **12**
down to Hades, because they made an uprising against God's
servant Moses. Because of jealousy David was envied not only **13**
by the Philistines but was persecuted even by Saul, king of
Israel.

But to pass from ancient examples, let us come to those who **5**
have most recently proved champions; let us take up the noble
examples of our own generation. Because of jealousy and envy **2**
the greatest and most upright pillars of the church were persecuted and competed unto death. Let us bring before our eyes **3**
the good apostles!—Peter, who because of unrighteous jealousy **4**
endured not one or two, but numerous trials, and so bore a
martyr's witness and went to the glorious place that he deserved.
Because of jealousy and strife Paul pointed the way to the **5**
reward of endurance; seven times he was imprisoned, he was **6**

exiled, he was stoned, he was a preacher in both east and west,
and won great renown for his faith, teaching uprightness to the
7 whole world, and reaching the farthest limit of the west, and
bearing a martyr's witness before the rulers he passed out of the
world and was taken up into the holy place, having proved a very
great example of endurance.

6 With these men who had lived holy lives has been gathered a
great multitude of God's chosen, who have set a splendid example among us in enduring many humiliations and tortures on
2 account of jealousy. On account of jealousy women have been
persecuted and made to endure dreadful and unholy insults, as
Danaids and Dirces, and reached the sure goal in the race of
faith and won the true prize, weak in body though they were.
3 Jealousy has estranged wives from their husbands, and nullified
the words of our forefather Adam, "This now is bone of my bones,
4 and flesh of my flesh." Jealousy and strife have overthrown great
cities and uprooted great nations.

7 We write this, dear friends, not only to warn you, but also to
remind ourselves, for we are in the same arena, and the same con-
2 test is before us. Therefore let us give up idle, vain considera-
tions, and let us turn to the renowned and solemn standard that
3 has come down to us, and see what is good and pleasant and
4 acceptable in the sight of our Maker. Let us fix our eyes on the
blood of Christ and learn how precious it is to his Father, because
it was shed for our salvation, and brought the blessing of repent-
5 ance to the whole world. Let us survey all the generations and
learn that in generation after generation the Master has offered
6 those who wished to turn to him an opportunity to repent. Noah
7 preached repentance and those who obeyed were saved. Jonah
warned the men of Nineveh of destruction, but they repented
of their sins and besought God and were forgiven and saved,
although they were aliens from God.

8 The ministers of the favor of God through the holy Spirit
2 told about repentance, and the Master of all things himself spoke

of repentance with an oath: "For as I live, said the Lord, I do not desire the sinner's death so much as his repentance," and he added a blessed thought, "Repent of your iniquity, house of 3 Israel. Say to the sons of my people, If your sins reach from earth to heaven, and if they are redder than scarlet and blacker than sackcloth, and you turn to me with all your hearts, and say 'Father!' I will listen to you as a holy people." And in another 4 place he speaks thus: "Wash yourselves and be made clean, put away the wickedness from your souls before my eyes. Cease from your wickedness, learn to do right, seek justice, deliver the oppressed, uphold the rights of the orphan, and do justice to the widow; and come, let us reason together, says the Lord; though your sins are like crimson, I will make them white as snow; though they are like scarlet, I will make them white as wool. And if you are willing, and listen to me, you will eat the good of the land, but if you are not willing and do not listen to me, the sword will devour you, for the mouth of the Lord has said this." So wishing to give all his beloved a share in 5 repentance, he has established it by his omnipotent decree.

Let us therefore obey his magnificent and glorious desire and 9 as suppliants of his mercy and goodness let us fall before him, and return to his compassion, forsaking labor that is in vain and strife and jealousy that lead to death. Let us look closely at those 2 who have perfectly served his sublime glory. Let us take Enoch, 3 who was found upright in obedience and was taken up, and did not experience death. Noah was found faithful and through his 4 service proclaimed rebirth to the world, and through him the Master saved the animals who entered in harmony into the ark.

Abraham, who was called "the friend," proved faithful when 10 he obeyed the commands of God. He went forth obediently from 2 his country and his kindred and his father's house, to leave a little country and a weak clan and a small household, and inherit what God promised. For he said to him, "Leave your country 3 and your kindred and your father's house for the land that I will

show you, and I will make you a great nation, and I will bless
you and make your name great, and you will be blessed. I will
bless those who bless you and curse those who curse you, and
4 all the families of the earth will be blest through you." And
again when he parted from Lot God said to him, "Raise your eyes
and look from the place where you now are north, south, east
and west, for all the land that you see I will give to you and
5 your descendants forever. And I will make your descendants like
the dust of the earth; if a man can count the dust of the earth,
6 your descendants can be counted." And again it says, "God
brought Abraham out and said to him, 'Look up at the heavens
and count the stars, if you can count them; so shall your
descendants be.' And Abraham had faith in God, and it was
7 credited to him as uprightness." Because of his faith and his
hospitality a son was given him in his old age, and in his
obedience he offered him in sacrifice to God on one of the
mountains he had shown him.

11 Because of his hospitality and piety Lot was saved from Sodom,
when all the country round was judged with fire and brimstone,
when the Master made it clear that he does not forsake those
that hope in him, but those that turn aside he consigns to pun-
2 ishment and torment. For when his wife, who had gone out with
him, changed her mind and disagreed with him, she was made a
symbol of this, and became a pillar of salt unto this day, to make
known to all that those who are dubious and doubtful about
the power of God are condemned and become a warning for all
generations.

12 Because of her faith and hospitality Rahab the harlot was
2 saved. For when the scouts were sent out to Jericho by Joshua
the son of Nun, the king of that country found out that they
had come to spy out their land, and he sent men to arrest them,
3 so that they might be taken and put to death. So the hospitable
Rahab took them in and hid them in the upstairs room under
4 the stalks of flax. And when the king's men came and said, "The

men who are spying out our land went in to your house; bring
them out, for those are the king's orders," she answered, "The
men you are looking for came to my house, but they went away
immediately and are going on their way," and pointed in the
wrong direction. Then she said to the men, "I am convinced that ⁵
the Lord God is going to give you this country, for the fear
and terror of you have fallen upon its inhabitants. So when it
comes about that you take it, you must save me and my father's
household." And they said to her, "It shall be done, just as you ⁶
have told us. So when you learn that we are coming, you must
gather all your people under your roof, and they will be saved;
for all that are found outside the house will perish." They also ⁷
gave her a signal, that she should hang a piece of scarlet from
her house, thus showing that all who believed and set their hope
on God should have redemption through the blood of the Lord.
You see, dear friends, that there was not only faith but prophecy
in this woman.

So let us be humble-minded, brethren, and put aside all pre- 13
tensions and conceit and folly and anger, and let us do what the
scripture says. For the holy Spirit says, "The wise man must not
boast of his wisdom, nor the strong man of his strength, nor the
rich man of his riches, but the man who boasts must boast of
the Lord, to seek him out and do justice and uprightness.
Especially remember the words of the Lord Jesus that he uttered
when he was teaching gentleness and patience. For this is what ²
he said: "Show mercy, that you may be shown mercy. Forgive,
that you may be forgiven. As you do, so it will be done to you;
as you give, so it will be given to you; as you judge, so you will
be judged; as you are kind, so kindness will be shown to you.
The measure you use will be used in measuring to you." With ³
this command and these orders let us strengthen one another
that we may live in obedience to his hallowed words, in humble-
mindedness. For the holy word says, "On whom shall I look but ⁴
on him that is humble and gentle and trembles at my words?"

14   It is right and proper then, brethren, for us to be obedient
to God rather than to follow those who in arrogance and disorder
2 are the instigators of detestable jealousy. For we shall incur no
ordinary injury but great danger if we recklessly surrender
ourselves to the purposes of these men who plunge into strife
3 and discord, to alienate us from what is right. Let us show
kindness to one another with the compassion and sweetness of
4 our Creator. For it is written, "The kind will be the inhabitants
of the land, and the innocent will be left upon it, but those who
5 transgress will be destroyed from upon it." And again it says, "I
saw the ungodly triumphing and towering aloft like the cedars of
Lebanon; but I went by and behold, he was not, and I looked
for his place, and could not find it. Keep watch of innocence, and
look at uprightness, for there is a posterity for the peaceable
man."

15   Let us therefore cling to those who keep the peace in piety, not
2 those who hypocritically wish for peace. For it says somewhere,
"This people honors me with the lips, but their heart is far from
3 me." And again, "They blessed with their mouth, but cursed
4 in their heart." And again it says, "They loved him with their
mouth, and with their tongue they lied to him, but their heart
was not straightforward with him, nor were they faithful to his
5 covenant." Therefore, "Let the deceitful lips be dumb that talk
of lawlessness against the upright," and again, "May the Lord
destroy all deceitful lips, the boastful tongue, men that say 'We
will magnify our tongue, our lips are with us: who is lord over
6 us?' For the wretchedness of the poor and the groaning of the
7 needy I will now arise, says the Lord, I will place him in safety,
I will deal boldly by him."

16   For Christ belongs to the humble-minded, not to those who
2 exalt themselves over the flock. The scepter of the majesty of
God, the Lord Jesus Christ did not come with the boast of
arrogance or pride, though he was able to do so, but in humble-
3 ness of mind, as the holy Spirit said of him, for it says, "Lord,

who has believed what we heard, and to whom has the arm of the Lord been revealed? We proclaimed him before the Lord as a child, as a root in dry ground. He has no comeliness or glory, and we saw him and he had no comeliness or beauty, but his appearance was insignificant, inferior to the beauty of men, a man of stripes and toil, who knew how to endure pain. For his face was turned away, he was dishonored and discountenanced. It was he that bore our sins and endured pain for us, and we **4** considered him as one in trouble, stripes, and affliction. But he **5** was wounded for our sins, and made to suffer for our iniquities. The chastisement of our peace was put upon him; through his stripes we were healed. We had all gone astray like sheep; each **6** one had gone astray by his own path; and the Lord gave him up **7** for our sins. And he did not open his mouth because of his ill-treatment. Like a sheep he was led away to be slaughtered, and as a lamb is dumb before its shearer, he did not open his mouth. His sentence ended in his humiliation. Who will tell the **8** story of his posterity? For his life is perished from the earth. **9** Because of the iniquities of my people he has gone to his death. And I will offer the wicked for his burial and the rich for his **10** death, for he did no iniquity, and no deceit was found in his mouth. And it is the Lord's will to cleanse him of his stripes. If **11** you make an offering for sin your soul shall see a long-lived posterity. And it is the Lord's will to take from the toil of his **12** soul, to show him light, and shape him with intelligence, to make upright an upright man who serves many well, and he himself will bear their sins. Therefore he will be the heir of **13** many, and share the spoils of the strong, because his life was given up to death and he was counted among the lawless. He **14** bore the sins of many, and because of their sins he was given up."

And again he says himself, "I am a worm and not a man, a **15** shame to mankind, and despised by the people. All who see me **16** mock me; they make mouths, they shake their heads: 'He hopes in the Lord! Let him deliver him; let him save him, since he is pleased with him!' "

17 You see, dear friends, what the example is that has been given us. For if the Lord was so humbled-minded, what are we to do who through him have come under the yoke of his favor?

17 Let us also be imitators of those who went about in the skins of goats and sheep, preaching the coming of Christ; I mean Elijah and Elisha, and Ezekiel too, the prophets, and besides 2 them the famous men. Abraham was far-famed, and called a friend of God, yet when he beheld the glory of God he said humbly, "I am but dust and ashes."

3 Of Job also it is written, "Now Job was upright and blameless, 4 true, godly, keeping himself from all evil." Why, he accuses himself, for he says, "No one is free from defilement, if he lives only a day."

5 Moses was called faithful in all God's house, and through his service God judged Egypt by the plagues and torments inflicted on them. But though he was so greatly glorified he did not boast, but when the oracle was given to him from the bush, he said, "Who am I, that you send me? I am weak-voiced and slow 6 of speech." And again he says, "I am but smoke from the pot."

18 And what are we to say of the famous David, of whom God said, "I have found a man after my own heart in David, the son 2 of Jesse; I have anointed him with eternal mercy." But he himself says to God, "Have mercy on me, O God, in your great mercy, and in the abundance of your compassion, wipe out my transgres-3 sion. Wash me thoroughly from my iniquity and cleanse me of my sin, for I know my iniquity and my sin is always before me. 4 Against you only have I sinned, and I have done what was evil in your sight, that you may be in the right when you speak and 5 prevail when you give judgment. For I was conceived in iniquity, 6 and my mother bore me in sin. For behold, you love truth; the secret and hidden matters of your wisdom you make known 7 to me. You shall sprinkle me with hyssop, and I will be cleansed;

you shall wash me, and I will be whiter than snow. You shall 8
make me hear joy and gladness; my humbled bones will rejoice.
Turn your face from my sins, and wipe out all my iniquities. 9
Create a clean heart in me, O God, and renew a right spirit 10
within me. Do not cast me out of your presence, and do not take 11
your holy Spirit from me. Give me back the gladness of your 12
salvation, and sustain me with your guiding spirit. I will teach 13
the lawless your ways, and ungodly men will return to you. Save 14
me from bloodguiltiness, O God, the God of my deliverance. My 15
tongue will rejoice in your uprightness. Lord, you shall open my
mouth, and my lips will declare your praise. For if you had 16
desired sacrifice, I would have given it; you will take no pleasure
in burnt offerings. The sacrifice for God is a broken spirit; a 17
broken and humbled heart God will not despise."

The humility and submission of so many men of such fame 19
have through their obedience made not only us but the generations before us better, as well as all who have received his
oracles in fear and truth. So since we have had a share in many 2
great and glorious deeds, let us run toward the goal of peace that
was given us from the beginning, and let us fix our eyes on the
Father and Creator of the whole world and cling to his splendid
and surpassing gifts of peace and benefits. Let us see him with 3
our mind and look with the eyes of the soul at his patient purpose. Let us consider how free from anger he is toward all his
creation.

The heavens are moved by his management and obey him in 20
peace. Day and night pursue the course fixed by him without 2
hindering each other. The sun and the moon and the troops 3
of stars roll harmoniously on their appointed courses under his
direction, without any divergence from them. By his will the 4
earth becomes fruitful and at the proper seasons produces ample
food for man and beast and all the living creatures on it, without
disagreement or changing any of his decisions. The unfathom- 5
able depths of the abysses and the indescribable verdicts of the

6 underworld are held together by the same decrees. The basin of the boundless sea was gathered by his creative action into its bodies and does not go beyond the barriers surrounding it but 7 does as he commanded it. For he said, "This far you shall come 8 and no farther, and your waves will break within you." The ocean, impassable to man, and the worlds beyond it are reg- 9 ulated by the same orders from the Master. The spring, sum- mer, autumn, and winter seasons peacefully succeed one another. 10 The winds from their respective quarters inoffensively perform their service at the proper times. Perennial springs, created for enjoyment and health, unfailingly offer their life-giving breasts to man, and the smallest of animals get together in harmony 11 and peace. All these things the great Creator and Master of the universe ordered to be in peace and harmony, in his kindness to all things and especially to us who have taken refuge in 12 his mercy through our Lord Jesus Christ, to whom be glory and majesty forever and ever. Amen.

21 Take care, dear friends, that his many benefits do not bring condemnation upon us, if we do not live worthily of him, and harmoniously do what is good and well-pleasing in his sight. 2 For it says somewhere, "The spirit of the Lord is a lamp that 3 searches the storerooms of the heart." Let us observe how near he is, and that none of our thoughts or of the reflections in which 4 we indulge escapes him. It is right therefore that we should 5 not be deserters from what he wills. Let us give offense to foolish and thoughtless men who exalt themselves and glory in 6 the arrogance of their speech, rather than to God. Let us revere the Lord Jesus Christ, whose blood was given for us, let us respect our rulers, let us honor our elders, let us train the young 7 in the fear of God, let us guide our wives to what is good. Let them exhibit the lovable quality of purity, let them display their sincere gentleness of disposition, let them show the forbearance of their tongues by their silence, let them bestow their affection not with partiality but in holiness upon all alike who fear God.

Let our children share in Christian instruction, let them learn 8
what power humility has with God, what pure love can do with
God, how good and great his fear is, and how it saves those who
live in it in holiness with a pure mind. For he is the searcher 9
of thoughts and desires; his breath is in us, and when he pleases
he will take it away.

Faith in Christ confirms all this, for he himself through the 22
holy Spirit invites us thus: "Come, children, listen to me, I will
teach you to revere the Lord. What man is there that desires life, 2
and loves to see good days? Keep your tongue from evil and your 3
lips from uttering deceit. Turn from evil, and do what is good. 4
Seek peace and pursue it. The Lord's eyes are on the upright, 5,6
and his ears are open to their appeal. The Lord's face is against
those that do evil, to destroy the memory of them from the earth.
The upright cries out, and the Lord hears him, and delivers him 7
from all his troubles. The scourgings of the sinner are many, but 8
mercy will surround those who hope in the Lord."

The all-merciful and beneficent Father has pity on those who 23
fear him, and kindly and lovingly confers his favors on those
who approach him with a sincere mind. Therefore let us not 2
waver, nor let our souls indulge in fancies over his surpassing
and glorious gifts. Far be that scripture from us where it says, 3
"How wretched are those who waver, who are of a doubting
heart, and say, 'We heard those things even in our forefather's
time, and here we have grown old, and none of them has happened to us.' You senseless people! Compare yourselves to a 4
tree; take a vine. First it sheds its leaves, then a shoot appears,
then a leaf, then a flower, and afterward a sour grape, then a
ripe grape." You see that in a short time the fruit of the tree
comes to maturity. In very truth his will will be quickly 5
and suddenly accomplished as the scripture also bears witness;
"He will come quickly and not delay, and the Lord will come
suddenly to his temple, and the Holy One for whom you look."

Let us consider, dear friends, how the Master is continually 24

proving to us that there is to be a resurrection, of which he
made the Lord Jesus Christ the first fruits when he raised him
2 from the dead. Let us observe, dear friends, the resurrection
3 that is regularly taking place. Day and night show us a resurrection; night falls asleep, day arises! day departs, night comes on.
4 Let us take the crops; how and in what way does the sowing
5 take place? The sower goes out and sows each seed in the
ground. They fall into the ground dry and bare, and decay;
then from their decay the greatness of the Master's providence
raises them up, and from a single grain many spring up and bear
fruit.

25   Let us observe the marvelous symbol that takes place in the
2 east, that is, in the region of Arabia. For there is a bird that
is called a phoenix. It is the only one of its kind, and lives five
hundred years. And when it approaches its time to depart and
die, it makes itself a nest of frankincense and myrrh and other
3 spices, and when the time has come it gets into it and dies. As its
flesh decays a kind of worm comes into being, which feeds upon
the moisture of the dead creature and becomes full-fledged. Then
when it is full grown it takes up the nest containing the bones
of its parent and succeeds in carrying them from the country
of Arabia all the way to Egypt, to the city called Heliopolis,
4 and in broad daylight, in the sight of all, it lights upon the altar
of the Sun and deposits them there and then starts back again.
5 So the priests consult their records of dates, and find that it has
come at the conclusion of the five hundredth year.

26   Do we, then, regard it as a great and marvelous thing for the
Creator of all things to bring about the resurrection of those
who have served him with holiness in the assurance of a good
faith, when even by a bird he shows us the greatness of his
2 promise? For it says somewhere, "And you will raise me up and
I will praise you," and "I lie down and sleep; I awake, for you
are with me." And again Job says, "And you will raise up this
flesh of mine, which has endured all these things."

With this hope, then, let our souls be bound to him that is **27**
faithful to his promises and upright in his judgments. He who **2**
has commanded us not to lie will much more not lie himself.
For nothing is impossible for God except lying. So let faith **3**
in him be rekindled in us, and let us consider that all things
are near him. With his majestic word he constituted all things, **4**
and with a word he can overturn them. Who can say to him, **5**
"What have you done?" or who can withstand the strength of
his might? When he pleases and as he pleases he will do every- **6**
thing, and none of the things he has decreed will pass away. All
things are in his sight, and nothing has escaped his will, since **7**
"the heavens are telling the glory of God, and the sky proclaims
the work of his hands. Day pours forth speech to day, and night
announces knowledge to night. There are no words, nor is there
any speech; their voices are not heard."

Since, then, all things are seen and heard, let us revere him, **28**
and give up low acts of foul desire, that we may be shielded by
his mercy from the judgments that are to come. For where **2**
can any of us fly from his mighty hand? And what world can
receive one who deserts from him? For the scripture somewhere
says, "Where shall I go and where shall I hide from your face? **3**
If I go up to heaven, you are there; if I go off to the ends of
the earth, there is your right hand. If I make my bed in the
abyss, there is your spirit." Where, then, can a man go or where **4**
can he escape from him who embraces all things?

Let us, then, approach him with holiness of spirit, lifting up **29**
to him hands that are pure and undefiled, loving our forbearing
and merciful Father who has made us his chosen portion. For **2**
thus it is written: "When the Most High divided the nations,
when he scattered the descendants of Adam, he fixed the boundaries of the nations in accordance with the number of the angels
of God. His people Jacob became the Lord's portion; Israel was
the allotment that fell to him." And in another place it says, **3**
"Behold the Lord takes from among the nations a nation for

himself, as a man takes the first fruits of his threshing floor, and out of that nation what is most holy will come."

30   So since we are a holy portion let us do all the things that belong to holiness, fleeing from evil-speaking, vile impure embraces, drunkenness and innovations and detestable desires,
2 wretched adultery and detestable pride. "For God," it says, "opposes haughty persons, but he favors humble-minded ones."
3 So let us join those to whom favor is given by God. Let us clothe ourselves with harmony, in humility and self-control, keeping ourselves far from all gossip and slander, and be justified by
4 deeds, not by words. For it says, "He who says much will hear
5 much in reply; or does the babbler think he is upright? Blessed is he that is born of woman and is short-lived. Be not profuse
6 in speech." Let our praise be with God and not from ourselves;
7 for God hates those who praise themselves. Let the testimony to our good deeds be given by others, as it was given to our
8 upright forefathers. Boldness and arrogance and audacity belong to those who are cursed by God, gentleness and humility and meekness are with those who are blessed by God.

31   Let us, then, cling to his blessing, and let us see what the ways to blessing are. Let us unroll the things that happened from
2 the beginning. Why was our forefather Abraham blest? Was it not because he attained uprightness and truth through faith?
3 With confidence Isaac knowing what would happen gladly let
4 himself be led to sacrifice. Jacob with humility withdrew from his country because of his brother, and went to Laban and served him, and the twelve scepters of the tribes of Israel were given him.

32   If one consider this sincerely in detail, he will recognize the
2 greatness of the gifts God has given. For from Jacob come all the priests and Levites that serve the altar of God. From him physically the Lord Jesus came. From him came kings and rulers and leaders in the line of Judah. And his other scepters enjoy no little glory, for God promised "Your posterity will be like

the stars of the sky." So they were all glorified and magnified 3
not through themselves or their deeds nor through the uprightness of their doings, but through his will. So we too, who by his 4
will have been called in Christ Jesus are made upright not
through ourselves or through our wisdom or understanding or
piety or deeds we have done in holiness of heart, but through
faith, by which Almighty God has made all men upright from
the beginning; to him be glory forever and ever. Amen.

What are we to do then, brethren? Are we idly to refrain 33
from doing good and forsake love? May the Master never allow
that to happen to us at least, but let us hasten earnestly and
eagerly to perform every good deed. For the Creator and Master 2
of all things himself rejoices in his works. For by his supreme 3
might he established the heavens and by his incomprehensible
understanding he organized them. He separated the earth from
the surrounding water, and established it upon the sure foundation of his own will, and the animals that roam over it he called
into being by his own command. The sea and the creatures in it
he prepared and shut in by his own power. Finally, with his 4
sacred and faultless hands he formed man, his pre-eminent and
greatest work, the impress of his own image. For thus God 5
spoke: "Let us make man in our image and likeness. And God
made man, male and female he made them." Then when he had 6
finished all these things, he praised them and blessed them and
said, "Increase and multiply." Let us observe that all the up- 7
right have been adorned with good deeds, and the Lord himself
when he had adorned himself with good works rejoiced. So hav- 8
ing this pattern let us accede to his will without delay, let us
do the work of uprightness with all our might.

The good workman boldly accepts the bread he has earned; 34
the lazy and careless one cannot look his employer in the face.
So we must be eager to do right, for all things come from him. 2
For he warns us, "Here comes the Lord, with his reward before 3
his face, to pay every man according to his work." So he urges 4

us to believe in him with all our hearts, and not to be idle or
5 careless about any good work. Let our glorying and our confidence be in him. Let us be obedient to his will. Let us consider how the whole multitude of his angels stand by and serve
6 his will. For the scripture says, "Ten thousand times ten thousand
stood by him, and thousands of times ten thousand served him,
and they cried, 'Holy, holy, holy is the Lord of hosts, all
7 creation is full of his glory.'" Let us too, therefore, gathered together in conscious harmony, cry to him earnestly as with one
8 voice that we may share his great and glorious promises. For it
says, "No eye has seen and no ear heard, nor has the human
mind imagined the things that God has provided for those that
wait for him."

35   How blessed and wonderful the gifts of God are, dear friends!
2 Life in immortality, splendor in uprightness, truth with boldness,
faith with confidence, self-control with sanctification, all these
3 things are within our understanding. Then what are the things
that are being provided for those that wait for him? The Creator
and Father of the ages, the Most Holy One himself knows their
4 number and beauty. Let us therefore strive to be found in the
number of those that wait for him, so that we may share in the
5 gifts he has promised. But how shall this be, dear friends?
If our mind is fixed believingly on God, if we seek what is pleasing and acceptable to him, if we perform acts that are in harmony
with his blameless will, and follow the way of truth, casting from
us all iniquity and wickedness, covetousness, quarreling, ill-nature
and deceit, gossip, slander, hatred of God, overbearingness and
6 boastfulness, vain glory and inhospitality. For those that do these
things are hateful to God, and not only those that do them, but
7 those that applaud them. For the scripture says, "But to the
sinner God says, 'Why do you recount my statutes and take my
8 covenant upon your lips? Yet you hate instruction, and cast my
words behind you! If you saw a thief, you ran off with him, and
you cast your lot with adulterers. Your mouth increased evil,

and your tongue wove deceit. You sat and spoke evil of your brother, and you slandered your mother's son. You did these 9 things, and I kept silent; you thought, sinful man, that I would be like you! I will rebuke you and set you before yourself.' So 10, 11 consider these things, you who forget God, that he may not seize you like a lion, and there be no one to save you! The sacrifice 12 of praise will glorify me, and there is a way by which I will show him God's deliverance."

This is the way, dear friends, by which we find our salvation, 36 Jesus Christ, the high priest of our offerings, the protector and helper of our weakness. Through him we fix our eyes on the 2 heights of heaven. In him we see mirrored God's faultless and sublime face; through him the eyes of our mind have been opened, through him our foolish, darkened understanding springs up to the light; through him the Master has willed that we should taste immortal knowledge. He, being the reflection of God's majesty, is as much greater than angels as his title is superior to theirs. "For thus it is written, 'He who makes his angels winds, 3 and his attendants a flame of fire.'" But of his Son, the Master 4 spoke thus, "You are my Son! I have today become your Father. Ask me, and I will give you the heathen for your inheritance, and the ends of the earth for your possession." And again he says 5 to him, "Sit at my right hand, until I make your enemies your footstool!" Who, then, are his enemies? Those who are bad and 6 oppose his will.

Let us therefore, brethren, campaign most strenuously under 37 his faultless orders. Let us observe those who campaign under 2 our rulers,—with what discipline, subordination, and obedience they execute their orders. They are not all generals or colonels 3 or captains or lieutenants, and so forth, but each one in his own rank carries out the orders given by the emperor and the rulers. The great cannot exist without the small, nor the small without 4 the great. There is a kind of blending among all, and there is an advantage in that. Let us take our body; the head is nothing 5 without the feet, just as the feet are nothing without the head. The smallest parts of our body are necessary and useful to the whole body. But they all coalesce and experience a common submission, in order to preserve the whole body.

38 So let our whole body be preserved through Christ Jesus, and let each one be subject to his neighbor, as he has been placed by
2 his spiritual gift. Let the strong care for the weak, and let the weak respect the strong. Let the rich provide for the poor, and let the poor give thanks to God, because he has given him one to supply his need. Let the wise man show his wisdom not in words but in good deeds. Let the humble-minded not bear witness to himself, but let himself have witness borne to him by others. Let him that is pure in the flesh not boast of it, knowing
3 that it is another who bestows on him his self-control. So let us consider, brethren, of what matter we were made, who we are, and what kind of beings we came into the world, from what a dark grave he that formed and created us brought us into his world, where he had prepared his benefits for us before we were
4 born. Since therefore we have received all this from him we ought to give him thanks for everything. To him be glory forever and ever! Amen.

39 Thoughtless, senseless, foolish, ignorant men mock and deride
2 us, wishing to exalt themselves in their imaginations. For what can a mortal man do? Or what strength has one who sprang from
3 the earth? For it is written, "There was no form before my
4 eyes, but I heard a breeze and a voice, 'What! Can a mortal be pure before the Lord? Or can a man be blameless for his deeds, if he does not believe in his servants, and finds some wrong
5 in his angels? Heaven is not clean in his sight; let alone, those that live in houses of clay, of whom are we ourselves, made of the same clay. He strikes them like a moth, and they do not last from morning till evening. Because they cannot help them-
6 selves, they perish. He breathed on them and they die, because
7 they have no wisdom.' If you call now, will anyone answer

you, or will you see one of the holy angels? For wrath destroys a foolish man, and jealousy puts to death one that is astray. I 8 have seen foolish men taking root, but their abode was immediately eaten up. May their sons be far from safety, may they be 9 derided at the gates of their inferiors, with no one to deliver them. For what has been prepared for them the upright will eat, and they themselves will not be delivered from evil."

Now that these things are clear to us, and we have looked 40 into the depths of the divine knowledge we ought to do in due order all the things the Master has commanded us to perform at appointed times. The sacrifices and services he has commanded 2 to be performed, and that it be not done unthinkingly or with disorder, but at fixed times and hours. Where and through whom 3 he wishes them to be performed he has himself determined by his supreme will, in order that they all might be done religiously with his approval and be acceptable to his will. So 4 those that make their offerings at the appointed times are acceptable and blessed, for since they follow the Master's regulations they cannot go wrong. For the high priest has been given his 5 own special services, and the priests have been assigned their own places and Levites have their particular duties. The layman is bound by the rules for laymen.

Let each one of you, brethren, please God in his own position, 41 with a good conscience, without going beyond the fixed rules of his ministry, and with reverence. Not everywhere, brethren, 2 but in Jerusalem alone are the perpetual sacrifices offered, or the free-will offerings, or the sin and trespass offerings, and there, they are not offered in every place, but at the altar before the sanctuary, after the offering has been inspected by the high priest and the attendants that have been mentioned. So those that do 3 anything contrary to what conforms to his will incur the penalty of death. You see, brethren, the greater the knowledge we have 4 been granted, the greater the risk we run.

42   The apostles received the gospel for us from the Lord Jesus
2   Christ; Jesus the Christ was sent from God. So Christ is from
God, and the apostles from Christ. Both came to pass regularly
3   by the will of God. So having received their instructions, and
having been reassured by the resurrection of our Lord Jesus
Christ, trusting in the word of God they set forth in the convic-
tion of the holy Spirit, preaching that the kingdom of God was
4   about to come. So as they preached from country to country
and from town to town, they appointed their first converts, after
testing them by the Spirit, as superintendents and assistants,
5   of those who were to believe. And this was no new thing; for
long before overseers and assistants had been written about.
For the scripture somewhere says, "I will appoint their superintendents in uprightness and their assistants in faith."

43   And what wonder, if those who in Christ were entrusted with
such a task appointed those just mentioned? When the blessed
Moses, also, "a faithful servant in all his house," noted down
in the sacred books all that had been enjoined upon him, being
followed by the rest of the prophets who bear witness with him
2   to his legislation. For when rivalry set in about the priesthood
and the tribes disagreed as to which of them was adorned with
the glorious title, he ordered the twelve tribal chiefs to bring
him staffs each marked with the name of a tribe, and he took
them and tied them together and stamped them with the seal
rings of the tribal chiefs, and he put them away in the Tent
3   of the Testimony on the table of God. And he shut the Tent
4   and put the seals on the keys as well as the staffs, and he said to
them, "The tribe whose staff buds is the one God has chosen to
5   be his priests and servants." Early in the morning he called all
Israel together, six hundred thousand men, and he showed the
seals to the chiefs of the tribes and he opened the Tent of the
Testimony, and brought out the staffs, and Aaron's staff was
6   found not only to have budded but to be bearing fruit. What do
you think, dear friends? Did not Moses know beforehand that

this would happen? Of course he knew. But he did this in order that there might be no disorder in Israel, that the name of the True and Only One might be glorified. To him be glory forever and ever. Amen.

Our apostles also knew through our Lord Jesus Christ that there **44** would be contention for the title of overseer. On this account, 2 as they had received full foreknowledge they appointed those already mentioned and later gave a supplement, in order that if they should fall asleep, other approved men should succeed to their duties. Those therefore that were appointed by them, 3 or afterward by other reputable men with the consent of the whole church, and have blamelessly served the flock of Christ, humbly, quietly, and disinterestedly, and for a long time have been universally approved—these men we consider are being unjustly removed from their ministry. For we will be guilty 4 of no small sin if we depose from the position of overseer those who have blamelessly and piously made the offerings. Blessed 5 are the elders who have gone before, who experienced a fruitful and perfect departure, for they have no need to fear that anyone will remove them from their appointed place. For we see that you 6 have dislodged some men who were conducting themselves well from the ministry they had blamelessly respected.

Be emulous, brethren, and zealous about the things that relate **45** to salvation. Study the holy scriptures, which are true, and given 2 by the holy Spirit. Be sure that nothing wrong or made up is 3 written in them. You will not find that upright men have been cast off by pious men. Upright men were persecuted, but it was 4 by lawless men. They were thrown into prison, but by impious men. They were stoned by transgressors. They were killed by those that had conceived a depraved and unjust jealousy. In 5 suffering these things, they endured them nobly. For what shall 6 we say, brethren? Was Daniel thrown into the den of lions by men who feared God? Or were Ananias and Azariah and Mishael 7 shut up in the fiery furnace by those who practiced the great and glorious worship of the Most High? Certainly not! Who, then, were the men that did these things? Detestable men, full of all evil, reached such a pitch of factious fury that they inflicted torture on men who were serving God with a pious and blameless purpose, not knowing that the Most High is the champion and defender of those who serve his most virtuous name with a clear conscience; to him be glory forever and ever.

8 Amen. But those that trustingly endured attained glory and honor; they were exalted and enrolled by God to be remembered by him forever and ever. Amen.

46,2 To such examples, brethren, we too must cling. For it is written, "Cling to those who are holy, for those who cling to them

3 will become holy." And again in another place it says, "With a guiltless man you will be guiltless, and with a chosen man you will be chosen, and with a crooked man you will deal craftily."

4 So let us cling to the guiltless and upright, for they are God's

5 chosen. Why is there quarreling and anger and faction and divi-

6 sion and war among you? Have we not one God and one Christ and one spirit of grace that has been poured out upon us? And

7 is there not one call through Christ? Why do we tear apart and rend the parts of Christ and revolt against our own body, and reach such a height of folly that we forget that we are parts of one another? Remember the words of our Lord Jesus,

8 for he said, "Alas for that man! It would have been better for him if he had never been born than to make one of my chosen fall! He might better have had a millstone hung around his neck and have been sunk in the sea than to pervert one of my

9 chosen." Your division has perverted many, it has plunged many into despondency, many into doubt, all of us into grief, and your rebellion still continues.

47,2 Take up the letter of the blessed Paul, the apostle. What did he first write to you, in the beginning of the preaching

3 of the gospel? Certainly he wrote you under the Spirit's influence about himself and Cephas and Apollos, for even then you had

formed parties. But those parties involved you in less sin, for 4 you were partisans of apostles of repute and of a man of whom they approved. But now think who have misled you and lessened 5 the repute of your far famed brotherly love. It is disgraceful, 6 dear friends, utterly disgraceful, and unworthy of Christian conduct to have it said that because of one or two people the old, established church of the Corinthians is in revolt against its elders. And this report has not only reached us but also those 7 who differ with us, so that because of your folly the name of the Lord is reviled and you yourselves are imperiled.

Let us therefore make haste to put a stop to this, and let us 48 fall down before the Master and implore him with tears to have mercy upon us and be reconciled to us, and restore us to our reverent and pure attitude of brotherly love. For it is a gate of 2 uprightness opening into life, as it is written, "Open for me the gates of uprightness; I will go in by them and thank the Lord. This is the gate of the Lord; the upright will go in by 3 it." So, while many gates stand open, the gate of uprightness 4 is the gate of Christ; blessed are all those that go in by it, and direct their course in holiness and uprightness, calmly accomplishing everything. Let a man be faithful, let him be able to 5 utter knowledge, let him be wise in his interpretation of what is said, let him be pure in conduct; the greater he seems to be, 6 the more humble-minded he should be, and the more disposed to seek not his own advantage but that of all.

Let him who in union with Christ has love, keep Christ's com- 49 mandments. Who can describe the bond of the love of God? Who 2,3 is equal to expressing the greatness of its beauty? The height to 4 which love lifts us is inexpressible. Love unites us to God, love 5 covers up a host of sins, love will bear anything, it is patient about everything. There is nothing vulgar, nothing vain, about love. Love knows no schism, love creates no discord, love does everything in harmony. By love all God's chosen have been made perfect. Without love nothing can please God. In love the Master 6 took us to himself. Because of the love he had for us, Jesus Christ our Lord by the will of God gave his blood for us, and his flesh for our flesh, and his life for our lives.

50 You see, dear friends, how great and wonderful love is, and
2 there is no describing its perfection. Who is fit to be found in it except those whom God deems worthy? So let us pray and beg of his mercy that we may be found in love, irreproachable, free
3 from human partiality. All the generations from Adam until this day have passed away, but those who by God's favor have been made perfect in love live in the abode of the godly, and they will be made manifest at the visitation of the kingdom of
4 Christ. For it is written, "Go into your chambers for a little while, until my wrath and anger pass, and I will remember a good
5 day, and will raise you up from your graves." How happy we are, dear friends, if we carry out the commandments of God in the harmony of love, that our sins may be forgiven through
6 love. For it is written, "How happy they are whose iniquities are forgiven and whose sins are covered up. How happy the man is whose sin the Lord will take no account of, and in whose mouth
7 there is no deceit." This blessing has come to those who have been chosen by God through Jesus Christ our Lord, to whom be glory forever and ever. Amen.

51 So for the things which we have gone astray and done through any intrusions of the adversary let us pray that we be forgiven. And those also who have been the instigators of dissension and
2 division ought to have regard for the common hope. For those who live in fear and love had rather suffer tortures themselves than have their neighbors do so, and they had rather bear condemnation themselves than have the harmony condemned which
3 has been honorably and uprightly handed down to us. For it is better for a man to acknowledge his transgressions than to harden his heart, as the heart of those was hardened who rebelled against Moses the servant of God. Their condemnation was made plain.
4 For "they went down alive into Hades" and "death will shepherd

them." Pharaoh and his host and all the rulers of Egypt, "the **5**
chariots and their riders," were engulfed in the Red Sea and
perished for no other reason than that their foolish hearts were
hardened after the signs and wonders had occurred in Egypt
through God's servant Moses.

The Master, brethren, is in no need of anything; he wants noth- **52**
ing of anyone but to give thanks to him. For David the chosen **2**
says, "I will give thanks to the Lord, and it will please him
more than a young calf with horns and hoofs. Let the poor see it
and rejoice." And again he says, "Offer to God the sacrifice of **3**
praise, and pay your vows to the Most High, and call upon me
in the day of your affliction, and I will deliver you, and you
will glorify me." For "the sacrifice of God is a broken spirit." **4**

For you know the sacred scriptures, dear friends, you know **53**
them well, and you have studied the oracles of God. So I write
these things to remind you of them. For when Moses went up on **2**
the mountain and spent forty days and forty nights in fasting and
self-abasement, God said to him, "Go down quickly from here,
for your people, whom you have brought out of the land of
Egypt, have disobeyed; they have gone astray from the way you
commanded them to follow, they have cast idols for themselves."
And the Lord said to him, "I have spoken to you once and again **3**
saying, I have seen this people, and behold, it is stiff-necked;
let me exterminate them, and wipe out their name from under
heaven, and I will make you a great, wonderful nation, much
larger than this one." And Moses said, "By no means, Lord! **4**
Forgive this people their sin, or wipe me also out of the book of
the living." What great love! What unsurpassable perfection! **5**
The servant speaks freely to his Lord, he begs forgiveness
for the multitude, or asks that he too be wiped out along with
them.

Who, then, among you is noble? Who is compassionate? **54**
Who is full of love? Let him say, "If on my account disorder **2**
and quarreling and divisions have arisen, I will leave, I will

go wherever you wish, and do whatever the majority commands; only let the flock of Christ be at peace with its appointed
3 elders." The man who does this will win himself great renown in
Christ, and every place will welcome him, for "the earth is the
4 Lord's and its fullness." This is what those who follow the divine
way of life that brings no regrets have done and will do.

55 To offer some examples from the heathen also, many kings
and rulers, in times of pestilence, in response to an oracle have
given themselves up to death in order by their own blood to
save their townsmen. Many have removed from their own cities,
2 so that they would rebel no more. We know that many among
us have given themselves up to bondage in order to ransom others.
Many have given themselves up to slavery and used the price
3 paid for themselves to feed others. Many women, strengthened
4 by the favor of God, have done heroic deeds. The blessed Judith,
when the city was besieged, asked the elders to permit her to
5 go out to the camp of the foreigners. So she exposed herself to
danger and went out for her love of country and of her besieged
people, and the Lord delivered Holophernes into a woman's hand.
6 To no less danger Esther also, in perfect faith, exposed herself,
in order to save the twelve tribes of Israel when they were on the
point of perishing, for by fasting and humiliation she implored the
all-seeing Master, the God of the ages, and he, seeing her
humility of soul, delivered the people for whom she had faced
danger.

56 So let us also intercede for those involved in any transgression,
that forbearance and humility may be granted them, so that they
may submit, not to us, but to the will of God. For so they will
have a fruitful and perfect remembrance with compassion, in the
2 sight of God and his people. Let us accept correction, dear
friends, over which no one should feel annoyed. The warning that
we address to one another is good and extremely beneficial, for
3 it unites us to the will of God. For the holy word says, "The
Lord has disciplined me severely, and he has not given me up to

death. For it is he whom the Lord loves that he disciplines, and 4
he chastises every son that he acknowledges. For the upright," 5
it says, "will discipline me in mercy and reprove me, but let not
the oil of sinners anoint my head." And again it says, "How 6
happy the man is whom the Lord reproves; do not refuse the
warning of the Almighty; for he causes pain, and restores again;
he strikes, and his hands heal. Six times he will rescue you from 7,8
distress, and the seventh time, no harm will befall you. In famine 9
he will deliver you from death, and in war he will free you from
the power of the sword. He will hide you from the scourge of the 10
tongue, and when evils come you will not be afraid. You will 11
laugh at unrighteous and lawless men, and you will not be
afraid of wild beasts. For wild animals will be at peace with you. 12
Then you will know that your house will be in peace, and the life 13
of your tent will not fail. And you will know that your posterity 14
will be many, and your children like all the herbage of the
field. And you will come to the grave like ripe wheat harvested 15
in season, or like a heap on the threshing floor gathered together
at the right time." You see, dear friends, what protection is given 16
those who are disciplined by the Master, for as a good father he
disciplines us so that through his holy discipline we may receive
mercy.

You therefore who laid the foundation of the disorder must 57
submit to the elders and be disciplined so as to repent, bending
the knees of your hearts. Learn to subordinate yourselves, laying 2
aside the boastful and haughty willfulness of your tongue, for
it is better for you to occupy a small but reputable place in the
flock of Christ than while seeming to be pre-eminent to be cast
out of your hope of him. For this is what the most excellent 3
Wisdom says: "Behold, I will utter to you the speech of my
Spirit, and will teach you my word. Because I called and you 4
would not obey, and I put forth words and you paid no heed,
but made my counsels futile and disobeyed my reproofs, therefore I will laugh at your ruin, I will exult when destruction

comes upon you and when confusion suddenly overtakes you, and catastrophe comes like a whirlwind, or when persecution or
5 siege befalls you. For it shall be, when you call upon me, that I will not listen to you; the evil will seek me and they will not find me. For they hated wisdom, and did not choose the fear of the Lord, and they would not heed my counsels, but mocked
6 my reproofs. Therefore they will eat the fruits of their own way,
7 and be filled with their own impiety. For because they wronged infants they will be slain, and examination will destroy the ungodly. But he who listens to me will live secure in his hope, and will be quiet with no fear of any evil."

58   Let us, then, obey his most holy and glorious name, and escape the threats uttered long ago by Wisdom against the disobedient, so that we may pitch our tents trusting in the most sacred name
2 of his majesty. Take our advice, and you will not regret it. For as God lives, and the Lord Jesus Christ lives, and the holy Spirit, who are the faith and hope of God's chosen, the man who humbly, with constant forbearance, and without cause for regret carries out the decrees and commands ordained by God, will be registered and enrolled in the number of those who are saved through Jesus Christ, through whom is glory to him forever and ever. Amen.

59   But if any disobey what has been said by him through us, let them know that they will involve themselves in no slight trans-
2 gression and danger. But we will be guiltless of this sin, and we will ask with earnest prayer and supplication that the Creator of all may keep unbroken the number that has been counted of his chosen in all the world through his beloved child Jesus Christ, through whom he called us from darkness to light, from ignorance
3 to the recognition of the glory of his name, to hope in your name, which is the source of all creation, opening the eyes of our mind to know you, who alone are most high among the highest, remaining holy among the holy, who humble the insolence of the haughty, who destroy the calculations of the heathen, who set the humble on high and bring the lofty low, who make rich

and make poor, who kill and make alive, the only benefactor of spirits, and God of all flesh, who look into the abysses, the observer of the works of man, the helper of those in peril, the savior of those in despair, creator and guardian of every spirit; who multiply nations on the earth and have chosen from all men those that love thee through Jesus Christ your beloved child, through whom you have trained, sanctified, and honored us.

We beseech you, Master, to be our helper and protector. Save 4 those of us who are in affliction. Lift up the fallen, show yourself to those in need, cure the sick, bring back those of your people who have gone astray, release those of us who are in prison, raise up the weak, encourage the fainthearted. Let all the heathen know that you alone are God, and Jesus Christ is your child, and we are "your people, and the sheep of your pasture."

For you through your operations have revealed the everlasting 60 constitution of the universe; you, Lord, created the world. You who are faithful in all generations, wonderful in might and majesty, wise in creating and intelligent in establishing existing things, good in the visible world and kind to those that trust in you, merciful and compassionate, forgive us our sins and wrong-doings and transgressions and failings. Do not take account of 2 every sin of your slaves and maidservants, but cleanse us with the cleansing of your truth and direct our steps to walk in holiness of heart, and to do what is right and well-pleasing before you and before our rulers. Yes, Lord, make your face shine upon 3 us in peace for our good, that we may be shielded by your mighty hand, and delivered from every sin by your uplifted arm, and deliver us from those that hate us wrongfully. Grant harmony 4 and peace to us and to all who inhabit the earth, as you gave it to our fathers, when they called upon you reverently in faith and truth—being made obedient to your almighty and glorious name and to our rulers and governors on earth.

You, Master, have given them the authority to reign through 61 your transcendent and unutterable might that we may recognize the glory and honor given them by you, and be subject to them, offering no opposition to your will. Grant, Lord, to them health, peace, harmony, stability, so that they may without offense con-

2 duct the government you have given them. For you, heavenly Master, king of the ages, give the sons of men glory and honor and authority over those who are on the earth. Lord, direct their counsel by what is right and pleasing in your sight, so that, piously administering in peace and gentleness the authority you

3 have given them, they may experience your mercy. You who alone are able to do these good things and far more abundantly for us, we praise you through the high priest and guardian of our souls, Jesus Christ, through whom be glory and majesty to you, both now and for all generations and forever and ever. Amen.

62   About the things that befit our religion and are most helpful to those who wish to direct their way piously and uprightly to

2 a virtuous life, brethren, we have written you enough. For we have handled every subject relating to faith, repentance, genuine love, self-control, sober-mindedness, and patience, reminding you that you must please Almighty God with holiness, in uprightness and truth and long-suffering in a life of concord, without malice, in love and peace, with earnest forbearance, as our forefathers already mentioned pleased him, with their humility toward their

3 Father and God and Creator and toward all men. And we have been more glad to remind you of these things because we knew well that we were writing to men who were faithful and of high repute and who had studied the oracles of God's teaching.

63   It is right therefore that admitting such numerous examples we should bow our necks and take the attitude of obedience, so that suspending our futile disorder we may without any blame

2 reach the goal set before us in truth. For you will cause us joy and gladness if you are obedient to what we have written through the holy Spirit, and uproot the abominable anger of your jealousy, in response to the entreaty for peace and harmony that we

3 have made in this letter. And we send faithful, thoughtful men,

who have lived among us blamelessly from youth to old age, who will be witnesses between you and us. We do this so that 4 you may know that our whole concern has been and still is that you may speedily be at peace.

Finally, may the all-seeing God and Master of spirits and Lord **64** of all flesh, who chose the Lord Jesus Christ, and us through him for his own people, give to every soul that is called by his excellent and holy name, faith, fear, peace, patience, and long-suffering, self-control, purity and sober-mindedness, so that they may be well-pleasing to his name through our high priest and defender Jesus Christ, through whom unto him be glory and majesty, might and honor, both now and forever and ever. Amen.

Send back quickly to us in peace and with joy the men sent **65** from us, Claudius Ephebus and Valerius Bito, together with Fortunatus, so that they may the sooner bring word of your peace and harmony, so prayed for and longed for by us, so that we too may the sooner rejoice in your tranquillity.

The grace of our Lord Jesus Christ be with you and with all **2** men everywhere who have been called by God and through him, through whom to him be glory, honor, might and majesty, eternal dominion, from ages past forever and ever. Amen.

The So-called Second Letter of Clement

II Clement is a Christian sermon, probably of Roman origin, written about A.D. *150 to 165. It came to the attention of Western learning with the coming to England in 1628 of the Codex Alexandrinus, in which it immediately follows I Clement, which is designated as the "first letter of Clement." But Eusebius long before had mentioned it doubtfully as the Second Letter of Clement,* Church History *3.38.4. No more probable explanation of the document has been offered than that it is a sermon of Soter, Bishop of Rome,* A.D. *166-174, sent as a letter to the church at Corinth, and acknowledged by Dionysius, Bishop of Corinth, in a well-known letter preserved in Eusebius* (Church History *4.23.11). Dionysius says that the Corinthian church will preserve Soter's letter, and read it from time to time, and be able to draw advice from it, "as also from the former epistle which was written to us through Clement." This would explain the preservation of the homily as a companion of I Clement, both documents having been written at Rome and sent to the church at Corinth.*

*The sermon is an appeal to its hearers to repent and serve God with their whole hearts, to live upright lives, and hold fast to their resurrection hope. It shows acquaintance not only with the four Gospels and the Letters of Paul, but with I Peter, the Gospel of the Egyptians (*A.D. *130-140), and a mysterious prophetical book, also quoted in I Clement, which may be the lost Book of Eldad and Modat, mentioned in Hermas (*Vis. *ii.3.4) and evidently known and read in Rome.*

II Clement accompanied I Clement not only into the closing pages of the New Testament in the Codex Alexandrinus, but found a place with it in one Harclean Syriac New Testament manuscript, of the twelfth century. They are mentioned as belonging to the New Testament in the Apostolic Canons, *a Syrian book of about* A.D. *400, and Abu'l Barakat (†1363) in telling of Christian literature in Arabic speaks of them as in the New Testament.*

The So-called Second Letter
of Clement

Brethren, we must think of Jesus Christ, as we do of God, as 1
the judge of living and dead, and we must not think lightly
of our salvation. For when we think little of him, we also hope 2
to receive little. And those who listen as though to small matters
sin, and we sin, not knowing whence we were called, and by
whom, and to what place, and what sufferings Jesus Christ endured for us. What return, then, can we make to him, or what 3
fruit can we offer worthy of his gift to us? How many blessings
do we owe to him? For he has given us the light, as a Father 4
he has acknowledged us as sons, he saved us when we were perishing. What praise, then, can we give him, or what repayment 5
for what we have received? We were blind in mind, worshiping 6
stone and wood and gold and silver, the works of men, and our
whole life was nothing but death. So when we were enveloped
in darkness, with our sight so full of mist, we received our sight
back, and laid aside by his will the cloud that enveloped us. For 7
he has taken pity on us, and mercifully saved us, seeing in us
our great error and ruin, and that we had no hope of salvation
except from him. For he called us when we were no more, and 8
from not being he willed that we should come to be.

"Rejoice, barren woman, who have had no children; break 2
forth and shout, you who have not borne, for the desolate woman
has more children than the one that has the husband." When he

said, "Rejoice, barren woman, who have had no children," he
meant us, for our church was barren before she was given chil-
2 dren. And when he said, "Shout, you who have not borne," he
meant this: let us not grow weary, like women in childbirth, in
3 offering our prayers to God in sincerity. And when he said, "For
the desolate woman has more children than the one that has the
husband," it was because our people seemed to be deserted by
God, but now that we have believed we have become more
4 numerous than those who seemed to have God. And another
scripture says, "I did not come to invite the upright but the
5 irreligious." This means that those who are perishing must be
6 saved. For it is great and wonderful to strengthen not what
7 is standing up but what is falling down. So Christ also wished
to save what was perishing, and saved many, coming and calling
us just as we were perishing.

3   Since he has shown us such mercy, first that we who are living
do not sacrifice to those dead gods, and do not worship them,
but through him have come to know the Father of truth, what
is knowledge with reference to him if it is not refusing to deny
2 him through whom we have come to know him? And he himself
says, "Everyone that acknowledges me before men I will acknowl-
3 edge before my Father." This, then, is our reward, if we acknowl-
4 edge him through whom we were saved. But how shall we
acknowledge him? By doing what he says, and not disregarding
his commands, and honoring him not only with our lips, but
5 with our whole hearts and our whole minds. For it says in Isaiah,
"This people honors me with their lips, yet their hearts are far
away from me."

4   Let us therefore not only call him Lord, for that will not save
2 us. For he says, "It is not everyone who says to me 'Lord! Lord!'
3 who will be saved, but he who acts uprightly." So then, brethren,
let us acknowledge him with our acts, by loving one another,
by not committing adultery or speaking evil of one another, or
being jealous, but by being self-controlled, merciful, kind. And

we ought to be sympathetic with one another and not to love money. By these actions let us acknowledge him, and not by their opposites. And we must not fear men more, but God. Be- 4, 5 cause of this, if you do these things, the Lord said, "Even if you are gathered with me in my bosom, but do not do my commands, I will cast you off and say to you, Go away from me, I do not know whence you come, you doers of iniquity."

Therefore, brethren, let us turn our backs on our stay in this 5 world, and do the will of him who has called us, and let us not be afraid to go out of this world. For the Lord says, "You will 2 be like lambs among wolves." But Peter answered and said to 3 him, "What if the wolves tear the lambs to pieces?" Jesus said 4 to Peter, "Let the lambs have no fear of the wolves after their death, and do not you fear those who kill you and can do nothing more to you, but fear him who after you are dead has power over soul and body to cast them into the fiery pit." You must 5 know, brethren, that our stay in this material world is small and short, but the promise of Christ is great and wonderful; it is rest in the kingdom that is coming and in eternal life. What, then, 6 must we do to obtain them but lead a holy and upright life and think of the things of this world as not our own, and not desire them? For when we desire to get these things, we miss the way 7 of uprightness.

And the Lord says, "No servant can serve two masters." If 6 we want to serve both God and money, it is unprofitable for us. "For what good does it do a man to gain the whole world, 2 and yet part with his life?" This world and the world to come 3 are two enemies. This world means adultery and corruption, 4 and avarice and deceit, and that world bids these things good-bye. So we cannot be friends of both; we must bid this one 5 good-bye to enjoy the other. We think it is better to hate what 6 is here, for it is little and short-lived and perishable, and to love what is there, which is good and imperishable. For if we 7 do the will of Christ, we will find rest, but if we do not, nothing

can save us from eternal punishment, if we disregard his com-
8 mands. And the scripture also says in Ezekiel, "If Noah, Job
and Daniel rise, they will not save their descendants in the
9 captivity." But if even such upright men cannot by their uprightness save their descendants, what assurance have we, if we do
not keep our baptism pure and undefiled, of entering the kingdom of God? Or who will be our advocate, if we are not found
to have holy and upright works?

7   So then, my brethren, let us take part in the contest, knowing
that the contest is at hand, and that many are arriving by sea
for the corruptible contests, but that not all will be crowned,
2 but only those who have worked hard and competed well. So
3 let us compete, so that we may all be crowned victors. So let
us run the straight course, the incorruptible contest, and let many
of us sail to it, and compete, in order that we also may be
crowned victors, and if we cannot all be crowned victors, let
4 us at least come near the wreath. We must know that if one
who competes in the corruptible contest is caught cheating, he
5 is flogged and removed, and thrown out of the stadium. What do
you think? What will be done with the man who cheats in the
6 competition for the incorruptible? For of those who have not
kept the seal of baptism, it says, "Their worm shall not die, and
their fire shall not be quenched, and they shall be a spectacle
for all flesh."

8,2   So while we are on earth, let us repent. For we are clay in
the hand of the workman. For just as the potter, if he is making
a dish, and it becomes misshaped or broken in his hands, models
it over again, but if he goes so far as to put it into the firing
furnace, he cannot mend it any more, so let us also while we
are in this world repent with all our hearts of the wicked things
we have done in the flesh, so that we may be saved by the Lord,
3 while we still have time to repent. For after we leave the world,
4 we can there no longer confess or repent any more. Therefore,
brethren, if we do the Father's will, and keep the flesh pure,
5 and keep the Lord's commands, we will receive eternal life. For

the Lord says in the gospel, "If you have not guarded the small, who will give you what is great? For I tell you, the man who can be trusted in a very small matter can be trusted in a large one." What he means, then, is this, Keep the flesh pure and the seal 6 of baptism unstained, so that we may receive eternal life.

And let none of you say that the flesh is not judged and does 9 not rise again. You must know: in what state were you saved? 2 In what did you regain your sight, if not when you were in this flesh? So we must guard the flesh as a temple of God. For just 3,4 as you were called in the flesh, you will also come in the flesh. If Christ the Lord who saved us, though he was at first spirit, 5 became flesh and in that state called us, so we also will receive our recompense in this flesh. So let us love one another, so that 6 we may all enter the kingdom of God. While we have the op- 7 portunity to be cured, let us entrust ourselves to God, the physician, and give him his compensation. What compensation? 8 Repentance from a sincere heart. For he has foreknowledge of all 9 things, and knows what is in our hearts. So let us give him praise, 10 not only with our lips but from our hearts, so that he may welcome us as sons. For the Lord said, "These who do the will of 11 my Father are my brothers."

Therefore, my brethren, let us do the will of the Father who 10 has called us, so that we may live, and let us prefer the pursuit of virtue; but let us give up evil, as a forerunner of our sins, and let us flee from ungodliness, so that evil may not overtake us. For if we are eager to do good, peace will pursue us. This is 2,3 why it is impossible for men to find peace, when they introduce the fears of men, and prefer enjoyment here to what is promised for the future. For they do not know what great torment their 4 enjoyment here will bring, and what enjoyment the promise of what is to come will bring. And if they did these things by them- 5 selves, it might be borne, but as it is they keep teaching evil to innocent souls, not aware that they will receive a double sentence, for both themselves and their hearers.

Let us therefore serve God with a pure heart, and we will 11

be upright; but if because we do not believe God's promise, we
2 do not serve him, we will be miserable. For the prophetic word
says, "How miserable the double-minded are, who doubt in their
minds, and say, 'We heard this long ago, even in the times of our
forefathers, and though we have waited day after day we have
3 seen none of them.' Senseless people! Compare yourselves to a
tree; take a vine. First it sheds its leaves, then a shoot appears,
4 afterward a sour grape, then a ripe grape. So my people also
has had disturbances and afflictions; then it will receive bless-
5 ings." Therefore, my brethren, let us not waver, but let us hope
and endure, so that we may also receive our recompense. "For
6 he is faithful who has promised" to give each man his compen-
7 sation for his work. So if we do uprightness before God, we will
enter his kingdom and receive the promises, "which no eye has
seen, and no ear heard, nor has the human mind imagined."

12   Let us therefore from hour to hour wait in love and uprightness
for the kingdom of God, since we do not know the day when
2 God will appear. For the Lord himself, when he was asked by
someone when his kingdom would come, said, "When the two
shall be one, and the outside like the inside, and the male with
3 the female neither male nor female." Now the two are one, when
we tell one another the truth, and in two persons there is one
4 soul, with no dissimulation. And "the outside like the inside"
means this: the inside means the soul, and the outside means
the body. So just as your body is visible, let your soul also be
5 manifest in its good actions. And "the male with the female
neither male nor female" means this: that a brother when he sees
a sister should not think of her at all as female, nor she think
6 of him at all as male. When you do this, he says, my Father's
kingdom will come.

13   So, brethren, let us now at last repent. Let us be vigilant for
the good, for we are full of much folly and wickedness. Let us
wipe off from us our former sins, and let us repent with our
whole hearts and be saved. And let us not try to please men,

or wish to please only ourselves, but also the outsiders, by our uprightness, in order that the name may not be reproached because of us. For the Lord says, "My name is continually re- 2 proached among all the heathen," and again, "Woe to the man because of whom my name is reproached." Why is it reproached? 3 Because you do not do what I want. For when the heathen hear from our mouths the oracles of God, they wonder at them as beautiful and great; but afterward when they find out that what we do is unworthy of the things we say, they turn from it too and revile it, declaring it a myth and a delusion. For when they 4 hear us say that God says, "It is no merit in you if you love those who love you, but you have merit if you love your enemies and those who hate you"—when they hear that, they wonder at such extraordinary goodness; but when they see that not only do we not love those who hate us but not even those who love us, they laugh at us, and the name is reviled.

Therefore, brethren, if we do the will of God our Father, we 14 shall belong to the first church, that spiritual one, that was created before the sun and moon; but if we do not do the will of God, we shall be of those meant by the scripture that says, "My house has become a robbers' cave." So, then, let us choose to be part of the church of life, in order that we may be saved. I do not suppose you are unaware that a living "church is the 2 body of Christ"; for the scripture says, "God made man male and female." The male is Christ, the female is the church. Besides, the books and the apostles say that the church not only exists now, but has done so from the beginning. For she was spiritual as our Jesus also was, but he was revealed in the last days, to save us. And the church, which was spiritual, was revealed in 3 the flesh of Christ, showing us that if any of us guards her in the flesh and does not corrupt her, he will get her back again in the holy Spirit. For this flesh is a copy of the spirit. No one therefore who has spoiled the copy will share in the original. So what he means is this, brethren: preserve the flesh, so that

4 you may share in the spirit. But if we say that the flesh is the church and the spirit is Christ, then the man who outrages the flesh outrages the church. Such a man therefore will not share in the spirit which is Christ. Such is the life and immortality this flesh can share in, if it is joined to the holy Spirit, and no one can say or tell what the Lord has prepared for his chosen.

15 I think I have given no little advice about self-control, and anyone who takes it will have no cause to regret it, but will save both himself and me who have given it to him. For it is no small
2 remuneration to convert a soul that is astray and perishing. For this is the recompense we can pay to God who created us, if the man who speaks and the man who hears speak and hear
3 with faith and love. Let us therefore in uprightness and holiness stand by the things we have believed, in order that we may ask with confidence of God, who says, "Even while you are speaking,
4 I will say, 'Here I am.'" For this saying is an indication of a great promise; for the Lord means that he is more ready to give
5 than a man is to ask. So let us avail ourselves of such kindness and not begrudge ourselves the obtaining of such blessings. For however much pleasure these words bring to those who do them, they mean just as much condemnation for those who disregard them.

16 Therefore, brethren, since we have been given no small opportunity to repent, let us while we have time turn to God who has called us, while we still have one who is ready to receive
2 us. For if we bid these luxuries good-bye and win the victory over our souls by not carrying out its evil desires, we will share
3 in the mercy of Jesus. But be assured that the day of judgment is already coming like a burning oven, and some of the heavens will melt, and all the earth will be like lead melting in the fire, and then the secret and the open doings of men will appear.
4 Therefore charity is good, as well as repentance for sin; fasting is better than prayer, but charity than both. Love covers up a host of sins, but prayer with a good conscience delivers from

death. Blessed is every man who is found full of these, for charity removes the load of sin.

Let us therefore repent with all our hearts, so that none of us **17** may perish to no purpose. For if we have commands to do this also, to drag men away from idols and instruct them, how much more it is not right that a soul that already knows God should perish! So let us help one another to restore those also who are **2** weak in goodness, in order that we may all be saved, and convert and warn one another. And let us not only seem to believe and **3** give heed now, while we are being exhorted by the elders, but also when we get home let us remember the Lord's commands and not be dragged the other way by worldly passions, but let us come here more frequently and try to progress in the Lord's commands, in order that all of us may live in harmony and be gathered together to life. For the Lord said, "I am coming to **4** gather all the nations, tribes and languages." This means the day of his appearing, when he will come and redeem us, each according to what he has done. And the unbelievers "will see **5** his glory" and power, and they will be amazed when they see the sovereignty of the world in the hands of Jesus, and say, "Alas for us, for it was you, and we did not know it and did not believe, and did not obey the elders when they brought us news of our salvation." And "their worm shall not die, nor shall their fire be quenched; and they shall be a spectacle for all mankind." He means that day of judgment, when men will see those who **6** lived ungodly lives among us and distorted the commands of Jesus Christ. But the upright who have done right and endured **7** torture and hated the indulgences of the soul, when they see how those who have gone astray and denied Jesus by their words or by their acts are punished with dreadful tortures in unquenchable fire, will give glory to their God, saying, "There will be hope for him who has served God with all his heart."

Let us also therefore be of those who give thanks, those who **18** have served God, and not of the ungodly who are judged. For **2**

I myself too who am utterly sinful and have not yet escaped temptation, but am still in the midst of the devil's tools, am eager to pursue righteousness, in order that I may succeed at least in getting close to it, in fear of the judgment that is to come.

19 Therefore, brothers and sisters, after the God of truth (the scripture lesson), I have read you an appeal to give heed to what is written, so that you may save yourselves and him that does the reading before you. For as recompense I ask you to repent with all your hearts and give yourselves salvation and life. For if we do this, we shall set up a mark for all the youth who wish 2 to devote themselves to piety and the goodness of God. And let us, unwise as we are, not be displeased or take it ill when someone warns us and tries to turn us from unrighteousness to uprightness. For sometimes when we do wrong we do not know it, because of the doubt and unbelief that are in our breasts, 3 and we are darkened in understanding by vain desires. Let us therefore practice uprightness, so that we may finally be saved. Blessed are they that obey these commands; even though they are ill-treated a little while in this world, they will gather the 4 immortal fruit of the resurrection. So the godly man must not grieve if he is miserable in these present times; a time of happiness is awaiting him; he will live again above, with his forefathers, and rejoice through an eternity free from sorrow.

20 But do not let it trouble your minds that we see the unrighteous possessing wealth and the slaves of God in difficulties. 2 Let us therefore have faith, brothers and sisters. We are taking part in the contest of a living God, and we are being trained by the present life so that we may win the wreath in the life 3 that is to come. None of the upright has received his fruit 4 quickly, but waits for it. For if God paid the recompense of the upright promptly, we would immediately be engaged in business, not religion, for we would pretend to be upright when we were pursuing not religion but gain. For that reason the judgment

of God overtakes a spirit that is not upright, and loads it with chains.

To the only God, invisible, Father of truth, who sent forth 5 to us the Savior and prince of immortality, through whom he has shown us the truth and the heavenly life—to him be glory forever and ever. Amen.

The Shepherd of Hermas

The last decade of the first century witnessed the writing not only of the Revelation of John at Patmos, near Ephesus, but of a second Christian revelation, The Shepherd of Hermas, at Rome. Hermas was a Christian prophet, and was clearly acquainted with the Revelation of John, but its literary influence upon him was very slight, Vision iv.2.1. The book that had most definitely stirred him to write is the so-called Letter to the Hebrews, a message sent to Rome about A.D. 95, which roused the Roman church to do its duty in teaching the other churches, 5.12, through I Clement and I Peter, and now moved Hermas to write, by its stern doctrine of no forgiveness for apostasy, which he understood to mean no forgiveness for sin after baptism. Hermas maintains that a Christian may fall into sin once after baptism and be forgiven once, but only once. He casts his message chiefly in the form of interviews with the angel of repentance (the Shepherd, as he calls him), a form of revelation much like that in the Ezra Apocalypse in II Esdras, where Ezra questions the angel Uriel and records his answers. We cannot suppose that Hermas knew that Hebrew apocalypse, but it belongs to exactly his period, the end of the first century.

Hermas was a slave, or a freedman, in Rome. His work began with a series of four visions, emphasizing repentance. The second of these describes it as the business of Clement to send copies of the visions to other churches, and this part of the book may go back to the last years of his episcopate, which lasted from A.D. 88 to 97. If Hebrews created the situation he sought to correct, this part must have been written between A.D. 95 and 97. It is significant that Hermas expected his book to be circulated among the churches.

Three or four years later, Hermas produced a larger work, the Shepherd proper, in which the Shepherd appears and plays the leading part, teaching Hermas and answering his questions. It begins with a Revelation ("apocalypse"), which is followed by a series of twelve Commands, telling how the repentant Christian should live. They are followed by ten Parables, setting forth the workings of repentance. As a Christian prophet Hermas feels entirely free to lay down a new series of commands, without any reference to the Ten Commandments of Judaism, and to utter new parables, beside those of Jesus himself. But Hermas did not know the fourfold gospel, and he shows few reflections of the Old Testament.

In 1922 a third-century papyrus of the Shepherd (published in 1934 at Michigan by Campbell Bonner) came to light which when complete evidently had precisely these contents, beginning with the "revelation" which we know as Vision v, and containing the twelve Commands and the ten Parables. The statement quoted in Hippolytus (Refutation 9.13, English 9.8) from the Elkesaite Alcibiades that a new repentance was proclaimed in the Roman church in the third year of Trajan strongly suggests that this second work of Hermas, the Shepherd proper, appeared A.D. 100. It would naturally be described as proclaiming a new repentance.

Still later the two books were combined, the Visions preceding the Shepherd, making the form preserved in part in the Codex Sinaiticus, which contains about one fourth of the whole, and the Athos manuscript (part of which is now at Leipzig), which contains all but the last tenth. (The Michigan papyrus contains *almost one-fourth of the total text, but not the part missing from the Athos manuscript.) This, which may be called the "complete edition," is also found in the two Latin versions, and in the Ethiopic translation, published by d'Abbadie in 1860. A number of smaller pieces, parchment or papyrus, also have been found, some covering parts of what is missing from the principal Greek manuscripts.*

Hermas wrote in the simplest sort of vernacular Greek, now familiar to us from the documentary papyri. He was naïve, frank, and informal in expression, and possessed of an originality and a sincerity that gained him a wide hearing. His book was accepted as part of the New Testament by Clement of Alexandria, toward the end of the second century, and by Origen in the third, and stood at the end of the New Testament in the Codex Sinaiticus, about the middle of the fourth.. Tertullian at first accepted it, but later repudiated it. Irenaeus accepted it as scripture. Eusebius put it among the rejected writings, but Athanasius in A.D. 367, recommended it to new converts for private reading. It was popular not only in Egypt and Abyssinia, but later through the sect of the Manichaeans it was read as far east as Chinese Turkestan. And in Dante's Divine Comedy, *A.D. 1300, Beatrice and Vergil, his mediums of revelation, recall Rhoda and the Shepherd, who performed the same service for Hermas.*

The Shepherd of Hermas

THE VISIONS

VISION I

The man who brought me up sold me to a woman named 1
Rhoda in Rome. Many years later I met her again, and I began to
love her like a sister. Some time later, I saw her bathing in the 2
river Tiber, and I gave her my hand and helped her out of the
river. So when I saw her beauty I reflected in my mind and said,
"How happy I would be if I had a wife of such beauty and
disposition." That was the only thought I had; I had no other.
Some time later, as I was on my way to Cumae, glorifying God's 3
creatures, they are so great and beautiful and strong, as I walked
along I fell asleep. And a spirit took me and carried me off
through a pathless region that a man could not make his way
through; it was precipitous and broken by the waters. So when
I had crossed that river, I came to level ground, and knelt down
and began to pray to the Lord and to confess my sins. As I was 4
praying, heaven opened and I saw this woman, whom I had
desired, greeting me from heaven and saying,

"Good morning, Hermas!"

And I looked at her and said to her, 5

"My lady, what are you doing here?"

She answered,

"I have been taken up here to expose your sins to the Lord."

I said to her, 6

"My lady, are you now the ground of my accusation?"

"No," she said, "but listen to the words that I am going to say to you. God who dwells in the heavens and created out of nothing the things that are, and has increased and multiplied them for the sake of his holy church, is angry with you, because you sinned against me."

7   I answered her and said,

"Did I sin against you? Where or when did I ever utter a coarse word to you? Have I not always regarded you as a goddess? Have I not always respected you as a sister? Why do you falsely charge me, my lady, with this wickedness and impurity?"

8   She laughed at me and said,

"The desire for evil occurred to your mind. Don't you think it is an evil thing for an upright man if an evil desire occurs to his mind? It is a sin, and a great one," said she, "for the upright man has upright thoughts. So when his thoughts are upright, his reputation is recognized in heaven, and he finds the Lord favorable to him in everything he does. But those who think evil thoughts in their minds bring death and captivity on themselves, especially those who lay claim to this world and pride themselves on their wealth, and do not cling to the blessings that are

9   to come. Their souls will regret it; they have no hope, but they have despaired of themselves and their life. But you must pray to God, and he will heal your sins, and those of your whole household, and of all the saints."

2   After she had said these words, the heavens were closed, and I was possessed with horror and grief. I said to myself,

"If this sin is to be recorded against me, how can I be saved? Or how can I propitiate God for the sins I have committed? Or with what words shall I ask the Lord to be gracious to me?"

2   While I was considering and debating this in my mind, I saw before me a great white chair of snow-white wool and an aged woman in shining clothing came up with a book in her hands, and sat down by herself, and greeted me, saying,

"Good morning, Hermas!"

And grieving and weeping I said,
"My lady, good morning."
And she said to me,   3
"Why are you gloomy, Hermas? You who are so patient and good-natured, and always laughing, why do you look so downcast and far from cheerful?"
I said to her,
"Because of a very good woman, who says that I have sinned against her."
Then she said,   4
"Far be this thing from the slave of God! But at any rate a thought about her did occur to your mind. Such a design involves the slaves of God in sin. For it is an evil and shocking design for a devout and already approved spirit, if it desires to do an evil act, and especially for Hermas, the self-controlled, who refrains from every evil desire and is full of perfect simplicity and great innocence.

"Yet this is not why God is angry with you, but to lead you   3
to convert your family, which has sinned against the Lord and against you who are their parents. But you are so fond of your children that you have not corrected your family, but have allowed it to become corrupt. That is why the Lord is angry with you. But he will heal all your wrongdoings that have been committed in your family, for because of their sins and iniquities you have been corrupted by the matters of daily life. But the   2
great mercy of the Lord has taken pity on you and your family, and will make you strong and establish you in his glory. Only do not be idle, but take courage and strengthen your family. For just as the smith, hammering his work, masters the task that he desires, so the daily upright teaching overcomes all wickedness. So do not cease to correct your children, for I know that if they repent with all their hearts they will be enrolled with the saints in the books of life."
After these words of hers had ceased, she said to me,   3

"Do you want to hear me read?"

"Yes, my lady," I said.

She said to me,

"Then listen, and hear the glories of God."

I heard mighty and wonderful things, which I could not remember, for all her words were awful, such as man cannot endure. So it was her last words that I remembered, for they were good for us and gentle.

4 "Behold, the God of hosts, whom I love, who has by his mighty power and his great understanding created the world, and by his glorious design clothed his creation with beauty, and by his potent word fixed the heavens and founded the earth upon the waters, and by his own wisdom and foresight formed his holy church, which he has blessed—behold, he is removing the heavens and the mountains and the hills and the seas, and all things will be level for his chosen, so that he may fulfill to them the promise he made with great glory and joy, if they keep with great faith the commands of God which they have received."

4 So when she stopped reading and rose from the chair, four young men came and took the chair and went away toward the
2 east. And she called me to her, and touched my breast and said to me,

"Did my reading please you?"

And I said to her,

"My lady, these last words please me, but the first ones were hard and difficult."

And she said to me,

"These last ones are for the upright, but the first are for the heathen and the apostates."

3 As she was talking with me, two men appeared and took her by the arms and went away toward the east, where the chair was. And she went away cheerfully, and said to me as she was going,

"Act like a man, Hermas!"

VISION II

When I was going to Cumae, at the same season as in the 1
previous year, as I was walking along, I recalled the vision of
the previous year, and again the spirit took me and carried me
off to the same place as the year before. So when I reached the 2
place, I knelt down and began to pray to the Lord and to glorify
his name because he had thought me worthy and had made my
former sins known to me. But after I had risen from prayer, I 3
saw before me the elderly woman whom I had seen the year
before, walking and reading aloud from a little scroll. And she
said to me,

"Can you report these things to God's chosen?"

I said to her,

"My lady, I cannot remember so much, but give me the little
scroll, so that I can copy it."

"Take it," she said, "and give it back to me."

I took it, and went away to a place in the country, and copied 4
it all letter by letter, for I could not make out the syllables. So
when I had finished the letters of the little scroll, the little scroll
was suddenly snatched from my hand, but by whom I could
not see.

Fifteen days later, when I had fasted and earnestly asked the 2
Lord, the meaning of the writing was revealed to me. And this is
what was written:

"Your children, Hermas, have set God at naught and have 2
uttered blasphemy against the Lord, and through their great
wickedness have betrayed their parents, and have been called betrayers of parents, yet they have not benefited by betraying them,
but they have further added wantonness and a mass of wickedness to their sins, and so their iniquities have reached their
fullness. But make these words known to all your children, and 3
to your wife, who is to be as your sister, for she does not control
her tongue, but does wrong with it. But when she hears these

4 words she will refrain, and she will find mercy. After you have made known to them these words which the Master commanded me should be revealed to you, then all the sins which they have previously committed will be forgiven them, and all the saints who have sinned unto this day, if they repent with all their
5 hearts and drive the doubts from their minds. For the Master has sworn by his glory, about his chosen, that if after this day has been set there is any more sinning they will not find salvation. Repentance for the upright comes to an end, the days of repentance for all the saints are over, but for the heathen there
6 is still repentance until the last day. So you must tell the leaders of the church to rectify their ways in uprightness, so that
7 they may receive the promises in full, with great glory. Stand firm, therefore, you who do what is upright, and do not doubt, in order that you may be admitted among the holy angels. Blessed are you who endure the great persecution that is coming, and
8 who will not deny their life. For the Lord has sworn by his Son, that those who have denied Christ have renounced their own life, that is, those who are now going to deny him in the days to come, but on those who denied him before, he has had mercy, because of his compassion.

3   "But you, Hermas, must not hold a grudge against your children any more, nor let your sister have her way, so that they may be cleansed from their former sins. For they will be disciplined with just discipline, if you do not hold a grudge against them. Holding a grudge produces death. But you, Hermas, have had great troubles of your own, because of the trangressions of your family, because you paid no attention to them. Why, you
2 neglected them, and were absorbed in your wicked affairs. But you are saved by your not falling away from the living God and your sincerity and your great self-control. These have saved you, if you abide by them, and they save all who do such things, and they save all who live in innocence and sincerity. These will
3 prevail over all evil and will endure to eternal life. Blessed are

all who practice uprightness; they will never be destroyed. But **4** you must tell Maximus, 'Behold, persecution is coming; if it seems best to you, deny again!' The Lord is near those who turn to him, as is written in Eldad and Modat, who prophesied to the people in the desert."

Now a revelation was made to me, as I slept, brethren, by a **4** very good-looking young man, who said to me,

"Who do you think the elderly woman from whom you received the little scroll was?"

"The Sibyl," said I.

"You are wrong," he said, "it was not she."

"Then who was it?" said I.

"The church," said he. I said to him,

"Why, then, is she elderly?"

"Because," said he, "she was created first of all; that is why she is elderly; and it was because of her that the world was formed."

Afterward I saw a vision in my house. The elderly woman **2** came and asked me if I had given the scroll to the elders. I said I had not done so.

"You have done right," she said, "for I have some words to add. So when I finish all the words, they will be made known through you to all the chosen. So you must write two little scrolls and **3** you must send one to Clement and one to Grapte. Then Clement must send it to the cities abroad, for that is his function, and Grapte will exhort the widows and orphans. But you shall read it aloud to this city, with the elders who have charge of the church."

VISION III

The third vision that I had, brethren, was this. I had fasted **1,2** often and prayed the Lord to disclose to me the revelation he had promised to show me through that elderly woman, and that very night the elderly woman appeared to me and said to me,

"Since you are in such need and so eager to know everything,

go to the field where you raise spelt, and about ten o'clock I will
3 appear to you, and show you what you must see." I asked her,
"My lady, to what part of the field?"

"Wherever you please," she said. I chose a beautiful, secluded
place; but before I told her and mentioned the place, she said
to me,

"I will come wherever you please."

4 So I reached the field and counted the hours, and came to the
place where I had arranged with her to come, and I saw an
ivory couch placed there, and on the couch lay a linen cushion,
5 and on it was spread out a cloth covering of flaxen linen. When
I saw these things lying there, and no one at the place, I was
astonished, and a sort of trembling seized me, and my hair stood
on end, and a kind of shudder came over me, because I was
alone. So when I came to myself and remembered the glory
of God and took courage, I knelt down and confessed my sins
6 to the Lord again, as I had done before. Then she came, with
six young men, whom I had seen before, and she stood by me,
and listened while I prayed and confessed my sins to the Lord.
And she touched me and said,

"Hermas, stop saying all these prayers about your sins; pray
also for uprightness, so that you may take some part of it to
your family."

7 Then she raised me up by the hand and led me to the couch,
and said to the young men,

"Go away and build."

8 When the young men were gone and we were alone, she said
to me,

"Sit down here." I said to her,

"My lady, let the elders sit down first."

9 "Do what I tell you," she said, "sit down." Then when I wanted
to sit at her right, she would not let me, but motioned to me with
her hand to sit at her left. As I was pondering and grieving because she would not let me sit at her right, she said to me,

"Are you grieved, Hermas? The place at my right belongs to others, who have already pleased God and suffered for the name. But you are far from ready to sit with them. But continue as you do in your sincerity, and you will sit with them, and so will all who do what they have done and bear what they have borne."

"What," said I, "did they bear?"   2

"Listen," said she. "Scourgings, prisons, great persecutions, crosses, wild beasts, for the name. That is why the right side of the sanctuary belongs to them, and to everyone who suffers for the name. The left side belongs to the rest. But to both, those who sit on the right and those who sit on the left, the same gifts and the same promises belong; only, these sit on the right and have a certain glory. You earnestly desire to sit with them on the   2 right, but your defects are many. But you will be cleansed of your defects, and all who do not doubt will be cleansed of all their sins, up to this day."

When she had said this she meant to go away, but I fell at 3 her feet, and entreated her by the Lord to show me the vision that she had promised. And she took me by the hand again and 4 raised me up, and made me sit on the couch, at the left, and she sat down at the right. And she lifted up a shining staff and said to me,

"Do you see something great?" I said to her,

"My lady, I don't see anything." She said to me,

"Look! Do you not see right in front of you a great tower being built on the waters, of glistening square stones?" And a 5 tower was being built in a square by the six young men who had come with her, and tens of thousands of other men were bringing stones, some from the deep and others from the land, and passing them to the six young men, and they were taking them and building. All the stones that were dragged out of the deep they 6 set in the building just as they were, for they had been shaped and fitted the joints with the others, and they fitted one another

so closely that their joints did not show, and the tower building
7 looked as though it was built of a single stone. Of the other
stones, which were being brought from the dry land, they threw
some away, and some they put into the building, and others
8 they broke up and threw far away from the tower. Many other
stones were lying around the tower, and they did not use them
for the building, for some of them were scaly, and others were
cracked, and others were too short, and others were white and
9 rounded, and would not fit into the building. And I saw other
stones being thrown far from the tower and reaching the road
and not staying on the road but rolling from the road into the
pathless ground, and others falling into fire and burning, and
others falling near the water and unable to roll into the water,
although some wished them to roll on and reach the water.

3   When she had shown me these things, she wished to hurry
away. I said to her,

"My lady, what good does it do me to have seen these things
and not know what they mean?"

She answered and said to me,

"You're an artful fellow, wanting to find out all about the
tower!"

"Yes, my lady," said I, "so that I may report it to the brethren,
and they may be cheered, and when they hear this may come to
2 know the Lord in much glory." She said,

"Many will hear, but when they hear, some of them will rejoice
and some will weep, but even these, if they listen and repent,
will rejoice too. So hear the parables of the tower, for I will
reveal everything to you. And don't trouble me any more about
a revelation, for these revelations are at an end, for they have
been completed. But you will never stop asking for revelations,
for you are without shame.

3   "The tower that you see being built is myself, the church. I
have appeared to you now and previously. So ask whatever you
please about the tower, and I will reveal it to you, so that you
4 may rejoice with the saints." I said to her,

"My lady, since you have once thought me worthy to reveal everything to me, reveal it."

She said to me,

"Whatever can possibly be revealed to you will be revealed. Only let your heart be close to God, and do not doubt what you see."

I asked her,   5

"Why is the tower built on waters, my lady?"

"As I told you before," said she, "you do question closely. Well, if you question, you will find out the truth. Hear, then, why the tower is built on waters: it is because your life has been saved and will be saved by water. But the tower was founded by the command of the almighty and glorious name, and it is sustained by the invisible power of the Master."

"My lady," I answered, "this is a great and wonderful thing.   4
But who are the six young men who are building it, my lady?"

"These are the holy angels of God, who were first created, to whom the Lord committed his whole creation, to increase it and build it up and rule over the whole creation; so through them, the building of the tower will be finished."

"And who are the others, who are bringing the stones?"   2

"They too are holy angels of God, but these six are superior to them. So the building of the tower will be completed, and they will all rejoice together around the tower, and will glorify God because the building of the tower has been finished."

I asked her,   3

"My lady, I would like to know what becomes of the stones, and what they mean."

She answered and said to me,

"Not because you are worthier than all others to have it revealed to you, for there were others before you and better than you, to whom these visions ought to have been revealed. But in order that the name of God may be glorified, they have been and will be revealed to you, because of the doubters, who debate in their minds, whether these things are so or not. Tell them that all these things are true, and none of them is beyond the truth, but they are all potent, sure, and on a good foundation.

5   "Now hear about the stones that go into the building. The stones that are square and white and fit their joints are the apostles and bishops and teachers and deacons who have lived in the holiness of God, and have been bishops and teachers and deacons for God's chosen in purity and reverence. Some of them have fallen asleep, and others are still living. They always agreed with one another and were at peace with one another, and listened to one another; that is why their joints fit together in the building of the tower."

2   "But the ones that are dragged out of the deep, and put into the building, and that agree in their joints with the other stones already laid, who are they?"

"They are those who have suffered for the name of the Lord."

3   "But I want to know who the other stones are, that are brought from the dry land, my lady."

"Those that go into the building without being shaped, the Lord has approved, because they have lived in the uprightness of the Lord, and carried out his commands."

4   "But who are the ones that are brought and set in the building?"

"They are young in the faith, and faithful, but they are exhorted by the angels to do right, because wickedness has been found in them."

5   "But who are the ones that they were rejecting and throwing away?"

"They are the ones that have sinned and want to repent. That is why they were not thrown far from the tower, because they will be of use in the building if they repent. So those who are going to repent will be strong in the faith, if they repent now, while the tower is being built, but if the building is finished, they will no longer have an opportunity, but will be outcasts. The only thing they have is that they lie near the tower.

"But do you want to know who they are that were broken **6** up and thrown far away from the tower? They are the sons of disobedience; their faith was hypocritical, and no wickedness escaped them. That is why they have no salvation, for on account of their wickedness they are of no use in building. That is why they were broken in pieces and thrown far away, because of the Lord's anger, for they angered him. As to the others that you **2** saw lying about in such numbers, and not going into the building, the scaly ones are the ones that have learned the truth, but do not stand by it."

"But who are the ones that were cracked?" **3**

"They are those who are against one another in their hearts and are not at peace with one another, but keep up an appearance of peace, but when they leave one another, their wicked thoughts remain in their hearts. These are the cracks that the stones have. But the ones that are too short are those who have believed **4** and live for the most part in uprightness, but they have some fraction of disobedience; that is why they are too short and not perfect."

"But the white and rounded ones, that would not fit into the **5** building, who are they, my lady?"

She answered, and said to me,

"How long are you going to be foolish and stupid, and ask about everything and perceive nothing? They are those who have faith, but have also the riches of this world. When persecution comes, because of their riches and their business affairs they deny their Lord." I answered her and said, **6**

"My lady, when then will they be of use for the building?"

"When," she said, "their riches, which lead their souls astray, shall be cut off, then they will be useful to God. For just as the round stone cannot be made square unless it is cut off and loses some part of itself, so those also who have this world's riches cannot be of use to the Lord unless their riches are cut off. Learn **7** first from your own case; when you were rich, you were useless, but now you are useful and beneficial to life. Be useful to God, for you yourself also benefit from the same stones.

7 "As for the other stones that you saw thrown from the tower and reaching the road and rolling from the road into the pathless ground, they are those who have believed but because of their doubt leave their true way. So thinking they can find a better road, they go astray and trudge miserably over the pathless

2 ground. And the ones that fall into the fire and are burned are those who finally turn away from the living God and it no longer occurs to their minds to repent, because of their wanton passions

3 and the wickedness they have done. But do you want to know who the others are who fall near the water and cannot roll into the water? They are those who have heard the message and wish to be baptized in the name of the Lord, then when the purity of the truth comes to their remembrance, they change their minds

4 and follow their evil passions again." So she concluded the explanation of the tower.

5 Still unabashed I asked her whether all these stones that had been thrown away, and did not fit into the building of the tower, could find repentance and have a place in this tower.

"They can find repentance," she said, "but they cannot fit into

6 this tower. But they will fit into another place far inferior, and that only when they are tormented and fill out the days of their sins. And this is why they will be removed from it, because they have shared in the upright word. And then they will experience removal from their torments, because of the evil deeds that they have done. But if it does not occur to their minds, they will not be saved, because of their hardheartedness."

8 Then when I had stopped asking her about all these things, she said to me,

"Would you like to see something else?"

As I was very eager to see more, I was delighted that I was

2 to do so. She looked at me with a smile and said to me,

"Do you see seven women around the tower?"

"Yes, my lady," said I.

"This tower is supported by them, by the Lord's command. Now listen to their activities. The first of them, who is clasping 3 her hands, is called Faith; through her God's chosen are saved. The next one, who is dressed for work and acts like a man, is 4 called Self-control; she is the daughter of Faith. Whoever follows her will have a happy life, because he will refrain from all evil-doing, believing that if he refrains from every evil passion he will make sure of eternal life."

"And who are the others, my lady?" 5

"They are daughters one of another, and they are named one of them Sincerity, and the next Knowledge, and the next Innocence, and the next Reverence, and the next Love. So when you do all the deeds of their mother, you can attain life."

"I would like to know, my lady," said I, "what power each of 6 them possesses."

"Listen," she said, "to the powers that they possess. Their 7 powers are controlled by one another, and they follow one another, in the order in which they were born. From Faith springs Self-control, from Self-control, Sincerity, from Sincerity, Innocence, from Innocence, Reverence, from Reverence, Knowledge, from Knowledge, Love. So their deeds are pure, reverent, and divine. So whoever serves these, and has the strength to master 8 their deeds, will have his home in the tower, with the saints of God."

Then I asked her about the times, whether it is already the 9 end. But she cried out loudly,

"Foolish man! Can't you see that the tower is still being built? When the building of the tower is finished, the end will come. But it will be quickly built up. Don't question me any more. Let this reminder and renewing of your spirits suffice you and the saints. But these things have been revealed not for you alone, 10 but in order that you may show them to all, after three days, 11 for you must first understand it yourself. And I command you,

Hermas, first to utter all these things that I am going to tell you, in the hearing of the saints, so that they may hear and do them, and may be cleansed from their wickedness, and you also with them.

9 "Listen to me, children. I brought you up in great sincerity and innocence and reverence, by reason of the mercy of the Lord, who instilled uprightness into you, so that you might be made upright and be purified from all wickedness and all perversity. But you are not willing to be made to cease from your

2 wickedness. So now listen to me, and live at peace with one another, and look after one another and help one another, and do not partake profusely by yourselves of what God has created,

3 but share it also with those who are in want. For some by eating too much bring on bodily sickness and injure their bodies, while the bodies of those who have nothing to eat is injured because

4 they do not have enough food, and their body is destroyed. So this lack of solidarity is harmful to you who have and do not

5 share with those who are in want. Beware of the judgment to come! So you who have more must seek out those who are going hungry, while the tower is still unfinished, for after the tower is finished, you will want to do good and will have no oppor-

6 tunity. So take care, you who pride yourselves on your wealth, that those who are in want do not groan, and their groaning go up to the Lord, and you with your goods be shut outside the

7 door of the tower. So now I say to the leaders of the church and to those who take the front seats, do not be like the magicians. The magicians carry their potions in boxes, but you carry

8 your potion and poison in your hearts. You have become callous and are not willing to cleanse your hearts and mix your wisdom in a clean heart, so that you may obtain mercy from the Great

9 King. So take care, children, that these divisions do not defraud

10 you of your life. How do you propose to train the Lord's chosen, if you have no training yourselves? So train one another and live at peace with one another, so that I too may stand joyfully

before the Father and give an account for you all to the Lord."

So when she stopped talking with me, the six young men who **10** were doing the building came and carried her away to the tower, and four others picked up the couch and carried it also away to the tower. Of these last I did not see the faces, because they were turned away from me. But as she was going away, I asked **2** her to reveal to me about the three forms in which she had appeared to me. She answered and said to me,

"About these matters you must ask someone else for a revelation."

Now in the first vision last year, brethren, she appeared to **3** me as very aged, and sitting in a chair. In the second vision her **4** face was younger, but her skin and hair elderly, and she talked to me standing up, and she was more cheerful than before. But **5** in the third vision she was in all respects younger and exceedingly beautiful; only her hair was that of an elderly woman, and she was perfectly cheerful, and seated on a couch. I was deeply **6** grieved about this, wanting to learn this revelation, and in a vision of the night I saw the elderly woman saying to me,

"Every asking of a question requires humility. So fast, and you will receive what you ask from the Lord."

So I fasted for one day, and that very night there appeared **7** to me a young man, and he said to me,

"Why are you so ready to pray for revelations? Take care, or you will injure your body by so many requests. These revelations **8** are enough for you. Can you bear seeing mightier revelations than you have seen?"

I answered him and said, **9**

"Sir, this is all I ask, that there may be a full revelation about the three forms of the elderly woman."

He answered me and said,

"How long will you be incapable of understanding? Why, it is your doubts that make you unable to understand, and the fact that you do not turn your heart to the Lord."

10 I answered him again and said,
"But from you, sir, we shall learn them more definitely."

11, 2 "Hear," said he, "about the forms you ask about. Why did she appear to you in the first vision as elderly and sitting in a chair? Because your spirits are aged and already withered, and have

3 no power, because of your infirmities and doubts. For just as old men, who have no longer any hope of renewing their youth, have nothing to look forward to but falling asleep, so you also, softened by the matters of this life, have given yourselves up to apathy, and have not thrown your anxieties upon the Lord; but your spirit has been broken, and you have been made old by your sorrows."

"Why, then, I should like to know, did she sit in a chair, sir?"

"Because anyone who is weak sits in a chair because of his weakness, so that the weakness of his body may be supported. This is the meaning of the first vision.

12 "In the second vision, you saw her standing up, with a younger and more cheerful face than before, but with the skin and hair of

2 an elderly woman. Listen," said he, "to this parable also. When a man grows old, and has already given up all hope of himself, because of his weakness and poverty, and has nothing to look forward to but the last day of his life, then suddenly an inheritance is left to him, and when he hears of it, he gets up and is filled with joy, and is clothed with strength, and he no longer lies down but stands up, and his spirit which was previously broken by his former misfortunes is renewed, and he no longer sits down, but he acts like a man. It was so with you too when you

3 heard the revelation which the Lord made to you. For he had compassion on you and renewed your spirits and you put off your weakness, and strength came to you, and you were made mighty in faith, and the Lord rejoiced to see your access of strength, and this is why he showed you the building of the tower and will show you other things, if with all your hearts you live in peace with one another.

"But in the third vision you saw her as younger and beautiful **13** and cheerful and beautiful in form. For just as, if good news come **2** to someone in sorrow, he immediately forgets his former sorrows and thinks of nothing but the news he has heard, and he is made strong to do good in the future, and his spirit is renewed because of the joy that he has experienced, so you also have experienced the renewing of your spirits from seeing these blessings. As for **3** your seeing her sitting on a couch, it means that the position is secure, for the couch has four feet and stands firm, for the world too is sustained by four elements. So those who have fully repented **4** will be young and firmly founded,—those who have repented with all their hearts. Now you have the revelation in full. Do not ask anything about a revelation again, but if there is any need, a revelation will be made to you."

VISION IV

The fourth vision that I had, brethren, twenty days after the **1** preceding vision that had come to me, was a forecast of the persecution that is at hand. I was going into the country by the Campanian Way; the place is about ten furlongs off the highroad, and **2** is easily reached. So as I was walking along by myself, I prayed **3** the Lord to complete the revelations and visions that he had shown me through his holy church, that he might strengthen me and grant repentance to his slaves who had fallen away, so that his great, glorious name might be glorified, because he had thought me worthy to be shown his marvels. And as I was glori- **4** fying him and giving him thanks, what seemed a voice rang in my ears in answer,

"Do not doubt, Hermas."

I began to reason with myself and say,

"What reason have I to doubt, when I have been given such a foundation by the Lord and have seen such glorious things?"

And I went a little nearer, brethren, and here I saw a cloud of **5**

dust that seemed to reach to heaven, and I began to say to myself,
"Are there cattle coming and raising a cloud of dust?"

6   It was about two hundred yards away from me. As the cloud of
dust grew bigger and bigger, I suspected that it was something
from God. The sun shone out for a moment and here I saw a
huge beast something like a sea monster, and fiery locusts were
coming from its mouth. The beast was about a hundred feet long,
7   and it had a head like a wine jar. And I began to cry, and to ask
the Lord to deliver me from it. And I recalled the words I had
heard, "Do not doubt, Hermas."

8   So, brethren, I clothed myself in faith in the Lord, and remembered the great things he had taught me, and took courage and
faced the beast. The beast was coming on with such a rush that
9   it could devastate a city. I went up to it, and the huge sea monster
stretched itself on the ground, and only thrust out its tongue, and
10   did not move at all until I had gone by. And the beast had four
colors on its head, black, then flame and blood color, then gold,
then white.

2   After I had passed the beast, and gone on about thirty feet,
behold, a girl met me, dressed as if she were coming from a bridal
chamber, all in white, with white sandals, veiled up to her fore-
head, and on her head she wore a snood, but she had white hair.
2   I knew from my earlier visions that she was the church, and I
was greatly cheered. She greeted me, saying,
"Good morning, my man."
"Good morning, my lady," I greeted her in return.
3   She answered me and said,
"Didn't anything meet you?"
"Yes, my lady," I said to her, "a huge beast did, that could
destroy whole peoples, but by the power of the Lord and his
great mercy I escaped from it."
4   "You deserved to escape," said she, "because you cast your
care upon God, and opened your heart to the Lord, believing
that you cannot be saved by anything but his great and glorious

name. That is why the Lord sent his angel who has authority over the beasts, whose name is Thegri, and he stopped its mouth, so that it should not hurt you. Because of your faith you have escaped great affliction, and because when you saw such a huge beast you did not doubt. Go, therefore, and tell the Lord's chosen 5 his mighty deeds, and tell them that this beast is the symbol of the great persecution that is coming. If therefore you will prepare yourselves beforehand and will repent with all your hearts and turn to the Lord, you will be able to escape it, if your hearts become pure and blameless, and you serve the Lord blamelessly the rest of the days of your lives. Cast your cares upon the Lord, and he will remedy them. Have faith in the Lord, you doubters, 6 for he can do all things, and can turn away his wrath from you, and send forth plagues upon you doubters. Alas for those who hear these words and disobey them; it would have been better for them not to have been born."

I asked her about the four colors that the beast had on its head. 3 She answered me and said,

"You are curious again about such things!"

"Yes," I said, "my lady, tell me what they are."

"Listen," said she. "The black is this world, in which you live. 2 The fiery bloody color means that this world must be destroyed 3 in blood and fire. The gold part is you, who have fled from this 4 world. For just as gold is tested with fire, and made useful, so you also who live in it are being tested. Then those who endure and are tested by fire will be purified by it. Just as gold loses its dross, you also will cast off all sorrow and tribulation, and be purified and useful for the building of the tower. But the white 5 part is the age to come, in which God's chosen will live, for those who have been chosen by God for eternal life will be spotless and pure. So do not cease to speak in the hearing of the 6 saints. Now you have the forecast of the great persecution that is to come. But if you so will, it will be nothing. Remember what is already written."

With these words she went away, and I did not see where she went, for a cloud appeared, and I turned back in fear, thinking that the beast was coming.

REVELATION V

1 After I had prayed at home, and had sat down upon my bed, a man came in of splendid appearance, in the garb of a shepherd, wearing a white goatskin, with a bag on his shoulders and a staff 2 in his hand. He greeted me, and I in turn greeted him. He sat down at once beside me and said to me,

"I have been sent by the most reverend angel, to live with you the rest of the days of your life."

3 I thought he had come to tempt me, and I said to him,

"Well, who are you? For I know," said I, "to whom I was entrusted."

"Don't you recognize me?" he said to me.

"No," said I.

"I am the shepherd, to whom you have been entrusted," said he.

4 Even as he spoke, his appearance changed, and I recognized him as the one to whom I had been entrusted, and I was bewildered, and fear seized me, and I was completely overwhelmed with sorrow that I had answered him so wickedly and foolishly. 5 But he answered me and said,

"Do not be bewildered but find strength in my commands which I am going to give you. For I am sent," said he, "to show you again all the things you saw before, the main points, which are profitable for you. First of all, write down my commands and my parables, but the other things you shall write as I shall show them to you. That," said he, "is why I command you to write the commands and parables first, so that you may have them at hand to read, and may be able to keep them."

6 So I wrote down the commands and parables as he commanded

me. If, then, when you hear them you keep them and live by 7
them and carry them out with a pure heart, you will receive
from the Lord what he has promised you. But if when you hear
them you do not repent, but go on adding to your sins, you will
receive the opposite from the Lord. All these things the shepherd,
the angel of repentance, commanded me to write thus.

THE COMMANDS

COMMAND I

"First of all, believe that God is one, and he created all things, 1
and organized them and out of what did not exist made all things
to be, and contains all things, but alone is himself uncontained.
Trust him therefore and fear him, and fearing him, be self- 2
controlled. Keep this command, and you will cast away from yourself all wickedness, put on every virtue of uprightness, and you
will live to God, if you keep this command."

COMMAND II

He said to me,   1
   "Be sincere and simple-minded, and you will be like little children, who do not know the wickedness that destroys the life of
men. First, speak evil of nobody, and do not enjoy hearing anyone 2
do so. Otherwise you who hear will be involved in the sin of the
one who speaks the evil, if you believe the evil that you hear
spoken, for by believing it you yourself also will be holding a
grudge against your brother. So you will be involved in the sin

3 of the one who speaks the evil. Evil-speaking is wicked. It is a restless demon, never at peace, but always at home with dissension. Abstain from it, and you will always get on well with all
4 men. Clothe yourself in reverence, in which there is no evil cause for offense, but all is smooth and glad. Do right, and from your labors which God gives you give generously to all who are in need, not questioning to whom to give or to whom not to give. Give to all, for God wishes that from what he gives gifts should
5 be made to all. So those who receive will account to God as to why they have accepted it and for what purpose. For those who accept it because they are in distress will not be judged, but
6 those who accept it on false pretenses will pay the penalty. So he who gives is innocent, for as he received from the Lord a service to perform, he has sincerely performed it, without distinguishing to whom to give or not to give. So this service, sincerely performed, becomes glorious in the sight of God. So he
7 who renders it sincerely will live to God. So keep this command, as I have told you, so that your repentance and that of your family may be found sincere, and your heart clean and stainless."

COMMAND III

1 Again he said to me,
"Love truth, and let nothing but truth proceed from your mouth, so that the spirit which God made to dwell in this flesh may be found truthful in the sight of all men, and the Lord who dwells in you will thus be glorified, for the Lord is truthful in
2 every word and with him there is no falsehood. So those who lie set the Lord at naught and become defrauders of the Lord, for they do not return to him the deposit which they received. For they received from him a spirit free from deceit. If they give this back a lying one, they have defiled the Lord's command and become defrauders of him."

3 So when I heard this I cried bitterly. And when he saw me crying he said,

"Why are you crying?"

"Because, sir," said I, "I do not know whether I can be saved."

"Why?" said he.

"Because, sir," said I, "I have never in my life spoken a true word, but have always talked deceptively with everybody, and represented my lie as true to all men, and no one ever contradicted me but they believed my word. How then, sir," said I, "after doing this, can I live?"

"Your thinking," said he, "is right and true, for you ought 4 as God's slave to have lived in truth, and a bad conscience ought not to have dwelt with the spirit of truth, nor to have brought grief to the revered, true spirit."

"Never, sir," said I, "have I correctly heard such words."

"Well, now," said he, "you hear them. Obey them, so that the 5 lies you have told heretofore in your business affairs may themselves prove worthy of belief, now that what you now say has been found true. For they also can prove trustworthy. If you obey these words and henceforth tell nothing but the truth, you will be able to attain life for yourself, and whoever will hear this command, and abstain from the most wicked sin of lying, will live to God."

COMMAND IV

"I charge you," said he, "to observe purity, and let no thought 1 occur to your mind about another man's wife or about some immorality or about any such like evil things, for if you do so, you will commit a great sin. But if you always remember your own wife, you will never commit sin. For if this idea occurs to 2 your mind, you will sin, and if other things as bad occur to you, you commit sin. For this idea is a great sin for a slave of God, but if any man commits this wicked act, he brings death upon himself. So beware; abstain from this idea, for where earnestness 3 dwells, there disobedience ought not to occur to an upright man's mind."

4 I said to him,

"Sir, permit me to ask you a few questions."

"Do so," said he.

"Sir," said I, "if a man has a wife who believes in the Lord and detects her in an adultery, does the husband sin if he continues to live with her?"

5 "So long as he is unaware of it," said he, "he does not sin. But if the husband knows of her sin, and the wife does not repent, but persists in her immorality, and the husband continues to live with her, he becomes involved in her sin and a sharer in her adultery."

6 "What, then, sir," said I, "is the husband to do, if the wife persists in this attachment?"

"He must divorce her," said he, "and the husband must live by himself; but if after divorcing his wife, he marries someone else, he too commits adultery."

7 "If then, sir," said I, "after the wife is divorced, she repents and wishes to return to her own husband, will she not be taken back?"

8 "Certainly," said he, "if her husband does not take her back, he sins, and involves himself in great sin. Why, the sinner who repents must be taken back, but not often, for the slaves of God can have but one repentance. So for the sake of her repentance, the husband ought not to marry. This course of action is

9 incumbent on wife and husband. Not only," said he, "is it adultery if a man defiles his flesh, but whoever imitates the actions of the heathen commits adultery, so that if anyone persists in such practices and does not repent, keep away from him and do not

10 live with him; otherwise you also share in his sin. That is why you were commanded to live by yourselves, whether husband or wife,

11 for in such circumstances repentance is possible. I therefore," said he, "am not supplying an occasion for the matter's ending in this way, but that the one who has sinned may sin no more. As for his former sin, there is one who can provide a cure, for it is he who has power over all things."

I questioned him again, saying,   **2**

"Since the Lord has thought me worthy of having you live with me always, permit me to say a few more words, since I have no understanding and my heart has been hardened by my past deeds. Make me understand, for I am very foolish and understand nothing at all."

He answered me and said,   **2**

"I am in charge of repentance, and I give understanding to all who repent. Or do you not think," said he, "that this very repentance is itself understanding? To repent," he went on, "is great understanding. For the man who has sinned understands that he has done wrong in the sight of the Lord, and the thing that he has done comes to his mind, and he repents and no longer does wrong, but lavishes himself on doing good, and he humbles his soul and torments it, because he sinned. So you see that repentance is great understanding."

"This is why, sir," said I, "I inquire into everything so par-   **3** ticularly of you; first, because I am a sinner, so that I may learn what things to do in order to live, for my sins are many and various."

"You will live," said he, "if you keep my commands and observe   **4** them. And whoever hears these commands and keeps them, will live to God."

"Let me ask a further question, sir," said I.   **3**

He said to me, "Go on."

"I have heard, sir," said I, "from some teachers, that there is no other repentance than the one when we went down into the water and received the forgiveness of our previous sins."

"You have heard correctly," said he, "for that is so. For he who   **2** has received forgiveness of sins ought never to sin again but to live in purity. But since you inquire into everything so particu-   **3** larly, I will disclose this also to you, not as giving an excuse to those who are going to believe, or to those who have already believed in the Lord. For those who have already believed or are

going to believe have no repentance for sins, but have forgive-
4 ness for their previous sins. For those then who were called before
these days, the Lord prescribed repentance. For since the Lord
knows men's hearts and knows everything beforehand, he knew
the weakness of human beings and the cunning of the devil,
that he would do some evil to the slaves of God, and act wickedly
5 to them. So the Lord, being merciful, had mercy on what he had
made, and set up this repentance, and authority over this repent-
6 ance was given to me. But I tell you," said he, "if after this great
and holy invitation a man is severely tempted by the devil and
sins, he has one opportunity to repent. But if he sins continually
and repents, repentance is unavailing; it will be hard for him to
live."
7 I said to him,
"I have been restored to life again, when I heard these things
from you so definitely, for I know that if I do not add any more
to my sins, I will be saved."
"You will be saved," said he, "and so will all who do these
things."
4 I questioned him again, saying,
"Sir, since you have borne with me once, tell me this too
besides."
"Go on," said he.
"If, sir," said I, "a wife or again a husband falls asleep, and one
of them marries, does the one who marries sin?"
2 "He does not sin," said he, "but if he remains by himself he
wins greater honor for himself, and great glory with the Lord;
3 but even if he marries he does not sin. So preserve purity and
gravity, and you will live to God. From now on, from the day
you were put in my charge, observe these things that I tell you
4 and am going to tell you, and I will live in your house. Your
former sins will be forgiven, if you keep my commands, and all
men will be forgiven if they keep these commands of mine and
live in this purity."

COMMAND V

"Be patient," he said, "and understanding, and you will pre- 1
vail over all evil actions and do all uprightness. For if you are 2
patient, the holy Spirit that lives within you will be pure, not
being darkened by another, evil spirit, but living in a large room
it will rejoice and be glad with the body in which it lives, and
will serve God with great cheerfulness, for he is at peace
within. But if any anger enters, the holy Spirit, which is sensitive, 3
is immediately distressed, for it does not find the place clean,
and seeks to leave the place, for it is choked by the evil spirit,
and has no room to serve the Lord as it desires, for it is contaminated by anger. For the Lord dwells in patience, but the
devil in ill temper. So if both spirits live together, it is unfor- 4
tunate and bad for the man in whom they live. For if you take a 5
little wormwood and pour it into a jar of honey, is not all the
honey spoiled, and is not such a quantity of honey ruined by the
very little wormwood, and does it not destroy the sweetness of the
honey, and it no longer has the same favor with its owner, because
it has become bitter, and worthless? But if the wormwood is not
put into the honey, the honey is found sweet and is of use to its
owner. You see that patience is very sweet, more so than honey, 6
and useful to the Lord, and he lives in it. But ill temper is bitter
and useless. Then if ill temper is mixed with patience, patience is
contaminated, and its petition is no longer useful to God."

"I would like to know, sir," said I, "the operation of ill temper, 7
so that I may guard against it."

"By all means," said he; "if you do not guard against it, you and
your family, you have lost all your hope. But guard against it, for
I am with you. And all those who repent with all their hearts
will keep themselves from it. For I will be with them and keep
them safe, for they have all been made upright by the most
revered angel.

2   "Now listen," said he, "to the operation of ill temper, how wicked it is, and how it destroys my slaves by its operation, and how it leads them astray from uprightness. But it does not lead those astray who are filled with faith, nor can it operate upon them, for my power is with them, but it leads the foolish and

2   doubters astray. For when it sees such men standing firm, it inserts itself into that man's heart, and for no reason at all, the man or the woman is embittered about business affairs, or food, or some trifle, or about some friend, or about giving or accepting, or some such foolish matters, for all these things are foolish and

3   empty and meaningless and harmful to the slaves of God. But patience is great and strong, and possesses a power that is sturdy and thrives in great enlargement, it is joyous, exultant, free from care, glorifying the Lord at all times, with no bitterness in it, remaining always meek and quiet. So this patience lives with those who

4   possess a faith that is perfect. But ill temper is in the first place foolish, fickle and senseless. Then from fickleness comes bitterness, and from bitterness wrath, and from wrath anger, and from anger vengefulness. And this being composed of such great evils

5   becomes a great and incurable sin. For when all these spirits reside in one vessel, where the holy Spirit also dwells, that vessel

6   cannot contain them, but overflows. So the sensitive spirit, which is not accustomed to live with an evil spirit, nor with harshness, departs from such a man, and seeks to live with gentleness and

7   quiet. Then when it leaves that man where it was living, that man becomes void of the upright spirit, and being thereafter filled with the evil spirits, he is unsettled in everything he does, being dragged hither and thither by the evil spirits, and is utterly blinded to good intentions. This, then, is what happens to all

8   who are ill tempered. So abstain from ill temper, the most evil spirit, and clothe yourself in patience, and resist ill temper and bitterness, and you will find yourself with the holiness that is loved by the Lord. Take care therefore never to disregard this command, for if you master this command you will be able to

keep the rest of the commands that I am going to give you. Be strong in them, and filled with power, and let all those who want to live by them be filled with power.

COMMAND VI

"I commanded you," said he, "in the first command, to observe **1** faith and fear and self-control."

"Yes, sir," said I.

"But now," said he, "I want to show you their capabilities also, so that you may understand what capability and effectiveness each of them possesses. For their effects are twofold. So they relate to right and wrong. So trust what is right, do not trust **2** what is wrong. For uprightness has a straight way, but wrongdoing a crooked one. But follow the straight and level way, and leave the crooked one alone. For the crooked way has no paths, **3** but broken ground and many obstacles, and it is rough and thorny. So it injures those who follow it. But those who follow **4** the straight way walk smoothly and without stumbling, for it is neither rough nor thorny. So you see that it is better to follow this way."

"I am pleased," said I, "to follow this way."   **5**

"You shall do so," said he, "and whoever turns to the Lord with his whole heart will follow it.

"Now hear about faith," said he, "There are two angels with **2** man, one of uprightness and one of wickedness."

"How, then, sir," said I, "am I to know their operations, for **2** both angels live with me?"

"Listen," said he, "and you will understand them. The angel of **3** uprightness is sensitive and modest and gentle and quiet. So when this one comes into your mind, he immediately talks with you about uprightness, purity, reverence, self-control, and every upright act and every glorious virtue. When all these things occur to your mind, know that the angel of uprightness is with you.

So these are the things the angel of uprightness does. So believe
4 him and what he does. Now observe what the angel of wickedness
does. First of all, he is ill tempered and bitter and foolish, and
his acts are wicked, destroying the slaves of God. So when he
comes into your mind, know him by what he does."
5   "I do not understand, sir," said I, "how I am to recognize him."
"Listen," said he. "When ill temper comes over you, or bitterness, know that he is in you; then the desire for much business,
and extravagance in many kinds of food and drink and many
drinking parties and various improper foods, and the desire for
women, and covetousness and a great arrogance and ostentation
and everything like them and akin to them—when these things
occur to your mind, know that the angel of wickedness is in you.
6 So when you recognize his actions, get away from him, and do
not trust him, because his doings are wicked and harmful to the
slaves of God. Here you have the operations of both the angels.
7 Understand them, and trust the angel of uprightness. But get
away from the angel of wickedness, for his teaching is wicked
in all he does. For even if a man is a believer and the thought of
this angel occurs to his mind, that man or that woman is sure to
8 commit a sin. But again, even if a man or woman is very wicked,
and the doings of the angel of uprightness occur to his mind, he
9 must necessarily do something good. So you see," said he, "that
it is good to follow the angel of uprightness, and to bid the angel
10 of wickedness goodbye. This command tells what relates to faith,
in order that you may believe what the angel of uprightness does,
and through doing them may live to God. But believe that the
doings of the angel of wickedness are bad; so if you do not do
them, you will live to God."

COMMAND VII

1 "Fear the Lord and keep his commands," he said. "So if you keep
God's commands, you will be strong in every action, and your

doing will be beyond criticism. For if you fear the Lord, you will do everything well. This is the fear you must have to be saved. Do not fear the devil, for if you fear the Lord you will 2 master the devil, for there is no power in him. And where there is no power, there is no fear either; but where there is glorious power, there is fear too. For everyone who has power inspires fear; but he who has no power is despised by everybody. But 3 fear the doings of the devil, for they are evil. So if you fear the Lord you will not do them, but refrain from them. So there are 4 two kinds of fear; if you want to do wrong, fear the Lord and you will not do it. But if again you want to do right, fear the Lord and you will do it; so that the fear of the Lord is powerful, great, and glorious. So fear the Lord, and you will live to him, and all who fear him and keep his commands will live to God."

"Why, sir," said I, "did you say of those that keep his com- 5 mands, 'They will live to God'?"

"Because," said he, "all creation fears the Lord, but it does not keep his commands. So life with God belongs to those who fear him and keep his commands. But those who do not keep his commands do not have life in him, either."

COMMAND VIII

"I told you," said he, "that God's creatures are of a twofold 1 kind; for self-control too is twofold. For in some things we must practice self-control and in some things we must not."

"Inform me, sir," said I, "in what things we must practice self- 2 control, and in what we must not."

"Listen," said he. "Be self-controlled about what is wrong, and do not do it, but do not be self-controlled about what is right, but do it. If you are self-controlled about what is right, so that you do not do it, you commit a great sin. But if you are self-controlled about what is wrong, so that you do not do it, you practice great uprightness. So restrain yourself from all evil, and do right."

3   "What, sir," said I, "are the kinds of wickedness from which we must restrain ourselves?"

"Listen," said he. "From adultery and immorality, from lawless drunkenness, from wicked luxury, from many kinds of food, and extravagance of wealth, and boastfulness and haughtiness and pride, and from lying and evil speaking and hypocrisy, holding

4   grudges and all abusive language. These actions are the wickedest of all in the life of men. So from these actions the slave of God must restrain himself. For one who does not restrain himself from these cannot live to God. So listen to the things that follow them."

5   "But, sir," said I, "are there still more wicked actions?"

"Yes, there are many," said he, from which the slave of God must restrain himself—theft, lying, robbery, false witness, covetousness, lust, deceit, vainglory, ostentation, and everything like

6   them. Don't you think these things are wicked?"

"Yes, very wicked," said I, "for the slaves of God."

"From all these things, the man who is serving God must restrain himself. So restrain yourself from all these, so that you may live to God, and be enrolled among those who practice self-restraint in them. These, then, are the things from which you

7   must restrain yourself. But listen to the things in which you must not restrain yourself, but which you must do. Do not restrain yourself in what is right, but do it."

8   "Tell me, sir," said I, "what you mean by right things, so that I may live by them and serve them, so that by doing them I may be saved."

"Listen," said he, "to the deeds that are right, which you must

9   do, and not restrain yourself from. First of all, faith, fear of the Lord, love, harmony, upright speech, truthfulness, endurance; there is nothing in human life better than these. If a man observes these, and does not restrain himself from them, he will be blessed

10 in his life. Then hear the things that follow them: waiting on widows, looking after orphans and needy people, delivering the

slaves of God from distress, being hospitable (for doing good may be found in hospitality), nonresistance to anyone, being quiet, being more needy than all men, revering the aged, practicing uprightness, observing brotherhood, putting up with insolence, being patient, not holding a grudge, encouraging the weary in heart, not casting out those who have stumbled from the faith, but converting and encouraging them, not oppressing debtors and those in need, and whatever other actions are like these. Do you think these things are right?" said he.   11

"Why, sir," said I, "what can be better than these?"

"Then live by them," said he, "and do not restrain yourself from them, and you will live to God. So keep this command. If you do   12 right, and do not restrain yourself from it, you will live to God, and all who do so will live to God. And again, if you do not do wrong and restrain yourself from it, you will live to God. And all who keep these commands and live by them will live to God."

COMMAND IX

"Cast off doubt from yourself," he said to me, "and do not   1 hesitate at all to ask God for anything, or say in yourself, 'How can I ask anything from the Lord and receive it, when I have sinned so much against him?' Do not reason thus, but turn to the   2 Lord with your whole heart, and ask of him undoubtingly, and you will come to know his great mercy, that he will not desert you, but will fulfill the request of your soul. For God is not like   3 men, who hold grudges, but he is forgiving, and feels pity for what he has made. So cleanse your heart of all the vanities of this   4 world, and the things I have told you of, and ask the Lord, and you will receive everything, and not fail to receive any of your requests, if you ask the Lord without doubting. But if you doubt   5 in your heart, you will receive none of your requests. For those who doubt in their relation to God are the waverers and do not get any of their requests at all. But those who have perfect faith   6

ask for everything trusting in the Lord, and they receive it, for
they ask undoubtingly, without any wavering. For any man who
wavers, if he does not repent, can be saved only with difficulty.
7 So cleanse your heart of wavering, and clothe yourself in faith,
for it is strong, and trust God, that you will receive from him all
that you ask for, and if ever, when you have asked the Lord for
something, you are somewhat slow in receiving it, do not doubt,
because you did not receive your soul's request quickly, for surely
it is on account of some temptation or some transgression of
which you are unaware, that you are slow in getting what you
8 asked for. So do not stop making your soul's request, and you
will receive it, but if you grow weary and waver, blame yourself
9 and not him who gives to you. Beware of such wavering, for it is
wicked and foolish and uproots many from the faith, even men
who are very faithful and strong. For this doubt is the daughter
10 of the devil, and does the slaves of God great evil. So despise
wavering, and master it in every matter, clothing yourself in
strong and powerful faith, for faith promises all things, accom-
plishes all things, but doubt distrusts itself and fails in everything
11 it undertakes. So you see," said he, "that faith is from above, from
the Lord, and has great power, but doubt is an earthly spirit,
12 from the devil, and has none. So serve faith, which has power,
and keep away from doubt, which has none, and you will live to
God, and all who are so minded will live to God."

COMMAND X

1 "Put sadness from you," said he, "for it is the sister of doubt
and bad temper."
2   "How, sir," said I, "can she be their sister? For bad temper
seems to me to be one thing, and doubt another, and sadness
another."

"You are foolish, man," said he, "and do you not understand
that sadness is more wicked than all the spirits and most danger-

ous to the slaves of God, and beyond all the spirits it destroys the man, and wears out the holy Spirit, and again saves."

"Sir," said I, "I have no understanding, and cannot understand 3 these parables. For how it can wear out and save again, I cannot see."

"Listen," said he. "Those who have never searched for the 4 truth nor inquired about the deity, but have merely believed, and been involved in business and wealth and heathen friendships, and many other affairs of this world—all who are absorbed in these things cannot understand the parables of the deity, for they are darkened by these doings and ruined and have become dried up. Just as fine vineyards, when they are neglected, are made 5 barren by the thorns and weeds, so men who have believed and then get into these many activities that I have mentioned are drawn aside from their purpose, and lose all understanding of uprightness, but when they hear of deity and truth their mind is absorbed in their business, and they understand nothing at all. But those who have the fear of God, and inquire about deity and 6 truth, and have their hearts turned toward the Lord, perceive and understand what is said to them the more quickly, because they have the fear of the Lord within themselves, for where the Lord dwells, there is also great understanding. So hold fast to the Lord, and you will understand and grasp everything.

"Hear then," said he, "foolish man, how sadness wears out the 2 holy Spirit, and again saves. When the doubtful man undertakes 2 any enterprise and fails in it because of his doubt, this sadness comes into the man, and offends the holy Spirit and wears it out. Then again when ill temper clings to a man about some matter, 3 and he is greatly embittered, sadness again comes into the ill-tempered man's heart, and he is grieved about the thing that he has done, and repents because he has done wrong. So this sad- 4 ness seems to bring salvation, because when he had done wrong he repented. So both actions grieve the Spirit, doubt, because he did not succeed in what he undertook, and ill temper grieves the

Spirit, because he did wrong. So both, doubt and ill temper,
5 distress the holy Spirit. So cast sadness from you, and do not
distress the holy Spirit that dwells within you, that it may not
6 entreat God and depart from you. For the Spirit of God which
has been put in our flesh will not endure sadness or restraint.

3   "So clothe yourself in cheerfulness, which always finds favor
with God, and is acceptable to him, and delight in it. For every
cheerful man does good things and thinks good thoughts and de-
2 spises sadness. But the sorrowful man always does wrong. First,
he does wrong, because he grieves the holy Spirit which was
cheerful when it was given to the man; and, second, he does
wrong in grieving the holy Spirit, because he does not pray to the
Lord nor confess to him. For the petition of a man who is sad
never has power to ascend to the altar of God."

3   "Why," said I, "cannot the petition of the man who is sad
ascend to the altar?"

"Because," said he, "sadness is entrenched in his heart. So the
sadness, mingling with the petition, prevents the petition from
ascending in purity to the altar. For just as vinegar and wine
mixed together do not have the same pleasant taste, so sadness
4 mixed with the holy Spirit does not have the same appeal. So
cleanse yourself from this wicked sadness, and you will live to
God. And all who cast off sadness from themselves and clothe
themselves entirely in cheerfulness will live to God."

COMMAND XI

1 He showed me men sitting on a bench, and another man sitting
in a chair, and he said to me,

"Do you see those who are sitting on the bench?"

"I do, sir," said I.

"They are believers," said he, "and the man who is sitting in
the chair is a false prophet, who is destroying the understanding
of the slaves of God. But he destroys that of the doubtful, not of
2 the believers. These doubtful ones, then, come to him as to a

soothsayer, and ask him what will happen to them. And this false prophet, since he has no power of a divine spirit within himself, talks with them about their questions and in accordance with their wicked desires, and fills their souls, just as they wish. For 3 since he is empty himself, he gives empty people empty answers, for whatever he is asked, he answers according to the emptiness of the man who asks it. But he says some things that are true, for the devil fills him with his spirit, to see if he will be able to break down one of the upright. So all who are strong in the faith 4 of the Lord, being clothed with truth, do not join such spirits, but keep away from them. But all who are doubtful and repent often, practice soothsaying like the heathen, and bring upon themselves greater sin by their idolatry. For the man who consults a false prophet on any action is an idolater and void of the truth and foolish. For no spirit given by God needs to be con- 5 sulted, but having the power of deity, it says everything of itself, because it is from above, from the power of the divine Spirit. But 6 the spirit that is consulted and speaks according to men's desires is earthly and trifling, and has no power, and it does not speak at all unless it is consulted."

"How, then, sir," said I, "is a man to know which of them is a 7 prophet, and which a false prophet?"

"Hear," said he, "about both prophets, and in the way I am going to tell you, you can test the prophet and the false prophet. Test the man who has the divine spirit by his life. In the first 8 place, the man who has the spirit that is from above is gentle, quiet and humble, and abstains from all wickedness and the futile desire of this world, and makes himself more needy than all men, and when he is consulted gives no answer to anyone, and does not speak by himself nor does the holy Spirit speak when a man wishes to speak, but speaks when God wishes him to speak. So when the man who has the divine spirit comes into 9 a meeting of upright men who have faith in the divine spirit, and a petition is offered to God on the part of the company of these men, then the angel of the prophetic spirit which is assigned to

him fills the man, and the man when he is filled with the holy
10 Spirit speaks to the congregation as the Lord wills. In this way,
then, the spirit of the deity will be made plain. Whatever power
11 therefore attaches to the spirit of deity belongs to the Lord. Hear
now," said he, "about the earthly, futile spirit, which has no
12 power, but is foolish. In the first place, that man who thinks he
has the spirit exalts himself, and wants to have a front seat, and
he is immediately bold and shameless and talkative, and lives in
great luxury, and many other pleasures, and accepts pay for his
prophesying, and if he does not get it, he does not prophesy. Can
a divine spirit, then, accept pay for prophesying? It is impossible
for a prophet of God to do this, but the spirit of such prophets is
13 earthly. Then too, it does not come near a meeting of upright
men at all, but avoids them, and attaches itself to those who are
doubtful and vain, and prophesies to them in corners, and deceives them, saying everything to them falsely, in line with their
desires, for it is answering empty-minded men. For an empty
vessel put among empty ones does not break, but they harmonize
14 with one another. But when he comes into a meeting full of upright men who have the spirit of deity, and prayer is offered by
them, that man is emptied, and the earthly spirit flees from him
in fear, and that man is struck dumb, and is completely shattered,
15 unable to say anything. For if you store wine or oil in a storeroom
and put an empty jar among them, and again want to empty the
storeroom, you will find the jar that you put there empty, empty
still. So the empty prophets, when they come among the spirits of
upright men, are found to be just as they were when they came.
16 You now have the life of both kinds of prophets. So test the man
17 who says he is inspired, by his deeds and his life. But for your
part trust the spirit that comes from God and possesses power,
but do not trust the earthly and empty spirit at all, because there
18 is no power in it, for it comes from the devil. Listen, then, to the
parable that I am going to tell you. Take a stone and throw it up
to heaven; see if you can reach it. Or again, take a squirt of water

and squirt it toward heaven, see whether you can pierce heaven."

"How, sir," said I, "can these things be? For the things you 19 speak of are both impossible."

"So," said he, "just as these things are impossible, the earthly spirits are impotent and weak. Now take the power that comes 20 from above. Hail is a very small grain, yet when it falls on a man's head, what pain it causes! Or again take a drop, which falls on the ground from the roof and makes a hole in the stone. So you 21 see that the smallest things from above when they fall on the earth have great power. So the divine spirit also comes from above and is mighty. So trust that spirit, but keep away from the other."

COMMAND XII

He said to me, 1

"Cast off from yourself every evil desire, and clothe yourself in good and holy desire, for when you are clothed with this desire, you will hate evil desire, and will control it as you please. For 2 the evil desire is savage and hard to tame. For it is terrible, and by its savagery it destroys men utterly, and especially if a slave of God gets entangled in it, and has no understanding, he is terribly destroyed by it, and it destroys such as have not the garment of good desire, but are entangled with this world. These men, then, it delivers to death."

"What kind of acts, sir," said I, "are produced by the evil desire, 3 and deliver men to death?"

"Hear," said he, "by what kind of acts the evil desire puts the slaves of God to death.

"Above all is the desire for someone else's wife or husband, and 2 for the extravagance of wealth, and many needless things to eat and drink, and many other foolish luxuries. For every luxury is foolish and futile for the slaves of God. These, then, are the evil 2 desires and put the slaves of God to death. For this evil desire is a daughter of the devil. So you must keep away from evil desires,

3 so that by doing so you may live to God. But as many as are
mastered by them, and do not withstand them, will finally die,
4 for these desires are deadly. But clothe yourself in the desire for
uprightness, and arming yourself with the fear of the Lord, resist
them. For the fear of God dwells in the good desire. If the evil
desire sees you are armed with the fear of God, and resisting it,
it will flee far from you, and be seen by you no more, for fear of
5 your weapons. So when you have conquered and triumphed over
it, come to the desire for uprightness and give up to it the victory
you have won, and serve it, just as it wishes. If you serve the good
desire, and are subject to it, you will be able to master the evil
desire and control it, as you please."

3   "I would like to know, sir," said I, "in what ways I must serve
the good desire."

"Listen," said he. "Practice uprightness and virtue, truthfulness
and the fear of the Lord, faith and gentleness, and whatever
good things are like them. By doing these you will be an acceptable slave of God, and will live to him, and everyone who serves
the good desire will live to God."

2   So he finished the twelve commands, and he said to me,
"You have these commands; live by them, and exhort those
who hear you, that their repentance may be pure for the rest of
3 the days of their lives. Perform carefully this service which I am
entrusting to you, and you will accomplish much, for you will
find favor among those who are going to repent, and they will
obey your words, for I will be with you and will compel them to
obey you."

4   "Sir," I said to him, "these commands are great and good and
glorious, and able to gladden the heart of the man who can keep
them. But I do not know whether these commands can be kept
by man, for they are very hard."

5   He answered and said to me,
"If you set before yourself that they can be kept, you can easily
keep them, and they will not be hard. But if it once occurs to your

mind that they cannot be kept by man, you will not keep them. But now I say to you, if you do not keep them, but neglect them, 6 you will not have salvation, nor will your children nor your family, since you have already decided for yourself that these commands cannot be kept by man."

He said these things to me very angrily, so that I was con- 4 founded, and very much afraid of him, for his appearance changed so that a man could not endure his anger. But when he 2 saw that I was utterly confused and confounded, he began to speak to me more kindly and cheerfully, and said,

"Foolish man, without understanding and doubtful, don't you understand how great, mighty and wonderful the glory of God is, because he created the world for man's sake, and made his whole creation subject to man, and gave him complete authority to have dominion over all things under heaven? If, then," said he, "man is 3 master of all God's creatures, and has dominion over them all, is he not able to master these commands also? The man who has the Lord in his heart," said he, "is able to master all things and all these commands. But those who have the Lord on their lips, 4 while their hearts are hardened, and who are far from the Lord, find these commands hard and difficult. So you who are empty 5 and fickle in the faith put the Lord into your hearts, and you will know that there is nothing easier, sweeter, or more gentle than these commands. Be converted, you who live under the com- 6 mands of the devil, which are hard and bitter and savage and brutal, and do not fear the devil, because he has no power over you. For I will be with you, I, the angel of repentance, who can 7 control him. The devil causes only fear, but his fear has no force. So do not fear him, and he will fly from you."

I said to him,   5
"Sir, listen to a few words from me."
"Say what you please," said he.
"Sir," said I, "man is eager to keep God's commands, and there is no one who does not pray to the Lord to be strengthened in

his commands and obey them, but the devil is hard and gets control of them."

2 "He cannot," said he, "get control of the slaves of God, who hope in him with all their hearts. The devil can wrestle with them, but he cannot throw them. So, if you resist him, he will be beaten and fly from you in disgrace. But all who are not quite 3 full fear the devil as though he had power. When a man fills a great many jars with good wine, and among the jars a few are not quite full, he goes to the jars and pays no attention to the full ones, for he knows that they are full, but he takes notice of the ones that are not quite full, for he is afraid that they have turned sour. For jars that are not quite full soon sour, and the flavor of 4 the wine is spoilt. So the devil also comes to all the slaves of God to tempt them. All, then, who are filled with faith stoutly resist him, and he goes away from them, for he finds no place where he can get in. So then he goes to those who are not quite full, and does what he pleases in them, and they become his abject slaves.

6 "But I, the angel of repentance, say to you, Do not be afraid of the devil. For I have been sent," said he, "to be with you who repent with all your hearts, and to strengthen you in the faith. 2 So put your trust in God, you who because of your sins have despaired of your life, and added to your sins and weighed down your life, for if you turn to the Lord with your whole hearts and do what is upright the rest of the days of your lives, and serve him rightly in accordance with his will, he will provide a cure for your former sins, and you will have power to master the doings of the devil. Do not be at all afraid of the devil's threats, 3 for he is as powerless as a dead man's sinews. So listen to me, and fear him who can do all things, who can save and destroy, and keep these commands, and you will live to God."

4 I said to him,

"Sir, now I am strengthened in all the requirements of the Lord, because you are with me, and I know that you will break in pieces all the power of the devil, and we will master him and prevail over all his doings. And I hope, sir, that I can keep these commands that you have commanded, if the Lord gives me strength."

"You will keep them," said he, "if your heart is pure toward the 5 Lord. And all who cleanse their hearts of the vain desires of this world, will keep them, and will live to God."

THE PARABLES

THE PARABLES THAT HE TOLD ME

PARABLE I

He said to me,   1

"You know," said he, "that you slaves of God live in a foreign country, for your city is far from this city. So if," said he, "you know your city in which you are going to live, why do you prepare lands and expensive establishments and buildings and useless rooms here? So the man who prepares these things for this 2 city cannot return to his own city. Foolish, doubtful, wretched 3 man, don't you understand that all these things belong to someone else, and in the power of someone else? For the lord of this city will say, 'I do not want you to live in my city, but get out of this city, for you do not observe my laws.' So if you have lands 4 and dwellings and many other possessions, what will you do with your land and house and all the other things you have prepared for yourself, when you are put out by him? For the lord of this country can justly say to you, 'Either observe my laws or get out of my country.' So what are you going to do, when you have a 5 law in your own city? For the sake of your lands and your other property, are you going to repudiate your law altogether and live by the law of this city? Take care that it does not prove disadvantageous to repudiate your law. For if you make up your mind to return to your city, you will not be received, because you have repudiated the law of your city, and you will be shut out of it.

6 So take care; as one who is living in a foreign land, provide for yourself no more than an adequate competence, and be ready, so that when the master of this city wants to put you out of it for disobeying his law, you can leave his city and go to your city

7 and joyfully observe your own law, uninjured. So take care, you who serve the Lord and have him in your hearts; do the deeds of God, remembering his commands and the promises he has made,

8 and believe that he will fulfill them, if his commands are kept. So instead of lands buy distressed souls, as one is able, and look after widows and orphans, and do not neglect them, and spend your wealth and all your establishments on such lands and houses as

9 you have received from God. For this is why the Master has made you rich, that you may perform these services to him. It is far better to buy such lands and possessions as you will find in

10 your city when you go home to it. This extravagance is right and holy, and brings no sadness or fear, but brings joy. So do not practice the extravagance of the heathen, for it is bad for the

11 slaves of God. But practice your own extravagance, in which you can rejoice, and do not counterfeit or touch what belongs to someone else, or desire it, for it is wicked to desire what belongs to someone else. Do your own work and you will be saved."

PARABLE II

Another parable.

1   As I was walking in the country, and observing an elm tree and a vine and contrasting them and their fruits, the shepherd appeared to me, and said,

"What are you in search of, about the elm tree and the vine?"

"I am considering, sir," said I, "that they are very well suited to each other."

"These two trees," said he, "constitute a figure for the slaves of 2 God."

"I would like," said I, "to understand the figure of the trees, that you speak of."

"Do you see the elm tree and the vine?" said he.

"I see them, sir," said I.

"This vine," said he, "bears fruit, but the elm is an unfruitful 3 tree. But this vine unless it climbs up on the elm cannot bear much fruit, because it is spread on the ground, and what fruit it does bear is rotten, because it is not hanging on the elm. So when the vine is supported by the elm, it bears fruit both from itself and from the elm. So you see that the elm bears much fruit, not 4 less than the vine, but rather more."

"How, sir," said I, "does it bear more?"

"Because," said he, "the vine when it hangs upon the elm bears its fruit in abundance and in good condition, but when it is spread on the ground, it bears very little fruit, and rotten at that. So this parable applies to the slaves of God, to rich and poor."

"Show me how, sir," said I.   5

"Listen," said he. "The rich man has money, but in his relations to the Lord he is poor, for he is worried about his wealth, and he offers very little prayer and confession to the Lord, and what he offers is faint and small and has no other power. So when the rich man rests upon the poor, and supplies his needs, he believes that what he does to the poor man will be able to find its reward with God, for the poor man is rich in prayer and confession, and his prayer has great power with God. So the rich man unhesitatingly provides the poor man with everything. And the poor man, 6 being provided for by the rich man, prays to God and gives him thanks for his benefactor, and he is still more zealous about the poor man, that he may continue to live, for he knows that the prayer of the poor is acceptable and rich in the Lord's sight. So 7 they both perform their work; the poor man works with prayer, in which he is rich, which he has received from the Lord; he gives it back to the Lord who supplies him with it. And the rich man likewise unhesitatingly supplies the poor man with the wealth which he has received from the Lord. And this is a deed that is great and acceptable in the sight of God, because he understands about his wealth and works for the poor man with the

8 gifts of the Lord, and properly performs his service. To men therefore the elm tree does not seem to bear fruit, and they do not know or perceive that when there is a drought, the elm, holding water, sustains the vine, and the vine, having a constant supply of water, bears double the amount of fruit, both for itself and for the elm. So the poor also, praying to the Lord for the rich, fill out their wealth, and the rich again, supplying the needs of the

9 poor, fill out their prayers. So they are both partners in the upright work. So the man who does these things will not be deserted by God, but will be enrolled in the books of the living.

10 Blessed are those who have, and who understand that they are made rich by the Lord, for the man who understands this will be able to do some good service also."

PARABLE III

Another parable.

1 He showed me many trees which had no leaves, but seemed to me to be dried up; for they were all alike. And he said to me,

"Do you see these trees?"

"I see, sir," said I, "that they are alike and dried up."

He answered me and said,

"These trees that you see are the people who live in this world."

2 "Why, then, sir," said I, "do they seem to be withered, and alike?"

"Because," said he, "neither the upright nor the sinners are apparent in this world, but they are alike. For this world is winter for the upright, and they are not apparent, for they live with the sinners. For just as in winter, the trees, having shed their leaves, 3 are alike, and do not show which are the dried-up ones and which are alive, so in this world neither the upright nor the sinners are apparent, but they are all alike."

PARABLE IV

Another parable.

Again, he showed me many trees, some budding, and others 1 dried up, and said to me,

"Do you see these trees?" said he.

"I see them, sir," said I, "some budding, and some dried up."

"These trees," said he, "that are budding are the upright, who 2 are going to live in the world to come. For the world to come is summer for the upright, but winter for the sinners. So when the mercy of the Lord shines forth, those who serve the Lord will be disclosed to all. For just as the fruits of every single tree are dis- 3 closed by summer, so also the fruits of the upright will be disclosed, and they will all be known in that world because they are flourishing. But the heathen and the sinners, the dried-up trees 4 that you saw, such people will be found to be dried up and unfruitful in that world, and they will be burned up like dry wood, and they will be revealed, that their conduct in their lives was wicked. For the sinners will be burned, because they sinned and did not repent, and the heathen will be burned, because they did not know him who created them. Bear fruit therefore in yourself, 5 so that in that summer your fruit may be known. Avoid much business and you will make no mistake, for those who do much business also commit much sin, being involved in their affairs, and not serving their Lord. How, then," said he, "can such a man 6 ask anything of the Lord and receive it, when he does not serve the Lord? Those who serve him will receive what they ask for. But those who do not serve the Lord will receive nothing.

7 But if a man works at a single business, he can serve the Lord also, for his mind will not be corrupted and turned from the Lord, but he will serve him with his mind pure. So if you do this,

8 you can bear fruit for the world to come, and whoever will do this will bear fruit."

PARABLE V

Another parable.

1 As I was fasting, seated on a certain mountain, and thanking the Lord for all his dealings with me, I saw the shepherd sitting beside me, and saying,

"Why have you come here so early?"

"Because, sir," said I, "I am keeping a station."

2 "What," said he, "is a station?"

"I am fasting, sir," said I.

"What is this fast," said he, "that you are keeping?"

"I am fasting, sir," said I, "just as I have been accustomed to do."

3 "You do not know how to fast to God," said he, "and this useless fast that you are keeping to him is not a fast."

"Why do you say so, sir?" said I.

"I tell you," said he, "that this which you think you are keeping is not a fast, but I will teach you what a full and acceptable fast to the Lord is."

"Yes, sir," said I, "you will make me happy if I learn the fast that is acceptable to God."

4 "Listen," said he. "God does not want a futile fast like this, for if you fast to God in this way, you will effect nothing for up-

5 rightness. But keep such a fast as this to God: Do no evil in your life, but serve the Lord with a pure heart; keep his commands, and live by his orders, and let no evil desire occur to your mind. Believe God, that if you do this and fear him and restrain yourself from every wicked act, you will live to God; and if you do this, you will keep a great fast, and one that is acceptable to God.

"Listen to the parable I am going to tell you about fasting. A 2, 2
man had a field and many slaves, and he planted a part of the
field as a vineyard. And as he was going on a journey, he selected
a slave who was most reliable, whom he liked and respected,
and called him in, and said to him, 'Take this vineyard that I
have planted, and fence it, till I come, but do nothing else to the
vineyard. Carry out this command of mine, and you will be free
in my house.' And the master of the slave went on his journey.
And when he was gone, the slave took the vineyard and fenced it. 3
And when he had finished fencing the vineyard, he saw that the
vineyard was full of weeds. So he thought it over to himself, and 4
said, 'I have carried out that command of the owner; now I will
spade up the vineyard; it will look better after it is spaded up,
and having no weeds it will yield more fruit, because it will not
be choked by the weeds.' He took the vineyard and spaded it up,
and pulled up all the weeds that were in the vineyard, and that
vineyard became very pleasing and thriving, for it had no weeds
to choke it. After a while, the master of the slave and the field 5
came, and went into the vineyard. And when he saw that the
vineyard was nicely enclosed and besides was spaded up, and all
the weeds were pulled up and the vines were flourishing, he was
greatly pleased with the work of his slave. So he called in his 6
beloved son, who was his heir, and his friends, who were his advisers, and told them what he had ordered his slave to do, and
what he had found done. And they congratulated the slave on
the testimony his master gave to him. And he said to them, 'I 7
promised this slave his freedom, if he kept the command I gave
him. But he has kept my command and has done good work on
the vineyard besides, and has pleased me greatly. So in return
for this work that he has done, I want to make him joint heir with
my son, because when he thought of a good thing, he did not
neglect it but carried it out.' The master's son agreed with this 8
decision, that the slave should be joint heir with the son. A few 9
days later, he gave a dinner, and sent him many dishes from the

dinner. When the slave got the dishes sent him by his master, he took what was enough for him and distributed the rest to his
10 fellow slaves. His fellow slaves were glad to receive the dishes, and began to pray for him, that he might find still greater favor
11 with his master, because he treated them in this way. His master heard all this that had happened and was again greatly pleased with his conduct. The master called all his friends and his son together again and told them what the slave had done with the dishes he had received, and they all the more heartily approved the slave being made joint heir with his son."

3   "Sir," said I, "I do not know these parables, and I cannot understand them, unless you explain them to me."

2   "I will explain everything to you," said he, "and everything
3 that I shall talk with you about. I will show you his commands; and if you keep them, you will be pleasing to him, and be enrolled in the number of those who keep his commands; and if you do anything good beyond God's command, you will gain greater glory for yourself and be more honored in the sight of God than you would have been. So if while keeping God's commands you add these services also, you will be happy, if you observe them as I command."

4   I said to him,

"Sir, I will observe whatever you command me, for I know that you are with me."

"I will be with you," said he, "because you have the same zeal to do right, and I will be with all," said he, "who have this zeal.
5 This fast," said he, "of keeping the Lord's commands is very good. This, then, is the way you must keep this fast that you are going
6 to observe. First of all, guard against every evil word and every evil desire, and cleanse your heart from all the vanities of this
7 world. If you observe these things, your fast will be perfect. And this is what you must do: when you have completed what has been written above, on the day on which you fast, you must taste nothing but bread and water, and you must estimate the amount

of the cost for that day which you are going to observe of the articles of food you would have eaten and give it to a widow or an orphan or somebody who is in want, and so you will be humble minded, so that as a result of your humility the man who receives it may fill his soul and pray to the Lord for you. So if 8 you carry out your fast in the way I command you, your sacrifice will be acceptable in the sight of God, and this fast will be recorded, and the service carried out in this way is right and joyous and acceptable to the Lord. This is the way you must observe 9 these things, with your children and all your family, and if you observe them you will be blessed, and all who hear them and observe them will be blessed, and whatever they ask of the Lord they will receive."

I earnestly besought him to explain to me the parable of the 4 field and the owner and the vineyard and the slave who fenced the vineyard in, and the palings, and the weeds that were pulled up out of the vineyard, and the son and the friends who were the advisers, for I understood that all these things were a parable. He answered me and said, 2

"You are very insistent about asking questions. You ought not," said he, "to ask any questions at all, for if it is necessary to have it explained to you, it will be explained."

I said to him,

"Sir, all that you show me and do not explain, there is no use in my seeing, and not understanding what it means. In the same way, if you tell me parables and do not interpret them, there will be no use in my having heard you say something."

He answered me again and said, 3

"Everyone," said he, "who is a slave of God and has his Lord in his heart, can ask him for understanding, and get it, and interpret every parable, and the words of the Lord that are spoken in parables will be made known to him. But all who are weakly and sluggish in prayer hesitate to ask the Lord. But the Lord is 4 very compassionate and never fails to give to all who ask him.

But when you have been strengthened by the glorious angel, and had with him such conversation, and are not sluggish, why do you not ask the Lord for understanding, and get it from him?"

5   I said to him,

"Sir, when I have you with me, I must of necessity ask and question you, for you show me everything and talk with me, but if I had seen or heard them without you, I would have asked the Lord to have it explained to me."

5   "I told you just now," said he, "that you were unprincipled and persistent in asking for the explanations of the parables. But since you are so determined, I will explain to you the parable of the field and the rest of what followed, so that you can make them known to everybody. Listen now," said he, "and under-

2 stand them. The field is this world, and the owner of the field is he who created all things and perfected them and gave them power. The slave is the Son of God, and the vines are this people

3 which he himself planted. The palings are the holy angels of the Lord who hold his people together. The weeds which were pulled up from the vineyard are iniquities of the slaves of God, and the dishes that he sent to him from the dinner are the commands which he gave his people through his Son, and the friends and advisers are the holy angels who were created first, and the master's absence from home is the time that remains until his coming."

4   I said to him,

"Sir, it is all great and wonderful, and it is all glorious. Could I then," said I, "have understood this? Nor can any other man understand it, even if he is exceedingly intelligent. Further, sir," said I, "explain to me what I am going to ask you."

5   "Speak," said he, "if you want something."

"Why, sir," said I, "is the Son of God put in the guise of a slave, in the parable?"

6   "Listen," said he. "The Son of God is not given the guise of a slave, but he is given great authority and dominion."

"I do not understand how, sir," said I.

"Because God planted the vineyard," said he, "that is, created 2 the people, and he turned it over to his Son, and the Son appointed the angels over them, to protect them, and he himself cleansed their sins, after great labor and enduring much toil, for no vineyard can be spaded up without toil or hardship. So when 3 he had cleansed the sins of the people, he showed them the paths of life, and gave them the law which he received from his Father. You see," said he, "that he is the Lord of the people, having received all power from his Father. But hear why the Lord took his 4 Son and the glorious angels as counselors about the slave's inheritance. The pre-existent holy Spirit, which created all creation, 5 God made to live in such flesh as he pleased. So this flesh, in which the holy Spirit lived, served the Spirit well, living in holiness and purity, and did not defile the Spirit at all. So because it 6 had lived honorably and purely and toiled with the Spirit in every act, conducting itself with strength and courage, he chose it as a partner of the holy Spirit, for the conduct of this flesh pleased him, because while possessing the holy Spirit it had not been defiled on earth. So he took the Son and the glorious angels 7 as counselors, in order that this flesh also, after faultlessly serving the Spirit, should have some place to live, and not appear to have lost the recompense for its bondage. For all flesh in which the holy Spirit has lived, which has been found undefiled and unspotted, will receive a recompense. Now you have the explana- 8 tion of this parable also."

"I am glad, sir," said I, "to hear this explanation."   7

"Listen, now," said he. "Keep this flesh of yours pure and undefiled, so that the Spirit that lives in it may bear witness to it, and your flesh may be made upright. Take care that the idea does 2 not enter your mind that this flesh of yours is mortal, and you misuse it with some defilement. If you defile your flesh, you defile the holy Spirit also, and if you defile the flesh, you will not live."

"But if, sir," said I, "there was a previous ignorance, before

3 these words were heard, how is the man who has defiled his flesh to be saved?"

"For the earlier acts of ignorance," said he, "it is possible for 4 God alone to give healing, for all power is his, but now keep it, and the Lord who is all-merciful will heal them, if henceforth you do not defile either your flesh or your spirit, for they are both connected, and one cannot be defiled without the other. So keep them both pure, and you will live to God."

PARABLE VI

1 As I was sitting in my house and glorifying the Lord for all that I had seen, and questioning about the commands because they were fine and joyous and glorious and able to save a man's soul, I said to myself, How blessed I will be if I live by these 2 commands! Everyone who follows them will be blessed. As I was saying this to myself, I suddenly saw him sitting beside me, and saying,

"Why do you doubt about the commands that I have given you? They are fine. Have no doubt, but put on faith in the Lord, and you will follow them, for I will make you strong in them. 3 These commands are beneficial for those who are going to repent, for if they do not follow them their repentance is vain. 4 So you who repent must lay aside the wickedness of this world which leads you astray, and putting on every upright virtue you will be able to keep these commands and not add any longer to your sins. So if you add nothing to them, you will cut off much of your former sins. So follow my commands and you will live to God. All these things have been told you by me."

5   After saying these things to me, he said to me,

"Let us go out in the country, and I will show you the shepherds of the sheep."

"Let us go, sir," said I.

And we came to a field, and he showed me a young shepherd

wearing a suit of clothes yellow in color. He was feeding a great 6
many sheep, and these sheep seemed to be well fed and were
frisking vigorously and were joyously skipping hither and thither.
And the shepherd himself was joyful over his flock, and the very
appearance of the shepherd was very joyful as he ran about
among the sheep.

And he said to me,   2

"Do you see this shepherd?"

"I do, sir," said I.

"This," said he, "is the angel of luxury and pleasure. So he perverts the souls of God's slaves who are empty, and turns them
away from the truth, beguiling them with wicked desires by
which they are destroyed. For they forget the commands of the 2
living God and follow pleasure and vain luxury and are destroyed
by this angel, some of them to death, and some to corruption."

I said to him,   3

"Sir, I do not know what 'to death' and 'to corruption' mean."

"Listen," said he, "the sheep that you saw very joyfully skipping about are those who have completely departed from God,
and have surrendered themselves to the desires of this world. So
for them there is no repentance leading to life, because they
have added to their sins and blasphemed against the name of
God. Their lot is death. But the ones that you saw not skipping 4
about but feeding in one place are those who have surrendered
themselves to luxury and pleasure, but have not uttered any
blasphemy against the Lord. So these have been corrupted from
the truth. For them there is hope of repentance, by which they
can attain life. So corruption has some hope of renewal, but
death means eternal destruction."

We went on a little further, and he pointed out to me a large 5
shepherd, who seemed savage in appearance, clad in a white
goatskin, with a bag on his shoulder, and carrying a very rough
and knotted staff and a great whip. And he had such a very
bitter look that I was afraid of him, he had such a look. This 6

shepherd was receiving from the young shepherd the sheep that were frisking and well fed, but not skipping about, and he put them in a precipitous place, full of thorns and briers so that the sheep could not extricate themselves from the thorns and

7 briers, but were entangled in the thorns and briers. So they were feeding entangled in thorns and briers, and were very miserable, being beaten by him, as he kept driving them about hither and thither, and giving them no rest, and these sheep had no peace at all.

3 When I saw them so flogged and so wretched I was sorry for them, because they were being so tormented, and had no relief at

2 all. I said to the shepherd who was talking with me,

"Sir, who is this shepherd who is so heartless and severe, and has no pity at all for these sheep?"

"That," said he, "is the angel of punishment. He is one of the

3 upright angels, but is in charge of punishment. So he takes charge of those who wander away from God, and have followed the desires and pleasures of this world, and punishes them as they deserve, with various terrible punishments."

4 "I would like to know, sir," said I, "what these different punishments are."

"Listen," said he, "to the different tortures and punishments. The tortures are in this life, for some are punished with losses and some with want, and some with various sicknesses, and some with utter disturbance, and some with insults from worthless

5 people and with many other sufferings. For many, being unsettled in their purposes, attempt many things, and nothing at all succeeds for them. And they say that they do not succeed in their undertakings, and it does not occur to their minds that they

6 have done wrong, but they blame the Lord. So when they are afflicted with every affliction, they are turned over to me for sound instruction, and they are strengthened in the faith of the Lord, and serve the Lord with pure hearts the rest of the days of their lives. So when they repent, it occurs to them that the things

that they have done were wrong, and then they glorify God, and say that he is an upright judge, and that they suffered justly, each for what he had done. And thenceforth they will serve the Lord with pure hearts, and succeed in everything they do, receiving from the Lord all that they ask. And then they glorify the Lord, because they were turned over to me, and they never again suffer any evil."

I said to him,   4

"Sir, explain this to me besides."

"What more have you to ask?" said he.

"Sir," said I, "are those who live in luxury and pleasure tormented for the same length of time as they spend in luxury and pleasures?"

He said to me,

"They are tormented for the same length of time."

"They are tormented very little, sir," said I. "For those who   2
live in luxury and forget God ought to be tormented seven times as long."

He said to me,   3

"You are foolish and do not understand the power of the torment."

"Well, if I did, sir," said I, "I would not have asked you to explain it to me."

"Listen," said he, "to the power of both. The time of luxury   4
and pleasure is one hour, but an hour of torment has the power of thirty days. So if a man indulges in luxury and pleasure for one day, and is tormented for one day, the day of torment has the force of a whole year. So a man is tormented as many years as he lives days in luxury. So you see," said he, "that the time of luxury and pleasure is very short, but the time of punishment and torment is long."

"Since, sir," said I, "I do not yet understand at all about the   5
time of pleasure and indulgence and of torment; explain it to me more plainly."

2   He answered me and said,

"Your foolishness is persistent, and you do not want to purify your heart and serve God. Take care," said he, "that the time does not come and find you still foolish. So listen," said he, "so that

3 you may understand it, as you want to do. The man who lives in indulgence and pleasure for one day, and does what he pleases, has enveloped himself in great folly, and does not know what he is doing. For he forgets on the morrow what he did the day before. For indulgence and pleasure have no memories, because of the folly which envelops them. But when punishment and torment are fastened on a man, for a single day, he is punished and tormented for a year, for punishment and torment have

4 long memories. So when a man is tormented and punished for a whole year, he remembers his indulgence and pleasure, and knows that it is because of them that he is suffering these evils. So every man that lives in indulgence and pleasure is tormented thus, because though they had life, they have given themselves up to death."

5   "What kinds of indulgence, sir," said I, "are harmful?"

"Everything a man likes to do," said he, "is indulgence for him. For an ill-tempered man indulges himself when he yields to his temper, and the adulterer and the drunkard and the slanderer and the liar and the covetous man and the robber and the man who does such things each yields to his disease. So he

6 indulges himself in what he does. All these indulgences are harmful to the slaves of God. So because of these pleasures those

7 who are punished and tormented suffer. But there are indulgences that save men, for many indulge in doing good, being carried away by their own pleasure. So this indulgence is advantageous to the slaves of God, and wins life for the man. But the harmful indulgences already mentioned bring torments and punishments upon them, and if they persist in them and do not repent, they bring death on themselves."

PARABLE VII

A few days later I saw him in the same field where I had seen **1**
the shepherds, and he said to me,

"What are you looking for?"

"I am here, sir," said I, "so that you may command the punishing shepherd to leave my house, for he is distressing me too
much."

"You have to be distressed," said he, "for so the glorious angel
gave orders about you. For he wants you to be tested."

"Why, sir," said I, "what have I done so bad that I should be
turned over to this angel?"

"Listen," said he, "your sins are numerous, but not so great **2**
that you should be turned over to this angel, but your family
has committed great sins and iniquities, and the glorious angel
has been incensed at their doings, and that is why he has given
orders that you should be distressed for a while, so that they too
may repent, and cleanse themselves from every desire of this
world. So when they repent and are purified, the angel of punishment will leave you."

I said to him,   **3**

"Sir, even if they have done such things as to enrage the glorious
angel, what have I done?"

"They cannot be distressed in any other way than if you, who
are the head of the family, are distressed. For if you are distressed,
they will necessarily be, but as long as you are prosperous, they
cannot experience any distress."

"But look, sir," said I, "they have repented with all their **4**
hearts."

"I too know," said he, "that they have repented with all their
hearts; then do you think that the sins of those who repent are
immediately forgiven? Not at all! But the man who repents must
torment his own soul, and be extremely humble in all that he does,
and be distressed with all kinds of afflictions. And if he bears the

afflictions that overtake him, the creator and sustainer of all
things will certainly take pity on him and give him some healing.
5 This, of course, if he sees that the heart of the repentant man is
pure from any evil thing. But it is good for you and your family
to be distressed now. But why do I say so much to you? You
must be distressed, as that angel of the Lord who turned you
over to me has ordered. And thank the Lord for this, that he
has thought you worthy of being shown the distress beforehand,
so that knowing it is coming you may bear it bravely."

6   I said to him,
     "Sir, be with me, and I will be able to bear any distress."
     "I will be with you," said he, "and I will ask the punishing
angel to afflict you more lightly. But you will be distressed for a
little while, and you will be restored again to your place. Only
continue to be humble minded and to serve the Lord with a
pure heart, with your children and your family, and follow my
commands which I give you, and your repentance will be able
7 to be strong and pure. And if you keep these commands with
your family, all distress will leave you, and distress will leave all
who follow these commands of mine."

PARABLE VIII

1   He showed me a great willow tree that overshadowed plains
and mountains, and all who were called by the name of the
2 Lord came under the shelter of the willow. And an angel of the
Lord, glorious and very tall, stood beside the willow, with a
great sickle, and he was cutting branches from the willow, and
giving them to the people who were in the shade of the willow;
3 he gave them little sticks, about eighteen inches long. After
they had all got the sticks, the angel put down the sickle, and
4 the tree was as sound as when I had first seen it. And I wondered and said to myself, How can the tree be sound after so
many branches have been cut off? The shepherd said to me,

"Do not wonder that the tree has remained sound after so many branches have been cut off; see it all," said he, "and it will be made clear to you what it means."

The angel who had given the sticks to the people asked them 5 back again, and in the order in which they had received them, they were called to him and each one of them gave back the sticks. And the angel of the Lord received them and examined them. From some he received the sticks dry and apparently 6 moth-eaten. The angel ordered the ones who had given up such sticks to stand by themselves. And others gave them up dry, 7 but they were not moth-eaten. He ordered them also to stand by themselves. And others gave them up half dry, and these stood 8 by themselves. And others gave the sticks up half dry and cracked; 9 and these stood by themselves. And others gave their sticks up 10 green and cracked, and these stood by themselves. And others gave 11 their sticks up half dry and half green, and these stood by themselves. And others brought their sticks up two-thirds of the 12 stick green and one-third dry, and these stood by themselves. And others gave them up two-thirds dry and one-third green, 13 and these stood by themselves. And others gave up their sticks 14 all but a little green, but a very little of their sticks was dry, at the very tip, and they had cracks in them; and these stood by themselves. And of others there was very little green, and 15 the rest of each stick was dry, and these stood by themselves. And others came bringing their sticks green, just as they had got 16 them from the angel; most of the people gave up such sticks, and the angel rejoiced exceedingly over them, and they stood by themselves. And others gave up their sticks green and budded, 17 and these stood by themselves; and the angel rejoiced exceedingly over them. And others gave up their sticks green and 18 budded, and their buds seemed to have some fruit. And the men whose sticks were found in this condition were very glad. And the angel rejoiced over them, and the shepherd was very glad about them.

2   And the angle of the Lord gave orders that crowns be brought. And crowns were brought apparently made of palm leaves, and he crowned the men who had given up the sticks that had buds and some fruit, and he sent them off into the

2   tower. And he sent to the tower the others also who had given up their sticks green and budded but with no fruit on the buds,

3   and he gave them a seal. And all those who went into the tower

4   had the same clothing, as white as snow. And he sent those who had given up the sticks green, just as they had received them, and he gave them white clothes and a seal.

5   After the angel had concluded this, he said to the shepherd, "I am going away, but you must send these men inside the walls, in so far as anyone deserves to live there. But examine their sticks closely, and then send them on; but examine them closely. See that no one slips by you," said he, "but if anyone does, I will test them at the altar." After saying this to the shepherd, he went away.

6   And after the angel had gone away, the shepherd said to me, "Let us take the sticks from all of them and plant them; perhaps some of them will be able to revive."

    I said to him,

    "Sir, how can these dry things revive?"

7   He answered me and said,

    "This tree is a willow, and by nature tenacious of life. So if the sticks are planted and given a little moisture, many of them will live, and then I will try to pour water on them. If any of them can live, I will rejoice with them, and if none revives, I will not be found to have been negligent."

8   The shepherd ordered me to call them, just as each of them stood. They came up by groups, and gave up the sticks to the shepherd, and he planted them in rows, and after planting them he poured plenty of water on them, so that the sticks disappeared

9   in the water. And after he had watered the sticks he said to me, "Let us go, and come back in a few days and look at all the

sticks, for the creator of this tree wishes all who have received branches from this tree to live, and I too hope that these sticks now that they have received moisture and been watered will most of them live."

I said to him,   3

"Sir, tell me what this tree is, for I am perplexed about it, because, though so many branches have been cut off, the tree is sound and nothing at all appears to have been cut from it. So I am perplexed about this."

"Listen," said he. "This great tree that overshadows plains 2 and mountains and all the earth is the law of God, which has been given to all the world. And this law is the Son of God, who has been preached to the ends of the earth. And the peoples under the shade of it are those who have heard the preaching and believed it. And the great, glorious angel is Michael, who 3 has authority over this people and guides them, for it is he who puts the law into the hearts of those who believe. So he observes those to whom he has given the law, to see whether they have kept it. But you see the sticks of each one, for the sticks 4 are the law. So you see many of the sticks made useless, and you will know that they are all men who have not kept the law; and you will see each one's dwelling."

I said to him,   5

"Sir, why did he send some off into the tower, and leave others to you?"

"Those," said he, "who had transgressed the law they had received from him he has left under my authority, with a view to repentance. But those who have satisfied the law and kept it, he keeps under his own authority."

"Who, then, sir," said I, "are those who are crowned and go into 6 the tower?"

"The ones who are crowned," he answered and said to me, "are those who have grappled with the devil and conquered him. They are the ones who have suffered for the law. The others 7 who themselves also gave up their sticks green and budded, but with no fruit, are those who have been persecuted for the law

8 but did not suffer death, or deny their law. And those who gave them up green just as they had received them, are holy and upright and have lived with an exceedingly pure heart and kept the Lord's commands. The rest you will learn when I examine these sticks that have been planted and watered."

4 A few days later we went to the spot, and the shepherd sat down in the great angel's place and I stood beside him. And he said to me,

"Fasten a towel about your waist and wait on me."

2 1 put on a clean towel made of sackcloth. And when he saw that I had put it on and was ready to wait on him, he said,

"Call the men whose sticks have been planted, in the order in which each one gave up his stick."

And I went back to the field and called them all, and they all

3 stood in rows. He said to them,

"Let each one pull up his own stick and bring it to me."

4 The first to give them up were those who had had them dry and worm-eaten, and when they proved to be dry and worm-

5 eaten, he ordered them to stand by themselves. Then those who had them dry and not worm-eaten gave them up, and some of them gave up their sticks green and some dry and apparently moth-eaten. So those who had given them up green he ordered to stand by themselves, and those who had given them back dry

6 and worm-eaten he ordered to stand with the first ones. Then those who had had the half-dry and cracked ones gave them back, and many of them gave them back green and free from cracks, and some green and budded, and with fruit on the buds, such as those who had gone into the tower crowned had had. And some gave them up dry and worm-eaten, and some dry and not eaten, and some were as before half dry and cracked. He ordered them to stand each one by himself, some in their own rows and some by themselves.

Then those who had had their sticks green but cracked gave 5 them up. All these gave them up green, and took their stand in their own row. And the shepherd rejoiced over them, because they were all changed and had lost their cracks. And those also 2 who had had them half green and half dry gave them back. So the sticks of some were found entirely green, of some half dry, of some dry and worm-eaten, and of some green and budded; all these were sent off each to his appointed place. Then those who 3 had had them two-thirds green and one-third dry gave them back. Many of them gave them back green, and many half dry, and others dry and worm-eaten. These all stood each in his appointed place. Then those who had had sticks two-thirds dry and one- 4 third green gave them up. And many of them gave them up half dry, and some dry and worm-eaten, and others half dry and cracked, but a very few green. All these took their stand in their appointed place. And those who had had their sticks green, 5 but a very little dry, and cracked, gave them up. Some of these gave them up green, and some green and budded; these also went to their appointed place. Then those who had had them a 6 very little green and the rest dry gave them up; their sticks were found to be for the most part green and budded and with fruit in the buds, and others were entirely green. The shepherd rejoiced exceedingly over these sticks, because they were found in this condition. And these went off each to his appointed place.

After the shepherd had examined the sticks of all of them, he 6 said to me,

"I told you that this tree was tenacious of life. Do you see," said he, "how many have repented and been saved?"

"I do, sir," said I.

"Observe," said he, "that the Lord's compassion is great and glorious, and he has given the spirit to those who were worthy of repentance."

"Why, then, sir," said I, "have not all repented?"   2

"He has granted repentance," said he, "to those whose hearts he saw would be clean, and who would serve him with all their hearts. But to those whose guile and wickedness he saw, who pretend to repent, he did not grant repentance, so that they might not again profane his name."

3   I said to him,

"Now, sir, explain to me what sort of person one of those who have given up their sticks is, and where they live, in order that those who have believed and have received the seal, and have broken it, and have not kept it whole, when they hear it may realize what they have done and repent, and receive a seal from you, and glorify the Lord because he has had mercy on them, and has sent you to renew their spirits."

4   "Listen," said he. "Those whose sticks were found dry and moth-eaten are the apostates and traitors to the church, and men who blasphemed the Lord through their sins, and besides have been ashamed of the Lord's name by which they were called. So these have utterly perished to God. And you see that not one of them has repented, although they have heard the words that you have spoken to them, which I commanded you. From such men 5 life has departed. And those also who gave up the sticks that were dry and undecayed are close to them, for they were hypocrites and brought in strange teachings, and led the slaves of God astray and especially those who had sinned, not allowing them to repent, but persuading them by their foolish teachings.

6   These, then, have a hope of repentance. And you see that many of them have repented since you told them my commands, and more will repent. But those who will not repent have lost their lives. But those of them that have repented have become good, and have found their home inside the first walls, and some of them have even gone up into the tower. So you see," said he, "that repentance for sins brings life, but failing to repent brings death.

7   "And those who gave them up half dry and with cracks in them, hear about them too. Those of them whose sticks were half

dry are doubters, for they are neither alive nor dead. And those 2 who had them half dry and with cracks in them are doubters and slanderers and never at peace with one another, but are always causing dissensions. But repentance," said he, "is open to them also. You see," said he, "that some of them have repented already. And for them," said he, "there is still hope of repentance. And those of them," said he, "who have repented will have their 3 homes in the tower, and those of them who have been slower to repent will live inside the walls, and those who do not repent, but persist in what they are doing, will surely die.

"And those who gave up their sticks green and cracked have 4 always been faithful and good, though they had some jealousy of one another about pre-eminence and about some distinction. But they are all foolish, to be jealous of one another about pre-eminence. But they also, when they heard my commands, puri- 5 fied themselves and quickly repented, for they were good. So they found their home in the tower. But if one of them turns back to creating dissension, he will be cast out of the tower and will lose his life. Life belongs to all who keep the Lord's com- 6 mands, but there is nothing in the commands about pre-eminence or any distinction, but about a man's patience and humility. So the life of the Lord is in such men, but in creators of dissension and transgressors there is death.

"But those who gave up their sticks half green and half dry 8 are the ones who are absorbed in business and do not associate with God's people; that is why one-half of them is alive, and one-half dead. Many, then, when they heard my commands repented. 2 So the home of those who repented is in the tower. But some of them deserted entirely. So they have no repentance. For on account of their business they blasphemed the Lord and denied him. So they have lost their lives because of the evil they have done. And many of them doubted. These can still have repentance 3 if they repent quickly, and their home will be in the tower. And if they repent slowly, they will live inside the walls. But if they do not repent, they too have lost their lives. And the ones who 4

gave them up two-thirds green and one-third dry are those who
5 have denied with many denials. So many of them have repented
and gone into the tower to live, but many have fallen away
from God utterly; these have utterly lost their lives. And some of
them have doubted and created dissension. So repentance is still
open to them, if they repent quickly and do not persist in their
pleasures, but if they persist in what they are doing they also
bring death upon themselves.

9   "And those who gave up their sticks two-thirds dry and one-
third green are the ones who have been faithful but have become
rich and honored among the heathen; they have assumed great
haughtiness and grown arrogant and forsaken the truth, and have
not associated with the upright but have lived among the
heathen, and this way was pleasanter to them. But they did not
fall away from God, but remained in the faith, though they did
2 not do the things the faith does. So many of them have repented
3 and found their home in the tower. But others, living entirely
with the heathen and being corrupted by their vanities, have
fallen away from God and lived heathen lives. These have been
4 rated as heathen. And others of them have doubted, and given
up the hope of being saved, on account of the things they had
done. And others have doubted and made divisions among themselves. So for those who have doubted because of what they
had done there is still repentance, but they must repent quickly,
so that their home may be in the tower. But death is close to those
who do not repent but persist in their pleasures.

10   "But those who gave up their sticks green, but with the very
tips dry and cracked, are the ones who have always been good
and faithful and glorious in the sight of God, but they have sinned
a very little because of small desires and grudges against one
another, but when they heard my words the greatest part of them
quickly repented, and they have found their home in the tower.
2 But some of them have doubted and some of them in their doubt
have created greater dissension. So in their case there is hope

of repentance, because they have always been good; one of them can hardly die. And those who gave up their sticks dry, with a 3 very small part green, are the ones who have only believed, but have done wicked things. But they have never fallen away from God, and have gladly borne the name, and gladly welcomed the slaves of God into their homes. So, hearing of this repentance, they have unhesitatingly repented, and are doing all that is virtuous and right. But some of them are also afraid, for they 4 know the things that they have done. So all these will have their home in the tower."

After he had concluded the explanations of all the sticks, 11 he said to me,

"Go and tell all men to repent and live to God, for the Lord in his compassion has sent me to give them all repentance, although some do not deserve to be saved, because of what they have done. But as he is long-suffering, the Lord wants those who were called through his Son to be saved."

I said to him, 2

"Sir, I hope that all, when they hear them, will repent. For I am convinced that each one when he realizes what he has done and fears God will repent."

He answered me and said, 3

"Those who repent with their whole hearts and cleanse themselves from their wickednesses that have been mentioned, and no longer add anything to their sins, will receive healing from the Lord for their past sins, if they do not doubt about these commands, and they will live to God. But those," said he, "who add to their sins, and follow the desires of this world, will condemn themselves to death. But you must follow my commands, 4 and you will live to God, and those who follow them and do right will live to God."

When he had showed me these things, and told me all this, he 5 said to me,

"The rest I will explain to you in a few days."

PARABLE IX

1 After I had written the commands and parables of the shepherd, the angel of repentance, he came to me and said to me,

"I want to show you what the holy Spirit which talked with you in the form of the church showed you; for that spirit is the
2 Son of God. For since you were too weak in the flesh, it was not shown you by an angel. So when you had been strengthened through the spirit, and become strong in your strength, so that you could even see an angel, then the building of the tower was revealed to you through the church. You have seen it all well and reverently, as revealed by a girl. But now you see it by an
3 angel, through the same spirit. But you must learn it all more exactly from me. For it was for this that I was assigned by the glorious angel to come to live in your house, so that you might see it all as well as possible, with none of the fear you had before."

4 And he led me off to Arcadia, to a rounded mountain, and made me sit down on the top of the mountain, and he showed me a great plain, and around the plain twelve mountains, each with a different appearance.

5 The first was black as soot, and the second was bare, without
6 any vegetation, and the third was full of thorns and briers. The fourth had half-dry vegetation, green at the top but dry at the roots, and some of the vegetation, when the sun had scorched it,
7 was turning dry. The fifth mountain had green vegetation and was rough. The sixth mountain was entirely full of fissures, some small and some large, and the fissures contained vegetation, but the vegetation was not very flourishing but looked rather
8 withered. The seventh mountain had gay vegetation, and the whole mountain was flourishing, and all kinds of cattle and birds were feeding on this mountain, and the more the cattle and the wild fowl ate, the more the vegetation of this mountain flourished. The eighth mountain was full of springs, and every

kind of creature of the Lord was watered from the springs of
that mountain. The ninth mountain had no water at all and was 9
all desert, but it had wild animals on it and deadly reptiles that
destroyed men. The tenth mountain had huge trees and was all
shady, and under the shelter of the trees sheep lay resting and
chewing their cud. The eleventh mountain was thickly wooded, 10
and these trees were laden with fruit, adorned one with one fruit
and another with another, so that anyone who saw them wanted
to eat of their fruits. The twelfth mountain was all white, and
its appearance was gay, and the mountain itself was very
beautiful.

In the middle of the plain he showed me a great white rock 2
that had risen from the plain. The rock was higher than the
mountains, square, so that it could hold the whole world. And the 2
rock was old, and had a gateway carved out of it, but the carving-
out of the gateway seemed to me to be recent. The gateway
shone more brightly than the sun, so much so that I wondered
at the brightness of the gateway. And around the gateway stood 3
twelve girls. The four who stood at the corners seemed to me
to be the most glorious, but the others were glorious too, and
they stood on the four sides of the gateway, two girls in the
middle of each side. They were dressed in linen garments and 4
were becomingly dressed for work, with their right shoulders
bare, as though about to carry some load. So they were ready,
for they were very gay and eager. On seeing this, I wondered 5
to myself, for I was seeing great and glorious things, and besides
I was at a loss about the girls, because though they were so
dainty, they stood manfully as though they were ready to carry
the whole heaven.

And the shepherd said to me,   6

"Why do you reason with yourself and perplex and trouble
yourself? Do not attempt, as though you were intelligent, to
understand things you cannot understand, but ask the Lord that
you may receive intelligence and understand them. You cannot 7

see what is behind you, but what is before you can see. So let what you cannot see alone, and do not distress yourself, but master what you can see, and do not waste your strength on the rest. I will explain to you everything that I show you. So look at the rest."

3 I saw that six men had come, tall and splendid, and looking alike, and they called a multitude of men, and those who came were also tall men, very handsome and strong. And the six men ordered them to build a tower upon the rock. And there was a great tumult of those men who had come to build the tower,
2 as they ran this way and that around the gateway. And the girls who were standing around the gateway told the men to hurry to build the tower, and the girls held out their hands as though
3 they were going to receive something from the men. And the six men ordered stones to come up from some deep place, and go into the building of the tower. And ten gleaming square stones
4 came up, unhewn. And the six men called the girls and ordered them to pick up all the stones that were to go into the building of the tower, and to pass through the gateway, and give them
5 to the men who were to build the tower. And the girls put the first ten stones that had come up from the deep place on one another and together they carried them, one at a time.

4 And just as they had stood together around the gateway, the ones who seemed to be strongest picked it up and stooped under the corners of the stone. And the others stooped at the sides of the stone, and in this way they carried all the stones. And they brought them through the gateway as they had been ordered to do, and gave them to the men for the tower, and when they had
2 the stones they set to building. The tower was built on the great rock, and above the gateway. So those ten stones were fitted together, and they covered the whole rock, and they formed the foundation of the building of the tower, and the rock and the
3 gateway supported the whole tower. And after the ten stones twenty other stones came up from the deep place, and these

were fitted into the building of the tower, being brought by the
girls like the former stones. And after these thirty-five came up,
and these were fitted in like manner into the tower. And after
them forty other stones came up, and all these were put into the
building of the tower. So there were four courses in the foundations of the tower. And they stopped coming up from the deep 4
place, and the builders also stopped for a little while. And again
the six men ordered the multitude of the people to bring stones
from the mountains for the building of the tower. So they were 5
brought from all the mountains, of different colors, quarried out
by the men, and they were given to the girls, and the girls carried
them through the gateway, and handed them over for the
building of the tower. And when the stones of various colors
were put into the building, they all alike became white and
changed their various colors. But some stones were handed over 6
by the men for the building and did not turn bright, but were
found just as they were put in. For they had not been handed
over by the girls, or brought in through the gateway. So these
stones were out of place in the building of the tower. And the six 7
men, seeing the stones that were out of place in the building,
ordered them removed and taken down to their place from which
they had been brought. And they said to the men that were bring- 8
ing the stones,

"Do not put any stones at all into the building, but put them
by the tower, so that the girls may carry them through the gateway, and hand them over for the building. For if," said they,
"they are not brought through the gateway by the hands of
these girls, they cannot change their colors. So do not labor in
vain," they said.

And the building was ended on that day, but the tower was 5
not finished, for it was going to be built upon again. And there
was a delay in the building. And the six men ordered all the
builders to withdraw for a little while and rest, but they instructed
the girls not to go away from the tower. It seemed to me that

2 the girls were left to guard the tower. But after all the men had gone away and rested, I said to the shepherd.

"Why is it, sir, that the building of the tower has not been finished?"

"The tower," said he, "cannot be finished yet, unless its owner comes and tests this building, so that if some stones are found to be bad he can change them, for the tower is being built to meet his wishes."

3 "I would like to know, sir," said I, "what this building of the tower means, and about the rock and the gateway and the mountains and the girls and the stones that came up from the deep place and were not shaped but went into the building just as they 4 were; and why first ten stones were laid for the foundation, then twenty, then thirty-five, then forty, and about the stones that went into the building and were taken out again and put back in their place. Set my mind at rest about all these matters, sir, and make them known to me."

5 "If," said he, "you do not prove idly curious, you will know them all. For in a few days we will come here and you will see the rest of the things that will happen to this tower and will understand all the parables fully."

6 A few days later we went to the place where we had sat, and he said to me,

"Let us go to the tower, for the owner of the tower is coming to examine it."

So we went to the tower, and there was no one near it at all, 7 except the girls only. And the shepherd asked the girls whether the master of the tower had come, and they said that he was going to come, to examine the building.

6 And here a little later I saw a great body of men coming, and in the midst of them was a man so tall that he was taller 2 than the tower. And the six men who had charge of the building walked with him at his right and at his left, and with him were all who had worked on the building, and many other

glorious beings were about him. And the girls who watched the tower ran up to him and kissed him, and began to walk beside him around the tower. This man examined the building so 3 closely that he felt of each stone. And he had a stick in his hand, and struck each stone that had been put into the building. And 4 when he struck them, some of them turned as black as soot, and some scaly, and some cracked, and some were too short, and some neither black nor white, and some rough and not fitting the other stones, and some badly spotted; these were the kinds of defective stones that were found in the building. So he ordered 5 all these removed from the tower and placed beside the tower, and other stones brought and put in their places. And the builders 6 asked him from which mountain he wanted the stones brought and put in their places, and he did not order them brought from the mountains, but he ordered them brought from a place that was near by. And the plain was dug up, and fine square stones 7 were found, though some were round. And all the stones that were anywhere in that plain were brought and carried through the gateway by the girls. And the square stones were shaped and 8 put in the places of the ones that had been taken out, but the round ones were not set in the building, because they were hard to shape and slow to fashion, but they were put by the tower, as though they were going to be shaped and put into the building, for they were very fine.

So when the glorious man, the owner of the whole tower, had 7 finished these things, he called the shepherd to him and turned over to him all the stones that were lying beside the tower, which had been removed from the building, and said to him,

"Clean these stones carefully, and put the ones that can fit the 2 rest into the structure of the tower, and throw the ones that do not fit far from the tower."

After giving the shepherd these orders, he left the tower, with 3 all those with whom he had come, but the girls stood around the tower, guarding it. I said to the shepherd,   4

"How can these stones go back into the structure of the tower after being rejected?"

He answered me, saying,

"Do you see these stones?" said he.

"I do, sir," said I.

"The largest part of these stones," said he, "I will shape and put into the building, and they will fit with the rest of the stones."

5   "How," said I, "can they fill the same space after they have been cut down?"

He answered and said to me,

"Those that are found too small will be thrown into the middle of the structure, and those that are larger will be put on the outside and will hold them together."

6   After telling me this, he said to me,

"Let us go, and after two days let us come and clean these stones and put them into the building. For all around the tower must be cleaned, so that the master may not come suddenly and find things dirty about the tower and be incensed, and these stones will not get into the structure of the tower, and I will seem to the master to be negligent."

7   Two days later, we went to the tower, and he said to me,

"Let us examine all these stones and see which ones can go into the building."

I said to him,

"Sir, let us examine them."

8   And to begin with, we first examined the black stones, and they proved to be just as they were when they were taken out of the building. And the shpherd ordered them removed from the tower

2   and carried off. Then he examined the scaly ones, and he took many of them and shaped them and ordered the girls to take them and put them into the building. And the girls took them and put them into the building of the middle of the tower, and the rest he ordered put with the black ones, for they also were

3   found to be black. Then he examined the ones that were cracked,

and many of them he shaped and ordered taken back by the girls into the building; and they were put on the outside, because they were found to be stronger. But the rest could not be shaped, because there were so many cracks. So for that reason they were rejected from the building of the tower. Then he examined the 4 short ones, and many of them proved to be black, and some had developed great cracks, and he ordered these also put with the ones that were thrown away. The rest of them he cleaned and shaped and ordered put in the building. And the girls took them and fitted them into the midst of the structure of the tower, for they were so weak. Then he examined the ones that were half 5 white and half black, and many of them proved to be black, and he ordered them also taken away with the ones that were rejected. But all the rest were taken by the girls, for as they were white, they were fitted by the girls themselves into the building, and they were put on the outside, for they were found to be sound, so that they could hold the ones that were put in the middle, for not one of them was too short. Then he examined the rough, hard 6 ones, and a few of them were rejected, because they could not be shaped, for they proved to be too hard. But the rest of them were shaped, and taken by the girls, and fitted into the middle of the structure of the tower, for they were too weak. Then he examined 7 the ones that had spots, and a very few of them had turned black and were rejected and put with the rest, but the remainder proved to be bright and sound, and these were fitted into the building by the girls, and were put on the outside because of their strength.

Then he went to examine the round, white stones, and he 9 said to me,

"What are we to do about these stones?"

"How do I know, sir?" said I.

"Then do you notice nothing about them?"

"I do not possess this craft, sir," said I, "I am not a mason, nor 2 do I understand it."

"Do you not see," said he, "that they are very round, and if I want to make them square, a great deal must be cut off from them? But some of them must necessarily be put into the building."

3 "If, then, sir, it is necessary," said I, "why do you torment yourself, and not select the ones you want for the building, and fit them into it?"

He selected from them the largest, bright ones, and shaped them, and the girls took them and fitted them into the outside

4 of the building. And the rest that were left over were taken and put back in the plain from which they had been brought. But they were not rejected,

"For," said he, "there is still left a little of the tower to be built and the master of the tower wants all these stones fitted into the building, because they are very bright."

5 And twelve women were called, very beautiful in form, dressed for work, with their shoulders bare and their hair down, and these women seemed to me to be savage. And the shepherd ordered them to pick up the stones that had been rejected from the building and take them back to the mountains from which

6 they had been brought. And they picked them up gladly and took all the stones back and put them where they had been taken from. And after all the stones had been taken away, and not a stone lay around the tower any longer, the shepherd said to me,

"Let us go around the tower and see whether there is any imperfection in it."

7 And I went around it with him. And when the shepherd saw that the tower was beautifully built, he was very glad, for the tower was so built that when I saw it I coveted its building, for it was built as though it was made of one stone, without a single joint in it. The stone appeared to have been cut out of the rock, for it seemed to me to be all one stone.

10 And as I went with him I was glad to see such good things. And the shepherd said to me,

"Go and get some unslacked lime and a thin potsherd, so that I can fill up the prints of the stones that have been taken up and put into the building, for it must be smooth all around the tower."

And I did as he ordered, and brought them to him.   2

"Wait on me," said he, "and the work will soon be finished."

So he filled up the prints of the stones that had gone into the building, and ordered all around the tower swept and cleaned. And the girls took brooms and swept and removed all the dirt 3 from the tower, and sprinkled water about, and the location of the tower became gay and very attractive. The shepherd said to me,   4

"It has all been cleaned," said he. "If the owner comes to look the tower over, he will have nothing to blame us for."

With these words he was going to go away. But I took hold of 5 his wallet and began to adjure him by the Lord to explain to me what he had shown me. He said to me,

"I am busy for a while, and then I will explain it all to you. Wait here for me until I come."

I said to him,   6

"Sir, what am I to do here alone?"

"You are not alone," said he, "for these girls are with you."

"Then commend me to them," said I.

The shepherd called them to him and said to them,

"I entrust this man to you until I come."

And he went away. And I was alone with the girls and they 7 were very gay and were kind to me, especially the four of them that were the most glorious.

The girls said to me,   11

"The shepherd is not coming here today."

"What am I to do then?" said I.

"Wait for him until evening," they said, "and if he comes he will talk with you, but if he does not come, you must stay here with us until he comes."

I said to them,   2

"I will wait for him until evening, and if he does not come, I will go back to my house, and come back in the morning."

But they answered and said to me,

"You were entrusted to us; you cannot leave us."

3 "Where, then," said I, "am I to stay?"

"You shall sleep with us," they said, "as a brother, not a husband, for you are our brother, and in future we are going to live with you, for we love you dearly."

4 But I was ashamed to stay with them. And the one who seemed to be the foremost of them began to kiss me and embrace me. And the others seeing her embracing me began to kiss me

5 themselves, and to take me around the tower and play with me. I too seemed to have become young again, and began to play with them myself, for some were doing choral dancing, and others were dancing, and others were singing, and I walked around the tower with them in silence, and was happy with

6 them. When evening came, I wanted to go home, but they would not let me go but detained me, and I stayed with them

7 that night, and slept beside the tower. For the girls spread their linen garments on the ground and made me lie down in the midst of them, and they did nothing at all but pray, and I too prayed unceasingly with them, and I stayed there with the girls until eight o'clock the next morning.

8 Then the shepherd came, and he said to the girls,

"Have you done him any harm?"

"Ask him," they said.

I said to him,

"Sir, I enjoyed staying with them."

"What did you have for supper?" said he.

"Sir," said I, "I had the words of the Lord for supper all night long."

"Did they treat you well?" said he.

"Yes, sir," said I.

9 "Now," said he, "what do you want to hear first?"

"Just as you showed me from the beginning, sir," said I, "I ask you, sir, to explain them to me just as I ask you."

"Just as you please," said he, "I will explain them to you, and I will conceal nothing at all from you."

"First of all, sir," said I, "show me this: the rock and the gateway—who is it?" **12**

"This rock and gateway," said he, "are the son of God."

"How is it, sir," said I, "that the rock is old, but the gateway is new?"

"Listen," said he, "and understand, foolish man. The Son of **2** God is far older than all his creation, so that he was the Father's counselor in his creation. That is why the rock is old."

"But why is the gateway new, sir?" said I.

"Because," said he, "he was revealed in the last days of the **3** consummation; that is why the gateway is new, so that those who are going to be saved may enter the kingdom of God through it. Did you see," said he, "that the stones that came in **4** through the gateway were put into the building of the tower, but the ones that had not come in were put back in the place they came from?"

"I did, sir," said I,

"So," said he, "no one will enter the kingdom of God unless he takes this holy name. For if you want to enter a city, and **5** that city is walled around, and has a single gateway, can you enter that city except by the gateway that it has?"

"Why, sir," said I, "how can it be done in any other way?"

"Then if you cannot enter the city except by the gateway that it has, so," said he, "a man cannot enter the kingdom of God in any other way than through the name of his Son, who was beloved by him.

"Did you see," said he, "the crowd that was building the **6** tower?"

"I did, sir," said I.

"They are all glorious angels," said he, "so by them the Lord is walled about. But the gateway is the Son of God; this is the only entrance to the Lord. So no one can go in to him in any other

7 way than through his Son. Did you see," said he, "the six men, and in the midst of them the tall, splendid man who was walking about the tower and rejecting the stones from the building?"

"I did, sir," said I.

8 "The splendid man," said he, "is the Son of God, and the six are the glorious angels attending him on his right and left. None of these glorious angels," said he, "can enter God's presence without him. Whoever does not take his name cannot enter the kingdom of God."

13 "But who is the tower?" said I.

"This tower," said he, "is the church."

2 "And who are these girls?"

"These," said he, "are holy spirits, and a man cannot find his way into the kingdom of God in any other way than by being clothed by them with their clothing. For if you take the name only, and do not receive the clothing from them, you will get no benefit, for these girls are powers of the Son of God. If you bear the name, but do not bear his power, you will be bearing his name in vain.

3 "And the stones," said he, "that you saw rejected, are the ones that have borne the name, but did not put on the clothing of the girls."

"What kind of clothing have they, sir?" said I.

"Their very names," said he, "are their clothing. Whoever bears the name of the Son of God ought also to bear their names, for even the Son himself bears the names of these girls.

4 "All the stones," said he, "that you saw go into the building of the tower, handed over by their hands and remaining in the

5 building, are clothed with the power of these girls. That is why you see that the tower has become one stone with the rock. So those who have believed the Lord through his Son and clothe

themselves with these spirits will become one spirit and one body, and their garments will be of one color. And the home of such as bear the names of the girls is in the tower."

"Why then, sir," said I, "were the rejected stones rejected? 6 For they passed through the gateway and were put into the structure of the tower by the girls' hands."

"Since you are concerned about it all," said he, "and inquire closely, hear about the rejected stones. All these," said he, "took 7 the name of the Son of God, and they also received the power of these girls. So they received these spirits and were made strong and were with the slaves of God, and they had one spirit and one body and one clothing, for they were in agreement and did what was right. Then after a while they were seduced by the 8 women you saw clad in black clothing, who had their shoulders exposed and their hair down and were well formed. On seeing them they desired them and put on their power, and laid aside the clothing and power of the girls. So these men have been cast 9 out of the house of God and turned over to those women. But those who were not deceived by the beauty of these women stayed in the house of God. That," said he, "is the explanation of the ones that were rejected."

"What then, sir," said I, "if these men, being what they are, 14 repent and cast off their desires of these women, and return to the girls, and live in their power and acts? Will they not enter the house of God?"

"They will," said he, "if they renounce the acts of these 2 women, and take back the power of the girls and live in their ways. For that is why there was an interruption of the building, so that if they repent they may go back into the structure of the tower. But if they do not repent, then others will go in, and they themselves will be finally cast out."

I gave thanks to the Lord for all these things, because he has 3 had mercy on all those who call upon his name and has sent the angel of repentance to us who had sinned against him, and has renewed our spirit, and when we were already destroyed and had no hope of living, he has revived our life.

4   "Well, sir," said I, "show me why the tower was built not on the ground but on the rock, and on the gateway."

"Are you still stupid and foolish?" said he.

"I am obliged, sir," said I, "to ask you everything, for I cannot understand anything at all. For all great, glorious things are hard for men to understand."

5   "Listen," said he. "The name of the Son of God is great and incomprehensible and sustains the whole world. So if all creation is sustained by the Son of God, what do you think of those who have been called by him, and bear the name of the Son of God, 6 and live by his commands? Do you see, then, what kind of people he sustains? Those who bear his name with their whole hearts. So he has become their foundation, and gladly sustains them, because they are not ashamed to bear his name."

15   "Tell me, sir," said I, "the names of the girls and of the women who are wearing the black clothes."

"Hear the names," said he, "of the strongest girls who stood at 2 the corners. The first is Faith, the second, Self-control, the third, Strength, and the fourth, Patience. And the others who stood between them, bear these names: Sincerity, Innocence, Purity, Cheerfulness, Truth, Understanding, Harmony, Love. The man that bears these names and the name of the Son of God will be 3 able to enter the kingdom of God. Hear also," said he, "the names of the women with the black clothes. Of these also four are most powerful. The first is Unbelief, the second, Impurity, the third, Disobedience, and the fourth, Deceit. And the ones that follow them are called Grief, Wickedness, Wantonness, Ill temper, Falsehood, Folly, Slander, Hatred. The slave of God who bears these names will see the kingdom of God, but he will not enter it."

4   "But, sir," said I, "who are the stones that were fitted into the building from the deep place?"

"The first ones," said he, "the ten that were put into the foundations, are the first generation, and the twenty-five are the second generation of upright men, and the thirty-five are the prophets of God and his servants, and the forty are apostles and teachers of the preaching of the Son of God."

"Why, then, sir," said I, "did the girls hand over these stones 5 also for the building of the tower, after carrying them through the gateway?"

"Because," said he, "they were the first to bear these spirits, and did not part from one another at all, neither the spirits from the men nor the men from the spirits, but the spirits stayed with them till they fell asleep. And if they had not had these spirits with them, they would not have been of use for the building of the tower."

"Tell me still more, sir," said I.   16

"What more do you ask?" said he.

"Why, sir," said I, "did the stones come up from the deep place and why were they put into the building of the tower, though they had borne these spirits?"

"They had to come up through water," said he, "to be made 2 alive, for they could not enter the kingdom of God in any other way than by laying aside the deadness of their former life. So 3 even those who had fallen asleep received the seal of the Son of God, and entered the kingdom of God. For," said he, "before the man bears the name of the Son of God, he is dead, but when he receives the seal, he lays aside his deadness and receives life. So 4 the water is the seal. So they go down into the water dead, and they come up alive. So this seal was preached to them also, and they took advantage of it, in order to enter the kingdom of God."

"Why, sir," said I, "did the forty stones also come up with them 5 from the deep place, when they had had the seal already?"

"Because," said he, "these apostles and teachers who had preached the name of the Son of God, when they fell asleep in the power and faith of the Son of God, preached also to those who had previously fallen asleep, and themselves gave them the

6 seal of the preaching. So they went down with them into the water, and came up again. But these went down alive, and came up alive, but those who had previously fallen asleep went down

7 dead and came up alive. So they were made alive through them, and came to know the name of the Son of God. That is why they also came up with them, and were fitted together with them into the building of the tower, and were built together without being shaped. For they had fallen asleep in uprightness, and great purity, only they had not had this seal. That is the explanation of these things."

"It is, sir," said I.

17 "Now, then, sir, tell me about the mountains; why are their aspects some of one kind and some of another, and diverse?"

"Listen," said he. "These twelve mountains are the tribes that inhabit the whole world. So the Son of God was preached to them by the apostles."

2 "But tell me, sir, why the mountains are diverse, and one has one aspect and another another."

"Listen," said he. "These twelve tribes that inhabit the whole world are twelve nations, and they are diverse in thought and mind. So just as you saw that the mountains were diverse, there are diversities of mind and thought among these nations, and I will tell you the operation of each one."

3 "First, sir," said I, "tell me this: why, when the mountains are so diverse, when the stones from them were set in the building, they became bright, and of one color, like the stones that came up from the deep."

4 "Because," said he, "all the nations that live under heaven, when they have heard and believed, are called by the name of the Son of God. So when they have received the seal, they have come to have one thought and one mind, and to possess one faith and one love, and they have come to bear the spirits of the girls with the name. That is why the structure of the tower

became of one color, as bright as the sun. But since they went 5
in together and became one body, some of them have defiled
themselves, and been cast out of the race of the upright, and
again become as they were before, or rather even worse."

"How, sir," said I, "did they become worse, when they had 18
come to know God?"

"The man," said he, "who does not know God, and does wrong,
receives some punishment for his wrongdoing, but the man who
has come to know God ought not to do wrong, but to do right.
So if the man who ought to do right does wrong, does he not 2
seem to do much greater wrong than the man who does not know
God? That is why those who do not know God and do wrong
are condemned to death, but those who know God and have seen
his mighty acts, and yet do wrong, will be doubly punished and
die forever. So in this way the church of God will be purified.

"But as you saw the stones taken from the tower, and handed 3
over to the evil spirits and cast out of it (and there will be one
body of those who are purified, just as the tower became as
though made of one stone, after it had been purified), so the
church of God will be, after it has been purified, and the wicked
and hypocrites and blasphemers and doubters and doers of
different kinds of wickedness are cast out. After these have been 4
cast out, the church of God will be one body, one thought, one
mind, one faith, one love, and then the Son of God will rejoice
and be glad over them, when he has taken his people back pure."

"It is all great and wonderful, sir," said I. "In addition, sir," 5
said I, "tell me the force and function of each of the mountains,
so that every soul that trusts in the Lord may hear it, and glorify
his great, wonderful, glorious name."

"Listen," said he, "to the diversity of the mountains and of
the twelve nations.

"Those who believed from the first mountain, the black one, 19
are such men as these: apostates and blasphemers of the Lord,
and betrayers of the slaves of God. For them there is no repent-

ance, but there is death, and that is why they are black, for their race is lawless.

2   "And those who believed from the second mountain, the bare one, are such men as these: hypocrites and teachers of wickedness. So these are like the preceding ones, for they have no fruit of uprightness. For as their mountain was without fruit, so such men have the name, but are devoid of faith, and there is no fruit of truth in them. So there is repentance for these, if they repent quickly, but if they delay, their death will be with the preceding ones."

3   "Why, sir," said I, "is there repentance for these, but not for the first ones? For their actions are almost the same."

"This," said he, "is why these can have repentance—because they have not blasphemed their Lord, or been betrayers of the slaves of God, but because of their desire for gain they have acted hypocritically, and each taught to suit the desires of sinful men. But they will pay a penalty, though repentance is open to them, because they have not been blasphemers or betrayers.

20   "And those who believed from the third mountain, which had thorns and briers, are such men as these: some of them are rich, and some are involved in many business affairs; the briers are the rich, and the thorns those involved in different kinds 2 of business. So these who are involved in many different kinds of business do not associate with the slaves of God, but are choked by what they are doing, and led astray. And the rich find it hard to associate with the slaves of God, for they fear that they will ask them for something. So such men will find it hard to 3 enter the kingdom of God. For just as it is hard to walk barefooted among briers, it is hard for such men to enter the king- 4 dom of God. But there is repentance for all these, but speedy repentance, so that they may retrace the days and make amends for what they failed to do in former times, and accomplish some good. So if they repent and accomplish some good, they will live to God, but if they persist in their conduct, they will

be turned over to those women, who will put them to death.

"And those who believed from the fourth mountain, which **21** had much vegetation, which was green at the tops but dry near the roots, and some of it dried up by the sun, are such men as these: some are doubters, and others have the Lord upon their lips, but do not have him in their hearts. That is **2** why their foundations are dry and have no strength, and only their words are alive, but their actions are dead. Such men are neither alive nor dead. So they are like the doubters, for the doubters are neither green nor dry, for they are neither alive nor dead. For just as these plants when they saw the sun were **3** dried up, so the doubters, when they hear of persecution, because of their cowardice worship idols and are ashamed of their Lord's name. So such men are neither alive nor dead. But **4** these too, if they repent quickly, will be able to live. But if they do not repent, they are already turned over to the women who take away their lives.

"And those who believed from the fifth mountain, which had **22** green vegetation and was rough, are such men as these: they are believers, but are slow to learn, and self-willed and pleasing themselves, wanting to know everything, and yet they know nothing at all. Because of this self-will of theirs, understanding **2** has left them, and stupid folly has taken possession of them, and they praise themselves for having intelligence and want to be volunteer teachers, foolish as they are. So because of this **3** arrogance many through exalting themselves have been humbled, for self-will and overconfidence are a great demon. So many of these were rejected, but some repented and believed, and submitted to those who had understanding, perceiving their own foolishness. And for the rest of such people, repentance **4** is open, for they have not been wicked, but foolish and without understanding instead. So if these men repent, they will live to God, but if they do not, they will live with the women who mean to do them evil.

23 And those who believed from the sixth mountain, which had great and small fissures in it, and withered plants in the fissures,
2 are such men as these. The ones that hold the small fissures are those who hold grudges against one another, and they are withered in faith from their own slanders. But many of them have repented, and the rest will repent when they hear my commands. For their slanders are small, and they will soon
3 repent. And the ones occupying the large fissures are those who persist in their slanders and rage vengefully at one another. So these have been thrown away from the tower, and rejected
4 from the building of it. Such men will find it hard to live. If our God and Lord, who rules over all, and has authority over his whole creation, holds no grudge against those who confess their sins, but is merciful, can a man who is mortal and full of sins hold a grudge against a man, as though he could destroy
5 or save him? But I, the angel of repentance, tell you, all who hold this way of thinking must lay it aside and repent, and the Lord will heal your previous sins, if you cleanse yourselves from this demon. But if you do not, you will be handed over to him, to die.

24 "And those who believed from the seventh mountain, on which there were gay, green plants, and the whole mountain was flourishing, and all kinds of cattle and wild birds were feeding on the plants on this mountain, and the plants on which they fed became all the more luxuriant, are such men as these:
2 they were always sincere and without guile, and blessed, holding nothing against one another, but always rejoicing in the slaves of God and clad in the holy Spirit of these girls, and always feeling compassion for every man, and from their labors they provided for every man without reproach or hesitation.
3 So the Lord, seeing their sincerity and perfect innocence, prospered them in the labors of their hands and showed them
4 favor in all that they did. And I, the angel of repentance, tell you who are such men, continue to be such, and your descendants

will never be blotted out. For the Lord has tested you and has enrolled you in our number, and all your descendants will live with the Son of God, for you have partaken of his spirit.

"And those who believed from the eighth mountain, where **25** there were many springs and all the Lord's creation was watered from the springs, are such men as these: apostles and **2** teachers who have preached to the whole world, and have taught the word of the Lord reverently and purely and have kept nothing at all back for evil desire, but always lived in uprightness and truth, just as they had received the holy Spirit. Such men will go in with the angels.

"And those who believed from the ninth mountain, which was **26** desert, which had reptiles and wild animals that destroy men on it, are such men as these: the ones that were spotted are **2** deacons who served badly and plundered the living of widows and orphans, and made profit for themselves from the ministry they had accepted to perform. So if they persist in the same desire, they are dead and have no hope of life. But if they turn and perform their service purely, they will be able to live. And the ones that are scaly are those that have denied and **3** have not returned to their Lord, but have become barren and desert; in not associating with the slaves of God, but keeping to themselves, they are destroying their own souls. For just as a **4** vine left uncared for inside an enclosure is ruined and wasted by weeds and eventually becomes wild and is no longer of any use to its owner, so men such as these have despaired and growing wild have become useless to their Lord. So there is repent- **5** ance for these men, unless they are found to have denied from their hearts. But if anyone is found to have denied from his heart, I do not know whether he can live. And I do not say this **6** for these days, so that a man can deny, and obtain repentance, but repentance seems to be available for those who denied long ago. So if anyone is going to repent, let him be quick to do so before the tower is finished, or else he will be destroyed and put

7 to death by the women. And the short ones are deceivers and slanderers, and they are the wild animals that you saw on the mountain. For just as the wild animals with their poison destroy man and kill him, so such men's words destroy man and kill
8 him. So these men are short in their faith because of their behavior to one another, but some have repented and been saved. And the others who are of this kind can be saved if they repent, but if they do not repent, they will die at the hands of those women whose power they have.

27 And those who believed from the tenth mountain, where
2 trees were sheltering some sheep, are such men as these: bishops and hospitable men who were always glad to welcome the slaves of God into their homes without hypocrisy, and the bishops always unfailingly sheltered the needy and the widows by their
3 ministry, and always conducted themselves purely. So all these will always be sheltered by the Lord. So those who have done these things are in honor with God, and their place is already with the angels if they continue to serve the Lord to the end.

28 "And those who believed from the eleventh mountain, where there were trees full of fruit, one adorned with one fruit and
2 another with another, are such men as these: those who have suffered for the name of the Son of God, who have suffered willingly with all their hearts, and laid down their lives."
3 "Then why, sir," said I, "do all the trees have fruit, but the fruits of some of them are better-looking?"

"Listen," said he. "All who have ever suffered for the name are glorious in the sight of God, and the sins of all of them have been taken away, because they have suffered for the name of the Son of God. But hear why their fruits are of different kinds and
4 some superior to others. All," said he, "who, when brought before the authorities, have been questioned and have not denied but suffered willingly are in greater honor in the sight of God; the superior fruit is theirs. But of all those that were cowardly and hesitated, and debated in their minds whether they should deny

or confess, and suffered, the fruits are inferior, because this thought occurred to them, for it is a wicked thought that a slave should deny his master.

"Take care, then, you who have these thoughts, that this thought 5 does not remain in your minds and you die to God. But you who suffer for the name ought to glorify God because God has thought you worthy to bear this name and to have all your sins healed. So count yourselves happy, but consider that you have 6 done a great deed if one of you suffers for the sake of God. The Lord is offering you life, and you do not perceive it, for your sins have weighed you down, and if you had not suffered for the name of the Lord, you would have died to God on account of your sins. I say this to you who are in doubt about denying or con- 7 fessing: Confess that you have a Master, so that you may not deny him and be thrown into prison. If the heathen punish their slaves 8 if one of them denies his master, what do you suppose the Lord who has authority over all will do to you? Put these thoughts out of your minds so that you may live to God forever.

"And from the twelfth mountain, which was white, those who 29 believed are such men as these: They are like veritable babes, into whose minds no evil comes, and they do not know what wickedness is, but have always continued in innocence. Such 2 people therefore will undoubtedly live in the Kingdom of God, because they have not by any act profaned God's commands, but have continued in innocence all the days of their lives in the same attitude of mind. All of you, then, who will continue," said he, 3 "and will be like babes, with no wickedness, will be more glorious than all those who have been mentioned before, for all babes are glorious in the sight of God, and are foremost with him. So blessed are you who put off wickedness from yourselves, and put on innocence; you will be first of all to live to God."

After he finished the parables of the mountains, I said to him, 4

"Sir, now explain to me about the stones that were taken away from the plain and put in the building in place of the stones that were taken out of the tower, and the round stones that were put into the building, and those that are still round."

30   "Hear," said he, "about all these also. These stones of the plain that were taken and put into the building of the tower, in place of the ones that were rejected, are the roots of the white

2 mountain. So since those who believed from the white mountain were all found innocent, the master of the tower ordered them to be taken from the roots of this mountain to the building of the tower. For he knew that if these stones went into the building of the tower, they would remain bright and none of them would turn black. But if he had put in those from the other mountains, he would have had to visit the tower again, and to clean it. But all those who have believed and are going to believe have been found to be white, for they belong to the same

4 race. Blessed is that race, for it is innocent! Now hear about the stones that are round and bright. They too are all from the white mountain. Hear why they were found round. Their riches have clouded them a little from the truth and darkened them, but they have never forsaken God, and no evil word has gone out of their mouths, but it was all justice and the virtue of truth.

5 So when the Lord saw that their minds were able to favor the truth and to remain good, he ordered their wealth to be reduced, but not to be wholly taken away, so that they could do some good with what was left to them, and they will live to God, since they belong to the good race. So they have been cut down a little and put into the building of the tower.

31   "But the rest, which were still round and had not been fitted into the building, because they had not received the seal, were put back in their former place, for they were found to be quite

2 round. But this world and the vanities of their possessions must be cut off from them, and then they will be fit for the kingdom of God. For they must enter the kingdom of God, for this innocent race the Lord blessed. So no one of this race will perish. For although one of them, tempted by a most wicked devil, does

something wrong, he will quickly return to his Lord. I, the angel 3
of repentance, declare all of you happy who are as innocent as
babes, because your part is good and honorable in God's sight. But 4
I tell all of you who have received the seal, to preserve your
sincerity, and hold no grudges, and not to persist in your wickedness, or in the bitter memory of your offenses, but to be each one
of one spirit, and harmonize these evil divisions and put them
away from you, so that the owner of the flocks may rejoice in
them. And he will rejoice, if they are all found in good health, 5
and none of them scattered. But if some of them are found
scattered, alas for the shepherds! And if the shepherds themselves 6
are found scattered, what will they say to the owner of the flock?
That they have been scattered by the sheep? They will not be believed, for it is an incredible thing that a shepherd should be hurt
by the sheep. They will be punished for their lie, instead. I, too,
am a shepherd, and must most certainly give an account for you.

"Reform therefore while the tower is still being built. The Lord 32, 2
lives among peace-loving men, for peace is really dear to him, but
he is far from quarrelsome people and men abandoned to wickedness. So give your spirits back to him whole, as you received
them. For if you give a cleaner a new garment whole, and want 3
to get it back again whole, but the cleaner returns it to you torn,
will you accept it? Will you not immediately blaze up, and pursue him with abuse and say, 'I gave you a whole garment; why
did you tear it and make it useless? Because of the tear you have
made in it, it cannot be used.' Will you not say all these things
to the cleaner, just about a tear he has made in your garment?
If, then, you grieve so over your garment, and complain because 4
you do not get it back whole, what do you suppose the Lord will
do to you, who gave you the spirit whole, and you return it entirely useless, so that it cannot be of any use to its owner, for its
use began to be useless when it was spoiled by you. Will not the
owner of that spirit on account of this act of yours punish you
with death?"

5   "Surely," said I, "he will punish all those whom he finds cherishing the memory of their wrongs."

"Do not trample on his mercy," said he, "but honor him instead, because he is so patient with your offenses, and is not like you. Show a repentance that will profit you.

33   "All these things that are written above, I, the shepherd, the angel of repentance, have shown and told to the slaves of God. If therefore you believe and listen to my words and follow them and mend your ways, you will be able to live. But if you persist in wickedness and in holding grudges, no one of that kind will live to God. All these things that I had to tell you have been told you."

2   The shepherd himself said to me,

"Have you asked me everything?"

"Yes, sir," said I.

"Then why did you not ask me about the marks of the stones that were put in the building, why we filled up the marks?"

"I forgot, sir," said I.

3   "Then hear now," said he, "about them. They are those who have now heard my commands and have repented with all their hearts. And when the Lord had seen that their repentance was good and pure, and that they could continue in it, he ordered their former sins to be wiped out. For these marks were their sins, and they have been smoothed out so that they should not show."

PARABLE X

1   After I had written this book, the angel who had turned me over to the shepherd came to the house where I was, and sat down upon the couch, and the shepherd stood at his right. Then he called me and said to me,

2   "I have turned you and your household over to this shepherd," said he, "so that you may be protected by him."

"Yes, sir," said I.

"So if you want to be protected," said he, "from all annoyance and cruelty, and to succeed in every good work and word, and to have every upright virtue, live in accordance with his commands which I gave you, and you will be able to overcome all wickedness. For if you keep his commands, every desire and en- 3 joyment of this world will be subject to you, but in every good undertaking success will attend you. Take upon yourself his ripe understanding and restraint, and tell all men that he is greatly honored and esteemed with the Lord, and is a defender of great power and mighty in his authority. He alone has been given authority over repentance throughout the whole world. Does he seem to you to be powerful? Yet you despise his ripe understanding and the modesty that he shows toward you."

I said to him,   2

"Ask him himself, sir, whether since he has been in my house I have done anything against his orders, so as to offend him."

"I know myself," said he, "that you have not done anything and 2 will not do anything against his orders. And so I tell you this, so that you may keep on. For he has thought well of you, he tells me. But you must tell the others these things, so that they too who have repented or are going to repent, may think as you do, and he may give a good report of them to me and I may to the Lord."

"I myself, sir," said I, "tell every man the mighty deeds of the 3 Lord, but I hope that all who have sinned before, if they hear these things, will be glad to repent and regain life."

"Then continue in this service," said he, "and complete it. All 4 who carry out his commands will have life, and the man who does so will have great honor with the Lord. But all who do not keep his commands are fleeing from their own life and against him, and they do not follow his commands, but give themselves up to death, and every one of them is guilty of his own blood. But I tell you to keep his commands and you will have the curing of your sins.

3   "But I sent these girls to you to live with you, for I saw that they were agreeable to you. So you have them as helpers, so that you may be better able to keep these commands, for it is not possible that these commands be kept without these girls. I see moreover that they like to be with you, but I will instruct them not to

2   leave your house at all. Only you must make your house clean, for they will be glad to live in a clean house, for they are clean and chaste and industrious, and they all have favor with the Lord. So if they find your house clean, they will stay with you. But if any bit of impurity happens, they will leave your house at once, for these girls love no impurity at all."

3   "I hope I shall please them, sir," I said to him, "so that they will always be glad to live in my house, and just as he to whom you turned me over has no fault to find with me, they will not either."

4   He said to the shepherd,
"I know that the slave of God wants to live, and will keep these commands, and will support the girls in purity."

5   With these words he turned me over to the shepherd again, and calling the girls he said to them,
"Since I see that you like to live in his house, I entrust him and his house to you; do not leave his house at all." And they were glad to hear these words.

4   Then he said to me,
"Be brave in this service. Show every man the mighty deeds of the Lord, and you will find favor in this service. Whoever therefore follows these commands will live, and will be happy in his life, but whoever neglects them will not live, and will be un-

2   happy in his life. Tell all men who can do right not to stop; the practice of good deeds is good for them. Further, I declare that every man ought to be rescued from distress. For the man who is in want and suffers distress in his daily life is in great misery and

3   hardship. So the man who rescues such a soul from misery wins great joy for himself. For the man who is harassed by such dis-

tress endures such torture as a man does who is in chains. For many, on account of such calamities, when they cannot endure them, bring death upon themselves. So the man who knows of the misery of such a man and does not rescue him commits a great sin, and becomes guilty of his blood.

"So do good, all of you who have learned from the Lord, or 4 while you put off doing it the tower may be finished, for it is on your account that the work of building has been interrupted. So unless you make haste to do right, the tower will be finished and you will be shut out of it."

After he had talked with me, he got up from the couch, and 5 taking the shepherd and the girls went away, telling me, however, that he would send the shepherd and the girls back to my house.

The Letters of Ignatius

Early in the second century Ignatius, bishop of Antioch, was condemned to death and taken to Rome to be thrown to the lions in the Coliseum. As he passed through the province of Asia, he was welcomed by groups from the churches on his way, at Philadelphia and Smyrna, and churches on the alternative route through Tralles, Magnesia, and Ephesus sent delegations to Smyrna to greet him. To all these churches he later wrote letters of acknowledgement, urging them to combat the Docetic heresy then rife in Asia, and to stand by their bishops. The leading bishops, Onesimus of Ephesus and Polycarp of Smyrna, were active in cheering him on his way, and with an Ephesian deacon named Burrhus did all they could to help him with his letters. In fact, as Ignatius seems to have written nothing enduring before reaching Smyrna, or after parting with Burrhus at Troas, it seems likely that he wrote largely at their instance. Ephesus was in that generation the literary center of Christianity—consider probably Ephesians, the Pauline letter collection, the Revelation, the Gospel and Letters of John, the fourfold gospel—and it would be natural for them to encourage Ignatius to throw his great influence as a Christian confessor and prospective martyr against the most threatening heresy of their day. Not only did Onesimus bring Burrhus, evidently a competent scribe, from Ephesus to do Ignatius' writing for him, but Polycarp afterward made it his business to circulate what he wrote, as his Letter to

*the Philippians, written immediately after Ignatius' departure
from Smyrna, shows. The survival of the sevenfold corpus of
Ignatius' letters also points to such activity on the part of his
episcopal sponsors. And Ignatius' literary style is not at all that
of a man accustomed to written composition. Moreover, the
collection comes from the very time when the Christian public,
especially in Asia, was awakening to the enormous possibilities
of book publication in the promotion of their great enterprise.*

*From Smyrna Ignatius wrote letters of exhortation and instruc-
tion to the churches of Ephesus, Magnesia, and Tralles, which
had sent delegations to welcome and cheer him, and to the church
at Rome, to prepare its members for his coming, and urge them
to make no efforts for his release. The longest one, his letter to
the Ephesians, is about the length of Paul's Letter to the Colos-
sians. They reveal a man deeply attached to the basic realities
of Christian experience, heroically adjusting himself to the pros-
pect of certain, violent death, and warning the Asian churches
against the delusions of Docetism. Ignatius is also a strong
advocate of the threefold ministry, bishops, elders or presbyters,
and deacons.*

*Hurried on by his guards to Troas, but still accompanied by
the faithful Burrhus, he wrote from that port letters to the
Philadelphians, to the Smyrnaeans, and to Polycarp, the bishop
of Smyrna, who had so signally befriended him. From Troas he
was taken to Neapolis and Philippi, and there Ignatius finally
disappears from our view. Like so many others, he doubtless
suffered martyrdom in the Coliseum, Eusebius says in A.D.107-108,
but modern learning inclines to about A.D.110-117.*

*The letter written by Polycarp to the church at Philippi, soon
after Ignatius left there, indicates that while at Philippi Ignatius
suggested to the Philippians that copies of his letters, or some
of them, could be obtained from Polycarp at Smyrna, so that it*

is evident that the letters were not only sent to the churches addressed, but copies of them were preserved at Smyrna for wider distribution. That is to say, at least a limited publication of them took place at once, and it is decidedly probable that it was with this in view that Onesimus and Polycarp encouraged and helped Ignatius to write them, to aid in their campaign against the dangers of Docetism.

The seven Ignatian letters have had an extraordinary history, having been reduced in Syriac to three greatly abbreviated ones and, on the other hand, in Greek and Latin having been increased as a collection by the addition of six or more spurious letters, or individually expanded and interpolated, still accompanied by several spurious letters. But the list of seven given in Eusebius in A.D. 326, and known to us in the shorter Greek form, it is now generally agreed, is the original Ignatian corpus.

The Letters of Ignatius

To the Ephesians

Ignatius, also called Theophorus, to the deservedly happy church at Ephesus in Asia, blest in size by the full experience of God the Father, foreordained from eternity for enduring, unchanging glory for ever, unalterably united and chosen through true suffering by the will of the Father and Jesus Christ our God, heartiest greeting in Jesus Christ and in blameless joy.

I have through God approved your well-beloved name which 1 you bear by reason of your upright nature, by faith and love in Christ Jesus our Savior. You are followers of God's example, and rekindling your proper task by the blood of God, you have finished it perfectly. For when you heard that I was on my way from 2 Syria in chains for our common name and hope, in the hope of being permitted to fight wild beasts in Rome in order that by being permitted I might be able to be a disciple, you were eager to see me. Since therefore I have received your whole congrega- 3 tion in the name of God, in the person of Onesimus, a man of inexpressible love, and your bishop in the flesh, I pray that you will love him in Jesus Christ, and will all of you be like him. For blessed is he who has favored you, worthy as you are, with having such a bishop.

As to my fellow slave Burrhus, by the will of God your deacon 2 blessed in all things, I beg that he stay on with me, to the honor of yourselves and the bishop. And Crocus too, who is worthy of God and of you, in whom I have received an example of your love, has refreshed me in every way; may the Father of Jesus Christ refresh him so! With him came Onesimus and Burrhus and

2 Euplus and Fronto, in whom I have seen you all in love. May I have profit of you always, if I am worthy. So it is proper for you in every way to glorify Jesus Christ, who has glorified you, so that you may be united in a common subjection to the bishop and the body of elders, and be wholly sanctified.

3 I do not order you as though I were somebody. For though I am in chains for the name, I am not yet perfect in Jesus Christ. For now I am beginning to be a disciple, and I speak to you as my schoolmates. For I needed to be rubbed down by you with

2 faith, exhortation, endurance, patience. But since love does not allow me to be silent about you, I have on that account hurried to exhort you to run your race in harmony with the mind of God. For Jesus Christ, our inseparable life is the mind of the Father, just as the bishops who are appointed all over the world are in the mind of Jesus Christ.

4 Hence it is proper for you to run your race in harmony with the mind of the bishop, just as you are doing. For your deserving body of elders, worthy of God, is attuned to the bishop as the strings are to the harp. Therefore in your agreement and harmo-

2 nious love Jesus Christ is being praised. You must every man of you join in a choir so that being harmonious and in concord and taking the keynote of God in unison, you may sing with one voice through Jesus Christ to the Father, so that he may hear you and through your good deeds recognize that you are parts of his Son. So it is advantageous for you to be in blameless unity, so that you always share in God.

5 For if I in a short time have come to have such intimacy with your bishop, which was not human but spiritual, how much more do I think you happy who have been mingled with him as the church is with Jesus Christ and as Jesus Christ is with the Father,

2 so that all things may unite in harmony. Let no one deceive himself; unless a man is inside the altar, he is in want of the bread of

God. For if the prayer of one or two has such power, how much more that of the bishop and the whole church has! So the man 3 who does not come to church is proud already, and has separated himself. For it is written, "God opposes the proud." So let us be zealous not to oppose the bishop, so that we may be submissive to God.

And the more anyone sees the bishop silent, the more let him 6 revere him, for anyone whom the head of the house sends on business of his own we ought to welcome as we would the one who sent him. So it is clear that we must look upon the bishop as the Lord himself. So Onesimus himself praises highly your 2 good discipline in God, for you all live in the light of the truth, and no sect has any lodging among you; why, you will not even continue to listen to anyone, even though you do to Jesus Christ who speaks in truth.

For some are in the habit of making the name known in wicked 7 deceit, while they do some things unworthy of God. You must turn away from them as you would from wild beasts, for they are mad dogs, who bite by stealth. You must be on your guard against them, for they are hard to heal. There is one physician, 2 of flesh and of spirit, born and unborn, God become incarnate, true life in death, sprung from Mary and from God, first subject to suffering and then free from suffering, Jesus Christ our Lord.

So let no one deceive you, as indeed you are not deceived, for 8 you belong wholly to God. For when no quarrel, which might torment you, has gained a foothold among you, you are indeed living in God's way. I am your humble sacrifice, dedicated for you Ephesians, a church renowned forever. Those who are of the 2 flesh cannot do spiritual things, nor can those who are spiritual do the things of the flesh, just as faith cannot do the deeds of unbelief, nor unbelief the deeds of faith. But even what you do in the flesh is spiritual, for you do everything in union with Jesus Christ.

But I have learned that some men have visited you from out- 9

side, and brought you an evil teaching, though you did not allow them to scatter it among you, but closed your ears, so that you might not receive what they scattered, since you are like stones of a temple of the Father, prepared for the building of God the Father, hoisted up on high by the crane of Jesus Christ, that is, the cross, using the holy Spirit for a rope. Your faith is your wind-
2 lass and love is the road that leads up to God. So you are all traveling companions, carrying God and temple, and Christ and your sacred things, and being fully arrayed in the commands of Jesus Christ. In this I rejoice that I have been thought worthy through what I write to converse with you and congratulate you that following another way of life you love nothing but God alone.

10   Pray constantly for other men, also, for in their case there is a hope of repentance, that they may find God. Permit them to be
2 instructed by you, at least through your deeds. To their anger, be meek; to their boasts, be humble; to their abuse, utter your prayers; to their error, be steadfast in faith; to their savagery, be
3 gentle; not zealous to imitate them. Let us show ourselves their brothers by forbearance, and let us be zealous to imitate the Lord, to see who can be more wronged, defrauded, set at naught, so that no plant of the devil may be found in you, but with all purity and sobriety you may remain in union with Jesus Christ, in both flesh and spirit.

11   These are the last times; let us feel shame, let us fear the patience of God, that it may not result in our condemnation. For let us either fear the wrath that is to come or love the grace that now is, one or the other; only let us be found in union with
2 Christ Jesus, to live the true life. Let nothing attract you apart from him in union with whom I wear my chains, these spiritual pearls with which may I rise again through your prayer, in which may I always share, so that I may be found in the class of the Christians of Ephesus who were always in accord with the apostles, by the power of Jesus Christ.

I know who I am and to whom I am writing. I am condemned, **12**
you have received mercy. I am in danger, you are secure. You are **2**
the approach for those who are put to death on their way to God,
fellow initiates of Paul, who has been sanctified, and died a
martyr, deservedly happy, in whose footsteps may I be found
when I reach the presence of God; who in every letter recalls you,
in union with Christ Jesus.

So be zealous to meet together more frequently to give thanks **13**
to God and glorify him. For when you meet together frequently,
Satan's powers are destroyed and his destructiveness comes to
naught through the harmony of your faith. There is nothing better **2**
than peace, by which every war of beings in heaven or on earth
is nullified.

None of these things can escape you if you have perfect faith **14**
and love for Jesus Christ, which are the beginning and the end
of life; faith is the beginning and love the end. And when the two
are united they are God, and everything else that contributes to
character follows them. No one who professes faith sins, or who **2**
possesses love hates. The tree is known by its fruit, and similarly
those who profess to belong to Christ will be recognized by what
they do. For it is not a matter of what we now profess, but that
a man continue in the power of faith to the end.

It is better to be silent and be, than to talk and not be. It is **15**
good to teach, if the speaker does so. So there is one teacher, who
spoke and it was done, and even what he did silently was worthy
of the Father. The man who is really possessed of the word of **2**
Jesus can hear even his silence, so that he may be perfect, so
that he may act through what he says and be known through his
silence. Nothing is hidden from the Lord, but even our secrets are **3**
near him. So let us do everything with a sense that he is dwelling
within us, so that we may be his temples, and he be within us
our God, as he really is, and as will appear before our eyes from
the love we justly have for him.

16   Do not be misled, my brethren; adulterers cannot inherit the
2 kingdom of God. If, then, those who do these things in the flesh
are dead, how much more if by evil teaching a man corrupts faith
in God, for which Jesus Christ was crucified! Such a man, vile as
he is, will go to the unquenchable fire, and so will the man that
listens to him.

17   It was for this reason that the Lord let the ointment be put
upon his head—that he might breathe incorruptibility upon the
church. Do not be anointed with the foul smell of the teaching of
the ruler of this world, so that he may not capture us from the
2 life that lies before us. And why are we not all sensible, when we
have received the knowledge of God, which is Jesus Christ? Why
do we foolishly perish, ignoring the free gift which the Lord has
really sent us?

18   My spirit is a humble sacrifice to the cross, which is revolting
to unbelievers, but to us is salvation and eternal life. Where is
your philosopher? Your reasoner? Where is the boasting of the
2 so-called intelligent? For our God Jesus Christ was conceived
by Mary, by divine dispensation, of the line of David and of the
holy Spirit; he was born and he was baptized so that by his suffering he might purify the water.

19   And the maidenhood of Mary was hidden from the ruler of
this world, as were her giving birth and likewise the death of the
Lord—three secrets to be cried aloud, which yet were accom-
2 plished in the silence of God. How, then, was he shown to the
ages? A star blazed forth in heaven brighter than all the stars,
and its light was inexpressible, and its strangeness caused aston-
ishment, and all the rest of the stars, along with the sun and
moon, formed a chorus round the star, but it outshone them all;
and there was perplexity as to where this strange thing, so unlike
3 the rest, came from. In consequence of it all magic was dissolved,
and every wicked spell vanished, ignorance was abolished, the
old kingdom was destroyed, when God appeared in human form,
to bring us new, eternal life; and what God had prepared had

its beginning. Hence all things were in confusion, because the abolishing of death was being designed.

If Jesus Christ permits you through your prayer, and it is God's **20** will, in the second letter which I mean to write you, I will explain to you further the divine plan I have touched upon, as to the new man Jesus Christ, in his faith and in his love, in his suffering and resurrection; especially if the Lord reveals to me that you **2** all individually every one come together in grace, in one faith and in Jesus Christ, who was physically descended from David, the Son of man and Son of God, so that you may obey the bishop and the elders with an undisturbed mind, breaking one bread, which is the medicine of immortality, the antidote against death, to make us live forever in Christ Jesus.

My life is given for you and for those whom to do God honor **21** you sent to Smyrna, from which place I am writing to you, with thanksgiving to the Lord and love for Polycarp as well as for you. Remember me, as Jesus Christ remembers you. Pray for the **2** church in Syria, from which I am being led bound to Rome, though I am the last of the believers there, as I have been thought worthy to do honor to God. Farewell in union with God the Father and Jesus Christ our common hope.

To the Magnesians

Ignatius, also called Theophorus, to her that is blessed with the favor of God the Father, through Jesus Christ our Savior, in whom I greet the church that is at Magnesia on the Maeander, and wish her heartiest greeting in God the Father and in Jesus Christ.

When I learned how well disciplined you are in godly love, I **1** rejoiced and resolved in faith in Jesus Christ to address you. For **2** having been thought worthy of a most revered title, in the chains that I wear I sing the praises of the churches, in which I pray that there may be union of the flesh and spirit of Jesus Christ, our everlasting life, and of faith and love, than which nothing is better, and above all of Jesus and the Father. In union with him, if we endure the ill-treatment of the evil genius of this world, and escape, we will reach God.

2   Since therefore I have been permitted to see you in the persons of Damas your godly bishop and your worthy elders Bassus and Apollonius, and your deacon Zotion, my fellow slave, whose friendship may I enjoy, because he obeys the bishop as the grace of God and the board of elders as the law of Jesus Christ.

3   But it is right for you not to take advantage of the youth of the bishop but in view of the power of God the Father to show him all reverence, as I know the holy elders do, taking no advantage of his youthful appearance, but like men of godly prudence deferring to him, yet not to him, but to the Father of Jesus Christ,
2 to the bishop of all. In honor therefore of him who loved us it is right to be obedient without any hypocrisy. For it is not that a man deceives this bishop who can be seen, but that he tries to defraud the one who is invisible. In such a case one has to reckon not with flesh and blood, but with God who knows what is secret.

4   It is right, therefore, not just to be called Christians, but also to be such, just as some call a man bishop, but do everything without regard to him. Such men do not appear to me to be conscientious because they do not hold authorized meetings in accordance with the commandment.

5   Since, therefore, affairs come to an end, two things together lie before us, life and death, and each one is going to go to his own
2 place; for just as there are two coinages, the one that of God, the other that of the world, and each has its own stamp on it, the unbelieving bear the stamp of this world, and those who believe with love bear the stamp of God the Father through Jesus Christ, through whom, unless we choose to die in his suffering, his life is not in us.

Since, therefore, in the persons I have mentioned I have seen **6** in faith and have loved your whole number, I exhort you, be zealous to do everything in godly harmony, with the bishop presiding in the place of God, and the elders in the place of the council of the apostles, and the deacons too, who are so dear to me, entrusted with the service of Jesus Christ, who from eternity was with the Father and finally appeared. You must all therefore **2** assume God's attitude and respect one another, and let no one regard his neighbor materially, but in union with Jesus Christ always love one another. Let there be nothing among you that will be able to divide you, but be at one with the bishop and with the leaders, for an example and lesson of immortality.

So just as the Lord did nothing without the Father, since he **7** was united with him, either by himself or through the apostles, you must do nothing without the bishop and the elders. Do not try to make anything appear right for you by yourselves, but let there be one prayer in common, one petition, one mind, one hope in love, in faultless joy, which is Jesus Christ, than whom there is nothing better. Hasten all of you to come together as to one temple of God, as to one altar, to one Jesus Christ, who came forth from one Father and is in one and has gone to one.

Do not be led astray by strange doctrines or old fables, since **8** they are profitless. For if we are still practicing Judaism, we admit that we have not received God's favor. For the most divine **2** prophets lived in accordance with Jesus Christ. That is why they were also persecuted, being inspired by his grace, that the disobedient might be convinced that there is one God, who has manifested himself through Jesus Christ his Son, who is his Word that proceeded from silence, who in all things was pleasing to him that sent him.

If, then, those who lived in ancient ways attained a new hope, **9** no longer keeping the sabbath but observing the Lord's Day, on which our life too rose through him and his death (which some deny)—a mystery through which we came to believe, and be-

cause of this we endure, so that we may be found disciples of
2 Jesus Christ, our only teacher, how shall we be able to live without him to whom even the prophets, being his disciples in the
spirit, looked forward as their teacher? And therefore he whom
they waited for in uprightness, when he came raised them from
the dead.

10   Let us not therefore be insensible of his kindness. For if he
imitates us in what we do, we are lost. Let us therefore, since we
have become his disciples, learn to live our Christianity. For whoever is called by any other name than this does not belong to
2 God. So lay aside the bad yeast that has grown stale and sour, and
change to the new yeast, which is Jesus Christ. Be salted with
him, so that no one of you may be spoiled, for you will be con-
3 victed by the smell. It is wrong to talk of Jesus Christ and live
like the Jews. For Christianity did not believe in Judaism but
Judaism in Christianity, in which every language believed and
was brought together to God.

11   This I say, my dear friends, not because I know that any of you
are doing it, but as less than you, I want you to be on your guard
against falling into the snares of vainglory but be convinced of
the birth and suffering and resurrection which took place in the
time of the governorship of Pontius Pilate, which were truly and
certainly brought about by Jesus Christ our hope, from which
may none of you be turned aside.

12   May I have joy of you in every way, if I am worthy. For though
I am in chains, I cannot compare with one of you who are at
liberty. I know that you are not conceited, for you have Jesus
Christ within you. And all the more, when I commend you, I
know you that you feel ashamed, for the scripture says, "The upright is his own accuser."

13   Be zealous, therefore, to be firmly grounded in the edicts of
the Lord and the apostles in order that in everything you do you
may prosper in flesh and spirit, through faith and love, in the
Son and the Father and the Spirit, in the beginning and at the
end, along with your most esteemed bishop and the worthily

woven spiritual wreath of your board of elders, and the godly
deacons. Subordinate yourselves to the bishop and to one another, 2
as Jesus Christ in the flesh did to the Father, and the apostles did
to the Father and to Christ and the Spirit, so that there may be
union of both flesh and spirit.

Since I know that you are full of God, I have exhorted you 14
briefly. Remember me in your prayers, so that I may reach the
presence of God, and remember the church in Syria, to which I
am not worthy to belong. For I need your united prayer in God
and your love, that the church in Syria may be deemed worthy
of being bedewed by your church.

From Smyrna, from which place I am writing to you, the 15
Ephesians greet you; being here for the glory of God, like your-
selves; they have rested me, along with Polycarp, bishop of
Smyrna. The rest of the churches also greet you in honor of Jesus
Christ. Farewell in God's harmony, possessed of an undivided
spirit, which is Jesus Christ.

To the Trallians

Ignatius, also called Theophorus, to her that is beloved of God,
the Father of Jesus Christ, the holy church that is in Tralles in
Asia, chosen and worthy, outwardly and inwardly at peace
through the suffering of Jesus Christ, who is our hope through
our resurrection unto him; which church I greet in the full experience of God, in the apostolic fashion, and offer her heartiest
greeting.

I have learned that you have a disposition that is faultless and 1
unwavering in endurance, not from habit but by nature, as Po-
lybius your bishop has shown me, who by the will of God and
Jesus Christ has come to me at Smyrna, and so rejoiced with me,
in chains as I am in Christ Jesus, that I beheld in him your whole
company. So having received through him your godly kindness I 2
gave God glory, that I had found that you were imitators of God,
as I had heard.

2   For when you subordinate yourselves to the bishop as to Jesus Christ you appear to me to be living not in the human way, but after the manner of Jesus Christ, who died for us, in order that **2** by believing in his death you might escape death. It is necessary, therefore, as indeed you do, that you do nothing without the bishop, but subordinate yourselves also to the board of elders as to the apostles of Jesus Christ our hope, in union with whom we **3** shall be found, if we so live. And the deacons too, as ministers of the mysteries of Jesus Christ, must please all in every way. For they are not servers of food and drink, but servants of the church of God. So they must be on their guard against accusations as against fire.

3   In the same way all must respect the deacons as Jesus Christ, as they do the bishop also for he symbolizes the Father, and the elders as a council of God and a band of apostles. Without **2** these no body can be called a church. With all this I am sure that you agree. For I have received and still have with me in the person of your bishop a sample of your love. His very demeanor is a great lesson and his gentleness is power; I think even the un- **3** believers revere him. Because I love you, I spare you, though I might write more sharply on his behalf. But I do not think myself entitled, condemned as I am, to command you like an apostle.

4   Through union with God I have many ideas, but I take my own measure, so that I may not perish through boasting. For now I must more than ever be afraid and not pay attention to those who **2** flatter me. For those who talk to me scourge me. For I am glad to suffer, but I do not know whether I am worthy. For the jealousy is not apparent to many, but it makes war on me all the more. So I need humility, by which the ruler of this world can be destroyed.

5   Am I not able to write to you of heavenly things? But I am afraid that I may do you harm, for you are babies. So pardon me, or you may be choked, through being unable to take them in. **2** For I myself, though I am in chains and can understand heavenly things and the assignments of the angels and the relations of their rulers, and things seen and unseen, for all that am not yet a disciple. For we lack many things, that we may not come short of God.

I entreat you therefore—yet not I but the love of Jesus Christ— **6** use only Christian food and abstain from the herbage of others which is heresy. For they mix Jesus Christ with themselves, while **2** imposing on people with their pretensions of honesty, just as though they might give a deadly drug with honeyed wine, in ignorance of which a man gladly accepts death with fatal pleasure.

So be on your guard against such men. And you will be, if you **7** are not conceited but are inseparable from the god of Jesus Christ, and the bishop and the commands of the apostles. He who **2** is inside the altar is clean; but he who is outside the altar is not clean; that is to say, he who does anything without bishop and board of elders and deacon has not a clear conscience.

Not that I know of any such thing among you, but I am keep- **8** ing watch over you, since you are dear to me, for I foresee the snares of the devil. So take on meekness, and renew yourselves in faith, which is the Lord's flesh, and in love, which is the blood of Jesus Christ. Let no one of you hold a grudge against his **2** neighbor. Give the heathen no grounds for finding fault, so that the godly majority may not be abused on account of a foolish few. For alas for him through whom my name is abused among any.

Stop your ears, therefore, when anyone speaks to you apart **9** from Jesus Christ, who was descended from David, who was the son of Mary, who was truly born, who both ate and drank, was truly persecuted under Pontius Pilate, was truly crucified and died, in the sight of those in heaven and on earth and under the earth; who was also truly raised from the dead, when his Father **2** raised him, and his Father in like manner will raise us also who believe in him, through Christ Jesus, without whom we can have no true life.

10   But if, as some say, who are without God, that is, unbelievers, that he suffered only in semblance, though they are themselves only semblance, why am I in chains, and why do I pray to fight wild beasts? Then I am dying in vain. In that case I am speaking falsely of the Lord.

11   So flee from such evil offshoots, which bear a deadly fruit, and if a man tastes of it he immediately dies. For these are not
2 a planting of the Father. For if they were, they would be seen to be branches of the cross, and their fruit eternal—the cross by which through his suffering he calls you, since you are parts of him. Therefore the head cannot be born without the parts of the body, since God promises union, which is himself.

12   I send you greetings from Smyrna, as do the churches of God that are with me, who have rested me in body and spirit. My
2 chains exhort you, which I carry around with me for the sake of Jesus Christ, praying that I may reach the presence of God; continue to be harmonious and to pray with one another. For it is right that every one of you, and particularly the elders, should cheer the bishop, in honor of the Father and of Jesus Christ and
3 of the apostles. I pray that you may listen to me in love, so that I may not by having written become evidence against you. But pray for me too, for I need your love, by the mercy of God, so that I may be found worthy to obtain the lot which it is incumbent upon me to obtain, so that I may not be disqualified.

13   The love of the Smyrnaeans and Ephesians greets you. Remember in your prayers the church in Syria, in which I am not
2 worthy to be counted, for I am the last of them. Farewell in Jesus Christ, and subordinate yourselves to the bishop as God's command, and to the board of elders in the same way. Love one an-
3 other every one of you with undivided heart. My spirit offers itself for you not only now, but also when I shall reach the presence of God. For I am still in danger, but through Jesus Christ the Father can be counted on to answer my prayer and yours. May you be found faultless in union with him.

To the Romans

Ignatius, also called Theophorus, to her who has found mercy through the majesty of the Father Most High, and of Jesus Christ his only Son—to the church by the will of him who has willed all things that are, beloved and enlightened in faith and in love of Jesus Christ our God, which holds the chief place in the seat of the country of Rome, worthy of God, worthy of honor, worthy of felicitation, worthy of praise, worthy of success, worthily pure, and pre-eminent in love, named after Christ, named after the Father, which I greet in the name of Jesus Christ, Son of the Father; you who are united in body and spirit to every one of his commandments, unwaveringly filled with the grace of God, and strained clear of every alien color, hearty greetings free from blame in Jesus Christ our God.

Since in answer to my prayer to God I have been permitted **1** to see your godly faces, so that I have received even more than I asked—for I hope to greet you in chains for Christ Jesus, if it proves to be God's will that I should be found worthy to the end. For the beginning has been well arranged, if only I can find favor to obtain my inheritance unhindered. For I am afraid your very love will do me wrong, for it is easy for you to do what you please, but it is hard for me to reach the presence of God, if you do not let me alone.

For I do not want you to please men, but please God, just as **2** you are doing. For I will never have such an opportunity to reach the presence of God, nor can you, if you will be silent, put your names to a better deed. For if you are silent and let me alone, I will be a word of God; but if you are in love with my body, I will be just a voice again. Grant me nothing more than to be **2** poured out in sacrifice to God, while there is still an altar ready, so that you may form a chorus in love and sing to the Father through Jesus Christ, because God has deemed the bishop of Syria worthy to be found at the setting of the sun, summoning him from the sunrise. It is good to set from the world unto God, so that I may rise to him.

3   You have never envied anyone, you have taught others. And I want those things that you teach when instructing others to
2 hold good. Only pray that I may have inward and outward strength, so that I may not only say so but really desire it, that I may not only be called a Christian but be found to be one. For if I am found to be one, I can also be called one, and be faithful
3 when I am no longer visible to the world. Nothing visible is good. For our God Jesus Christ is more plainly visible now that he is in the Father. Christianity is not a matter of persuasion, but is greatest when it is hated by the world.

4   I am writing to all the churches and I charge all that I willingly die for God, if only you do not prevent it. I entreat you, do not be an ill-timed kindness to me. Let me be eaten by the wild beasts, through whom I can reach the presence of God. I am God's wheat, and I am ground by the teeth of the wild beasts, so that
2 I may be found pure bread of Christ. Instead, coax the wild beasts to be my grave, and to leave none of my body, so that when I have fallen asleep I may not be burdensome to anyone. Then I will really be a disciple of Jesus Christ, when the world will not see even my body. Pray to Christ for me, that through
3 these instruments I may be found a sacrifice to God. I do not command you, like Peter and Paul. They were apostles, I am a condemned man. They were free, I am still a slave. But if I suffer, I shall be emancipated by Jesus Christ, and I will rise in him, free. And now in chains I am learning to have no desires.

5   From Syria to Rome, I am fighting with wild beasts, on land and sea, night and day, bound to ten leopards, that is, a squad of soldiers, who get worse the better they are treated. Through their ill-treatment I am being made more and more a disciple,
2 but that does not prove that I am innocent. May I enjoy the wild beasts that are prepared for me, and I pray I may find them quick. I will coax them to devour me quickly, not as in the case of

some whom they were afraid to touch. If they will not of their own accord, I will force them to. Pardon me, I know what is 3 best for me. I am just beginning to be a disciple. May nothing, visible or invisible, envy my reaching the presence of Jesus Christ. Fire and cross and struggles with wild beasts, crushing of bones, mangling of limbs; grinding of my whole body, wicked torments of the devil—let them come upon me, only let me reach the presence of Jesus Christ.

The ends of the earth and the kingdoms of this world will do 6 me no good. It is better for me to die in Jesus Christ than to be king of the ends of the earth. I am in search of him who died for us. I want him who rose for our sake. Childbirth is upon me. Ex- 2 cuse me, brethren. Do not hinder my coming to life, do not wish me to die. Do not give to the world the man who wants to belong to God, nor delude him with mere matter. Let me receive the clear light. When I reach it, I will be a man indeed. Let me be an 3 imitator of the suffering of my God. If anyone has him within himself, let him understand what I want, and share my feeling, knowing what compels me.

The ruler of this world wants to take me captive and destroy 7 my purpose toward God. So let none of you who are present help him. Take my side, that is, God's, instead. Do not talk Jesus Christ, and desire the world. Envy must not live among you. 2 Even if when I come I beseech you, do not obey me, but obey this that I am writing to you, instead. For I write you alive, yet in love with death. My love has been crucified, and there is no material passion in me, but living water, speaking within me, saying to me from within, "Come to the Father." I do not enjoy 3 perishable food or the pleasures of this life. I want the bread of God, which is the flesh of Jesus Christ, who was descended from David, and for drink I want his blood, which is immortal love.

I no longer want to live a human life. And this can happen, if 8 you want it to. Want it, so that you too may be wanted. I am 2 asking you for it with a short letter; believe me! Jesus Christ will

show you that I am telling the truth when I say this. He is the
3 unerring mouth by which the Father has spoken truly. Pray for
me, that I may attain this. I write you not in terms of flesh and
blood but of the mind of God. If I suffer, you favored me; if I
am rejected, you hated me.

9   Remember in your prayers the church in Syria, which has God
for its pastor in my place. Jesus Christ alone will oversee it, to-
2 gether with your love. I am ashamed to be called one of them,
for I do not deserve it, for I am the last of them and born at the
wrong time, but if I reach the presence of God I have obtained
3 mercy to be somebody. My spirit sends you greeting, and so does
the love of the churches that have welcomed me in the name of
Jesus Christ not as a mere passer-by. For those that were not
actually on my way escorted me from city to city.

10   I write you this from Smyrna, by the hands of the deservedly
happy Ephesians. I have with me also, besides many others,
2 Crocus, a person dear to me. About those who have gone ahead
of me from Syria to Rome for the glory of God, I believe you
have had news; let them know that I am near. For they are all
worthy of God and of you, and it is right for you to refresh them
3 in every way. I write you this on the ninth day before the kalends
of September [August 24]. Farewell to the end, in the endurance
of Jesus Christ.

To the Philadelphians

Ignatius, also called Theophorus, to the church of God the
Father and the Lord Jesus Christ that is at Philadelphia in Asia,
that has found mercy and been established in godly harmony and
unwaveringly rejoices in the suffering of our Lord and in his
resurrection, being fully assured in all mercy; in the blood of
Jesus Christ I send greeting to her who is eternal and abiding joy,
especially if they be at one with the bishop and the elders and
deacons who are with him, appointed with the approval of

Jesus Christ, whom he has securely established in accordance with his will by his holy Spirit.

This bishop I know obtained his ministry, which is for the common good, not of himself or through men, nor through vanity, but in love of God the Father and the Lord Jesus Christ. I am amazed at his forbearance; he can do more by keeping silence than those who utter empty words. For he is tuned to the commandments as a harp is tuned to its strings. For that reason my soul blesses his attitude to God, recognizing it as virtuous and perfect, his steadfast and patient spirit too, with all the forbearance of the living God. **1** **2**

So as children of the light of truth, flee from division and false teachings; follow like sheep where the pastor is. For many plausible wolves take the runners in God's race captive with wicked pleasures, but in your unity they will find no place. **2** **2**

Keep away from evil pastures which Jesus Christ does not tend, for they are no planting of the Father. Not that I found any division among you, but a filtering process. For all who belong to God and Jesus Christ are with the bishop, and all who repent and return to unity with the church will also belong to God, in order to live in harmony with Jesus Christ. Do not be misled, my brethren. If anyone follows a schismatic, he cannot inherit the kingdom of God; if anyone holds alien views, he does not support Christ's suffering. **3** **2** **3**

Be zealous, therefore, to practice one giving of thanks, for there is one flesh of our Lord Jesus Christ, and one cup in token of union in his blood, one altar, as well as one bishop with the board of elders and the deacons, my fellow slaves, in order that whatever you do you do in accordance with the will of God. **4**

My brethren, I am altogether overflowing in love for you, and in the height of my exultation I am safeguarding you, yet not I, but Jesus Christ. Being in chains for him I am all the more afraid, as being still imperfect. But your prayer to God will perfect me, so that I may attain what I have been mercifully allotted, having **5**

taken refuge in the gospel as the flesh and blood of Jesus, and
2 in the apostles as the board of elders of the church. And we love
the prophets too, because they too announced the gospel, and
hoped in him and awaited him, through believing in whom they
were saved, being united with Jesus Christ—holy men worthy of
love and admiration, borne witness to by Jesus Christ, and numbered with us in preaching the good news of our common hope.

6   But if anyone expounds Judaism to you, do not listen to him.
For it is better to hear Christianity from a man who is circumcised than Judaism from one who is uncircumcised. But if both
do not talk of Jesus Christ, they are to me tombstones and graves
2 of the dead, on which only men's names are written. Flee, therefore, from the frauds and traps of the ruler of this world, in order
that you may not be distressed by his designs and weaken in your
3 love, but get together, all of you, with undivided heart. I thank
my God that I have a clear conscience about you, and no one
can boast in private or in public that I have been a burden to anyone in anything, great or small. And for all among whom I have
spoken, I pray that they may not find it a testimony against
themselves.

7   For even though some desired to lead me astray according to
the flesh, yet the spirit is not misled, for it is from God. For it
knows where it comes from and where it is going, and it exposes
secret things. I cried out when I was among you, I spoke with a
loud voice, the voice of God, Pay attention to the bishop and
2 the board of elders and the deacons. Some suspected me of saying
this because I knew beforehand that some had created division.
But he for whom I am in chains is my witness that I knew this
from no human flesh and blood. It was the spirit that was preaching, saying this: Do nothing without the bishop, keep your body
as the temple of God, love unity, avoid divisions, be imitators of
Jesus Christ as he was of his Father.

8   I therefore did my part as a man devoted to unity. But where
division and anger exist, God does not dwell. Now the Lord for-

gives all who repent, if in repentance they turn to union with God and the council of the bishop. I have faith in the grace of Jesus Christ, who will free you from every chain. I beg you to do noth- 2 ing from party spirit, but follow Christ's teaching. For I have heard some say, "What I cannot find in the records, I will not believe in the gospel." And when I said to them, "It is scripture," they answered me, "That is the question!" But my records are Jesus Christ, the incontestable records are his cross and death and his resurrection and faith through him; by these I want to be made upright through your prayers.

The priests too were admirable, but the high priest is greater, 9 who has been intrusted with what is most holy, who alone has been intrusted with the secrets of God, for he is himself the door to the Father, through which Abraham and Isaac and Jacob and the prophets and the apostles and the church enter. All these things contribute to union with God. But the gospel possesses 2 something distinctive in the coming of the Savior, our Lord Jesus Christ, his suffering and resurrection. For the beloved prophets in their preaching looked to him, but the gospel is the consummation of immortality. All these together are good, if you have faith with love.

Since through your prayers and the affection you have through 10 union with Christ Jesus, word has reached me that the church at Antioch in Syria is at peace, it is right for you as a church of God to appoint a deacon to go there as an ambassador of God to congratulate them when they are gathered together, and to glorify the Name. Blessed in Jesus Christ be he who shall be found 2 worthy of such a service; you too will be glorified. It is not impossible for you to do this for the sake of God, if you choose to, just as the neighboring churches have done, sending bishops, and others elders and deacons.

As to Philo, the deacon from Cilicia, a man of good repute, 11 who is still serving me in preaching the word of God, along with Rhaeus Agathopus, a choice man, who has accompanied me from

Syria, bidding his life goodbye, they bear you witness, and I thank God for you, because you welcomed them, as the Lord has welcomed you. But may those who showed them disrespect 2 be redeemed by the favor of Jesus Christ. The love of the brethren at Troas sends you greeting. From there I am writing to you, by the hand of Burrhus who was sent with me by the Ephesians and Smyrnaeans, to do me honor. Jesus Christ, in whom they hope in body, soul and spirit, in faith, love and harmony, will honor them. Farewell in union with Jesus Christ, our common hope.

To the Smyrnaeans

Ignatius, also called Theophorus, to the church of God the Father and the beloved Jesus Christ, which has found mercy with every spiritual gift, filled with faith and love, which is lacking in no spiritual gift, most revered and bearing the sacred vessels, that is at Smyrna in Asia, heartiest greetings in a blameless spirit and in the word of God.

1   I extol Jesus Christ, the God who has given you such wisdom. For I have observed that you are fixed in unshakable faith, as though you were nailed in body and spirit to the cross of the Lord Jesus Christ, and established in love by the blood of Christ, convinced about our Lord that he was in truth physically of the line of David, Son of God by the will and power of God, truly born of a virgin, baptized by John so that all uprightness might 2 be fulfilled by him; truly nailed for us in body under Pontius Pilate and Herod the governor, from the fruit of which we are, from his most blessed suffering, that he might through his resurrection raise a standard for the ages for his holy and faithful people, whether among Jews or among heathen, in the one body of his church.

2   For he suffered all these things for our sakes, in order that we might be saved. And he suffered really, just as he also really raised himself; it is not as some unbelievers say that he suffered seemingly, who themselves exist only seemingly, and as their

opinion is, will be their experience, for they will be disembodied and demon-possessed.

For I know and believe that even after the resurrection he **3** was in the flesh. And when he came to those who were with Peter, **2** he said to them, "Take me and feel of me, and see that I am no incorporeal phantom." And they immediately touched him and believed, being blended with his flesh and spirit. That is why they despised death, and showed themselves superior to death. And after the resurrection he ate and drank with them, as a being **3** of flesh and blood, though spiritually united with the Father.

But I give you these warnings, dear friends, though I know **4** you agree with me. But I am guarding you in advance against wild beasts in the shape of men, whom you must not only refuse to welcome but if possible even to meet, only you must pray for them, if somehow, difficult as it is, they may repent. Yet Jesus Christ, our true life, has power to bring it about. For if these **2** things were done by our Lord only seemingly, I am only seemingly in chains. And why did I give myself up to death, to face fire, sword, and wild beasts? But near the sword is near to God, in the midst of the wild beasts is in the midst of God, if only it is done for the sake of Jesus Christ. In order to suffer with him I can endure it all, since he who became perfect man gives me strength.

Some ignorantly deny him, or rather have been denied by him, **5** for they are advocates of death rather than of truth. They have not been convinced by the prophecies or the law of Moses, or as yet by the gospel, or our individual sufferings. For they have the **2** same idea about us. For what good does anyone do me, if he praises me, but reviles my Lord by not admitting that he wore flesh and blood? Whoever does not say this has completely denied him, for he is a mere corpse bearer. Their names, since they are **3** unbelievers, I have decided not to write down, but may I not even remember them until they repent about Christ's suffering, which is our resurrection.

Let no one be deceived. Even the heavenly beings and the glory **6** of the angels and the rulers visible and invisible if they do not believe in the blood of Christ will incur judgment. Let him accept it who can. No one must be exalted by position, for faith and love

2 are everything, and there is nothing superior to them. Observe how contrary to the mind of God they are who teach strange ideas about the favor of Jesus Christ that has come to us. They care nothing for love, for the widow, for the orphan, for the oppressed, for him who is in prison, or him who is released, for the hungry or the thirsty.

7   They keep away from Thanksgiving and prayer, because they do not admit that the Thanksgiving is the flesh of our Savior Jesus Christ, which suffered for our sins, and which the Father in his kindness raised up. So those who contradict the gift of God perish in their disputing. It would be better for them to love, in

2 order to rise. So it is right to keep away from such men, and not speak of them either in private or in public, but to pay attention to the prophets and especially to the gospel, in which the Lord's suffering has been shown us and the resurrection has been effected. Avoid divisions as the beginning of evils.

8   You must all follow the bishop, as Jesus Christ followed the Father, and you must follow the board of elders as you would the apostles, and revere the deacons as the command of God. Let no one do any of the things that have to do with the church, without the bishop. Let that be considered a valid Thanksgiving which is held under the bishop or someone authorized by him.

2 Wherever the bishop appears, let the people be, just as wherever Jesus Christ is, there is the universal church. It is not permissible to baptize or hold a religious meal without the bishop, but whatever he approves is also pleasing to God, so that everything you do may be secure and valid.

9   Finally, it is reasonable for us to come to our senses while we still have time to repent and turn to God. It is well to recognize God and the bishop. Whoever honors the bishop is honored by God. Whoever does anything without the bishop's knowledge

is serving the devil. So may everything abound to you through 2
grace, for you deserve it. You have rested me in every way, and
may Jesus Christ rest you. You have loved me when I was absent
and when I was present. God reward you! If you endure everything for his sake, you will reach his presence.

Philo and Rhaeus Agathopus, who accompanied me for God's 10
sake, you did well to welcome as deacons of Christ God. They
too thank the Lord for you, because you rested them in every
way. You will certainly not lose anything! My spirit is given for 2
you, and so are my chains which you did not despise or feel
ashamed of. And Jesus Christ, our perfect hope, will not be
ashamed of you.

Your prayer has gone to the church at Antioch in Syria. From 11
there I come bound with most revered chains, and I send greetings to all, though I am not worthy to be from there, for I am
the last among them. But by the will of God I have been thought
worthy not from any conscious act, but by the favor of God,
which I pray may be given me in full measure, in order that by
your prayers I may reach the presence of God. So in order that 2
your work may be completed, both on earth and in heaven, it is
right that in God's honor your church appoint an ambassador of
God to go to Syria and congratulate them because they are at
peace, and have regained their proper size and recovered their
proper proportions. So it seemed to me an act worthy of God for 3
you to send one of your own number with a letter to join in
glorifying the calm which by God's will has come to them, and
because they have now found a haven through your prayer. As
you are perfect, aim at what is perfect. For if you want to do
well, God is ready to help you.

The love of the brethren at Troas sends you greetings. From 12
there I am writing to you by the hand of Burrhus, whom you in
co-operation with your brethren the Ephesians sent with me,
and he has rested me in every way. I wish that all imitated him,
for he is a model of the ministry of God. Grace will fully repay

2 him. I send greetings to the godly bishop, and the revered board of elders, and my fellow slaves the deacons, and to you all individually and collectively, in the name of Jesus Christ and in his flesh and blood, in his suffering and resurrection, both physical and spiritual, in union with God and with you. Grace, mercy, peace, endurance be with you always.

13 I send greetings to the families of my brethren, with their wives and children, and to the unmarried women who are called widows. Goodbye in the Father's power! Philo who is with me

2 sends you greetings. I send greetings to the household of Tavia, and pray that she may be made steadfast in faith and love, in both body and spirit. I send greetings to Alce, one very dear to me, and to the incomparable Daphnus, and Eutecnus and each and all by name. Goodbye in the grace of God.

To Polycarp

Ignatius, also called Theophorus, to Polycarp, bishop of the church of the Smyrnaeans, or rather who has for his bishop God the Father and the Lord Jesus Christ, heartiest greetings.

1 I am so much pleased with your godly attitude, based as it is as though on immovable rock, that I glory exceedingly in having been permitted to see your blameless face; may I have joy

2 from it in God! I urge you, by the grace with which you are clothed, to press on in your race, and to urge all men to be saved. Justify your position, with all diligence of body and spirit. Pay attention to unity, for there is nothing better. Lift all men up, as the Lord lifts you up; bear with all men in love, just as you are

3 doing. Devote yourself to unceasing prayers. Ask for more understanding than you have. Be watchful, keeping your spirit awake. Speak to each individual, in God's way. Carry the sicknesses of all men, like a perfect athlete. Where there is more toil, there is much gain.

2 If you love good disciples, it is no credit to you; rather induce

the more troublesome to subjection by your gentleness. Not every wound is healed by the same plaster. Relieve paroxysms with moist applications. Be wise like a serpent in all things and 2 always guileless like a dove. This is why you are made of flesh and spirit—so that you may humor what is visible before your face; but ask that what is unseen may be shown you, so that you may lack nothing and abound in every gift. The time demands 3 you, as pilots demand winds and a storm-tossed man a harbor, in order to reach the presence of God. Be sober as God's athlete; the prize is immortality and eternal life, of which you also are persuaded. All in all, I am given for you, and so are my chains, which you have loved.

Men who seem plausible but teach strange doctrines must not 3 appall you. Stand firm like an anvil that is hammered. It behooves a great athlete to stand blows and yet win. Most of all, for God's sake we must endure anything, so that he too may endure us. Be more zealous than you are. Understand the times. 2 Wait for him who is above time, timeless, invisible, yet visible for our sakes, impalpable, incapable of suffering, yet he suffered for us; who in every way endured for our sakes.

Widows must not be neglected. After the Lord, you must be 4 their protector. Nothing must be done without your approval, and you must not do anything without God, as indeed you do not. Stand firm. Hold more frequent meetings. Seek all out by name. 2 Do not look down on men or women slaves, but they themselves must not be conceited, but be better slaves to the glory of God, in order that they may obtain from God a better freedom. They must not be in love with being freed at the cost of the church, or they may prove slaves of passion.

Flee from frauds, or rather preach about them. Tell my sisters 5 to love the Lord and be contented with their husbands in body and spirit. In the same way charge my brethren also in the name of Jesus Christ to love their wives as the Lord loves the church. If anyone is able to maintain chastity to the honor of the flesh 2 of the Lord, let him maintain it. If he boasts of it, he is lost, and if anyone besides the bishop knows it, he is ruined. It is right for men and women who are marrying to form their union with the approval of the bishop, in order that their marriage may be in accordance with the Lord's will and not to gratify desire. Let it all be done to the honor of God.

6 Pay attention to the bishop, in order that God may pay attention to you. I am giving myself for those who are obedient to the bishop, the elders, the deacons, and may I have my portion with them, in God. Toil together, struggle together, race together, suffer together, rest together, rise together, as God's managers,
2 assistants, and servants. Please him under whom you serve, from whom you receive your pay; let none of you be found a deserter. Let your baptism serve as shield, your faith as helmet, your love as spear, your endurance as full armor. Let your deeds be your deposits, so that you may get the savings due you. So be patient with one another in gentleness, as God is with you. Let me have joy of you always.

7 Since the church at Antioch in Syria is at peace, as has been reported to me, through your prayer, I myself have taken fresh courage, with God-given freedom from anxiety, if only, through suffering, I may reach the presence of God, so that at the
2 resurrection I may be found your disciple. It is your duty, most blessed Polycarp, to call a most holy council and to appoint someone who is greatly loved and resolute, who can be called God's messenger; command him to go to Syria and to glorify your
3 determined love, to the glory of God. A Christian has no authority over himself but devotes himself to God. This is God's work, and yours also, when you achieve it. For I trust in grace, that you are ready to do something good in the service of God. I have exhorted you in a few words, for I know the intensity of your sincerity.

8 So since I cannot write to all the churches, because I am sailing at once from Troas for Neapolis, as the Will ordains, you

must write to the churches ahead, as one who has the mind of God, to do the same thing, those who can sending messengers, the rest letters through those you send, so that you may be glorified by an everlasting deed, as you yourself deserve to be. I 2 send greetings to all by name, and to the wife of Epitropus with all her household and that of her children. I send greetings to my dear Attalus. I send greetings to the man who is to be directed to go to Syria. God's favor will be with him always, and with Polycarp who sends him. I bid you farewell always in our God 3 Jesus Christ. Abide in him, in the unity and oversight of God. I send greetings to Alce, a person beloved by me. Goodbye in the Lord.

The Letter of Polycarp to the Philippians

The letter of Polycarp to the Philippians is an early sequel to the letters of Ignatius. After Ignatius with his guard left Philippi for Rome, the Philippian Christians wrote as he had suggested to Polycarp at Smyrna, asking him to send them such letters of Ignatius as he had in his possession, and this he did with a covering letter of instruction and exhortation, which we know as Polycarp to the Philippians.

Polycarp urges them to be harmonious and steadfast, but does not stress the threefold ministry, as Ignatius had done, writing simply in the name of "Polycarp and the elders with him." He shows a wider knowledge of Christian literature than Ignatius, using not only Matthew, Luke-Acts, and the letters of Paul, but Hebrews and I Peter. He has had no news of the actual fate of Ignatius, and asks the Philippians if they have received any. So his letter must have been written a few weeks after Ignatius wrote the last of his letters at Troas and was taken across the Aegean to Macedonia.

Recent efforts to divide Polycarp's letter into two (P.N. Harrison, Polycarp's Two Epistles to the Philippians, *Cambridge, 1936)—one, chapters 13, 14, a covering letter to accompany the letters he was forwarding to Philippi, the other, 1-12, a later letter dealing with a crisis in the Philippian church about* A.D. *135 —lose sight of the fact that by that time Polycarp could not fail to show the influence of the fourfold gospel, published certainly*

237

by A.D. *120, and probably in nearby Ephesus. Indeed it is very likely that Polycarp was active in its publication.*

No complete Greek text of Polycarp's letter has yet been found. The eight Polycarp-Barnabas manuscripts contain almost nine chapters, and Eusebius, in the Church History, *3.36.13-15, supplies chapter 13. For the rest we are dependent upon the Latin version.*

The Letter of Polycarp to the Philippians

Polycarp and the elders who are with him to the church of God that is staying at Philippi, mercy and peace be granted you in abundance from God the Almighty and Jesus Christ our Savior.

I rejoice with you greatly in our Lord Jesus Christ that you wel- **1** comed the copies of true love and as you had opportunity set on their way the men who were encumbered with saintly chains, which are the diadems of those truly chosen by God and our Lord; and because the deep root of your faith, which has been **2** renowned from early times, still lasts and bears fruit to our Lord Jesus Christ, who for our sins endured even facing death, and whom God raised, setting aside the pains of death; on whom, **3** though you have not seen him, you believe with unutterable, triumphant joy which many desire to share, for you know that you have been saved by his favor, not by what you have done, but by the will of God through Jesus Christ.

Therefore prepare for action and serve God in fear and truth, **2** for you have forsaken fruitless talk and vulgar error, and believed on him who raised our Lord Jesus from the dead, and gave him glory and a throne on his right hand; to whom everything in heaven and on earth is subject, whom everything that has breath serves, who is to come as judge of the living and the dead, whose blood God will require from those who disobey him. He **2** who raised him from the dead will raise us also, if we do his will

and live by his commands, and love what he loved, refraining from all injustice, covetousness, love of money, evil-speaking, false witness; not returning evil for evil or abuse for abuse, or
3 blow for blow, or curse for curse, but remembering what the Lord said when he taught: "Do not judge, so that you may not be judged; forgive, and you will be forgiven, have mercy, so that you may be shown mercy; with the measure you use, men will measure back to you; and blessed are the poor and those who are persecuted for their uprightness, for the kingdom of God belongs to them."

3 I write you this, brethren, about uprightness, not taking it
2 upon myself, but because you first invited me to. For neither I nor anyone else like me can follow the wisdom of the blessed and glorious Paul, who when he was among you, face to face with the men of that time, carefully and steadfastly uttered his teaching about truth, and when he was absent wrote you letters, by poring over which you will be able to build yourselves up in
3 the faith that has been given to you. It is the mother of us all, followed by hope and led on by love to God and Christ and neighbor. For if a man is within these he has fulfilled the command of uprightness, for one who has love is far from any sin.

4 Love of money is the beginning of all troubles. So knowing that we brought nothing into the world, and can take nothing out of it either, let us put on the armor of uprightness and teach
2 ourselves first of all to follow the commands of the Lord, then teach your wives to live in the faith that has been given them and in love and purity, being devoted to their husbands in all sincerity and loving all alike with perfect chastity, and to bring
3 up their children in the fear of God. The widows must be sensible about the faith of the Lord, and pray constantly for all, refraining from all slander, evil-speaking, false witness, love of money and all evil, knowing that they are God's altar and that all offerings are examined and none of the thoughts or intentions or secrets of the heart escapes him.

Knowing, then, that God is not to be sneered at, we ought to **5** live in a way that is worthy of his command and glory. Similarly, **2** deacons must be blameless in the presence of his uprightness as servants of God and Christ, not of men; not slanderers, straightforward, not lovers of money, temperate in all things, tenderhearted, careful, living in accordance with the truth of the Lord, who became a servant of all. If we please him in this present world, we will receive the world to come also, even as he promised us to raise us from the dead, and if we conduct ourselves in a way worthy of him, we shall also reign with him, provided we have faith. Similarly, the younger men must be **3** blameless in all respects, caring for purity above all, and restraining themselves from all evil. For it is right to refrain from the passions in the world, for "every passion is at war with the Spirit," and "neither people who are immoral or sensual or given to unnatural vice will have any share in God's kingdom," nor those who do what is wrong. Therefore it is necessary to refrain from all these things, subjecting ourselves to the elders and deacons as to God and Christ. The virgins must live with a blameless and pure conscience.

The elders must be tenderhearted, merciful to all, bringing **6** back what has gone astray, visiting all the sick, neglecting neither widow nor orphan nor poor man, but always intending to do what is right in the sight of God and men, refraining from all anger, partiality, unfair judgment, keeping far from all love of money, not quick to believe anything against anyone, not severe in judgment, knowing that we all owe the debt of sin. If, **2** then, we beg the Lord to forgive us, we ought to forgive too, for we are before the eyes of the Lord and of God, and we must all stand at the judgment seat of Christ, and each give an account of himself. So let us serve him with fear and all concern, just **3** as he commanded us, and as did the apostles who evangelized us and the prophets who foretold the coming of our Lord. Let us be zealous for what is right, refraining from causing offense and from false brothers and from those who bear the name of the Lord in hypocrisy, and mislead foolish men.

7 "For anyone who does not acknowledge that Jesus Christ has come in the flesh is antichrist," and whoever does not accept the testimony of the cross is of the devil, and whoever perverts the sayings of the Lord to his own desires and says there is neither 2 resurrection nor judgment—he is the first-born of Satan. Therefore let us forsake the folly of the multitude and their false teachings, and return to the word that was handed down to us from the beginning, and be collected and prayerful and persevere in fasting, in our petitions beseeching the all-seeing God not to subject us to temptation, just as the Lord said, "One's spirit is eager, but flesh and blood are weak."

8 Let us therefore hold constantly to our hope, and to the guarantee of our uprightness, that is, Jesus Christ, who carried the burden of our sins in his own body on the cross, who committed no sin and deceit was never on his lips, but he endured it 2 all for us, so that we might live in union with him. So let us be imitators of his endurance, and if we suffer for his sake, let us glorify him. For he set us this example in himself, and this is what we have believed.

9 So I beg you all to obey the message of uprightness and to exhibit all endurance, such as you saw with your own eyes not only in the blessed Ignatius and Zosimus and Rufus, but also in others of your number, and in Paul himself and the rest of the 2 apostles, being assured that all these have not run in vain, but in faith and uprightness, and that they are in the place that they have deserved with the Lord, with whom they suffered. For they did not love the present world, but him who died for us and was raised up by God for our sakes.

10 So stand fast in these things, and follow the Lord's example, steadfast in faith and immovable, loving the brotherhood, devoted to one another, united in truth, giving way to one another in 2 the gentleness of the Lord, despising nobody. When you can do

good, do not put it off, for charity delivers from death. You must all subordinate yourselves to one another, and live irreproachable lives among the heathen, so that you may be praised for your good deeds, and the Lord may not be ill spoken of through you. But alas for him, on account of whom the name 3 of the Lord is ill spoken of. Therefore teach all men to be serious, and be so yourselves.

I am exceedingly sorry for Valens, who was once made an **11** elder among you, because he so fails to understand the position that was given him. I warn you therefore to abstain from covetousness and to be pure and truthful. Keep yourselves from all evil. But how can a man who cannot control himself in these 2 things preach self-control to someone else? If a man does not refrain from covetousness, he will be defiled by idolatry and will be judged as one of the heathen who are ignorant of the judgment of the Lord. Or do we not know that God's people are to be the judges of the world, as Paul teaches? But I have not found 3 or heard of any such thing among you, among whom the blessed Paul labored, and who are mentioned in the beginning of a letter of his. For he boasts of you in all the churches which alone had then come to know the Lord; we had not yet come to know him. Therefore, brethren, I am very sorry for Valens and for his 4 wife; may the Lord grant them true repentance! So be self-controlled in this matter, and do not look on such people as enemies, but call them back as ailing members, gone astray, so that you may save your whole body. For if you do this, you build one another up.

For I am sure that you are well trained in the sacred writings, **12** and nothing is hidden from you, but this has not been granted to me. Only, as it says in these scriptures, "Be angry, but do not sin," and "the sun must not go down upon your anger." Blessed is the man that remembers this, which I believe is the case with you. But may the God and Father of our Lord Jesus 2 Christ, and the eternal high priest himself, Jesus Christ, the Son of God, build you up in faith and truth, and in all gentleness and without anger and in patience and long-suffering and endurance and purity, and may he give you your part and lot with his saints, and to us with you, and to all who are under heaven who shall believe in our Lord Jesus Christ and in his Father

3 who raised him from the dead. Pray for all the saints. Pray also for emperors and authorities and rulers, and for those who persecute you and hate you and for the enemies of the cross, in order that your fruit may be manifest among all men, so that you may be perfect in him.

13   Both you and Ignatius wrote me that if anyone was going to Syria he should take your letter also. This I will attend to, if I find a good opportunity, either myself, or the man I send to repre-

2 sent you also. The letters of Ignatius that were sent us by him and the others that we had in our possession we send you as you instructed us to do; they are appended to this letter, and you will be able to derive great benefit from them. For they embrace faith, steadfastness, and all the edification that pertains to our Lord. And if you learn anything definite about Ignatius himself and those who are with him, let us know.

14   I write you this by Crescens, whom I recommended to you recently, and recommend now. For he has lived blamelessly among us, and I believe he will do so among you. But you will consider his sister recommended when she reaches you. Farewell in the Lord Jesus Christ with all your people. Amen.

The Martyrdom of Polycarp

On the 22nd of February, A.D. *156, Polycarp, the venerable and renowned bishop of Smyrna, suffered martyrdom. He was eighty-six years old, and had been bishop for fully forty years. He had only recently returned from a visit to Rome, where he had tried in vain to reach an agreement with Bishop Anicetus on the proper date for the celebration of Easter, when he was arrested, condemned, and brutally put to death.*

So great was the dismay and sorrow occasioned by this startling event that the church at Smyrna recorded it in detail in a letter, sent to the church at Philomelium, two hundred miles to the east, and this came to be circulated among the churches generally. It was a moving story, and marks the virtual beginning of the great literature of martyrdom, which eventually grew to vast proportions; the modern editions contain sixty-nine volumes. Such stories stirred Christians to hold the line in times of persecution.

When Irenaeus was a boy in Asia he had seen Polycarp, and he tells the story of his spirited encounter with Marcion. Eusebius copied most of the Martyrdom into his Church History, *4.15, though his text omits some of the few miraculous touches it contains. There are at least six Greek manuscripts of the Martyrdom, from the tenth to the thirteenth century, besides a Latin version, and Syriac and Coptic versions of the Eusebius extracts. The closing lines of the text throw interesting light upon its early transmission.*

The Martyrdom of the Holy Polycarp, Bishop of Smyrna

The church of God that is staying at Smyrna to the church of God that is staying at Philomelium and to all the congregations of the holy catholic church in every place, may the mercy, peace and love of God our Father and the Lord Jesus Christ be granted in abundance.

We write to you, brethren, the facts about the martyrs and 1 the blessed Polycarp, who as though setting a seal to it by his martyrdom brought the persecution to an end. For almost all the preceding events took place in order that the Lord might show us again the martyrdom of the Gospel kind. For like the 2 Lord he waited to be betrayed, in order that we also might become his imitators, not taking account of our own interests only, but of the interests of our neighbors. For it is a mark of true and constant love to wish that not only one's self but all the brethren also be saved.

Blessed and noble therefore are all the martyrdoms that have 2 taken place by the will of God. For we must be very careful to ascribe the power over all things to God. For who could fail to 2 admire their nobility and endurance and love for their Master? For when they were so torn by scourges that their physical structure was visible even to the inner veins and arteries, they endured it, so that even the bystanders pitied them and bewailed them. And others reached such a pitch of heroism that not one

of them sighed or groaned, showing all of us that at the very
time they were being tortured the noble martyrs of Christ were
absent from the body, or rather that the Lord stood by them and
3 talked with them. And giving heed to the favor of Christ, they
despised the world's tortures, at the cost of a single hour pur-
chasing eternal life. And the fire of their inhuman tormentors felt
cold to them, for they kept their eyes on escaping the eternal,
unquenchable fire, and with the eyes of their minds they looked
at the blessings reserved for those who are steadfast, "which no
ear ever heard and no eye ever saw, and never occurred to the
human mind," but they were shown by the Lord to them, for they
4 were no longer men but were already angels. In like manner those
condemned to the wild beasts endured terrible punishments,
being made to lie on beds of sharp shells, and subjected to other
forms of varied tortures, in order that if he could he might by
persistent punishment bring them to deny their faith.

3   For the devil used many devices against them, but, thank
God, he failed against them all. For the most noble Ger-
manicus reinforced them in their timidity by the endurance he
displayed, and fought gallantly with the wild beasts. For when
the governor wished to persuade him, and told him to have pity
on his youth, he forcibly drew the wild beast upon himself,
wishing to escape the sooner from their unjust and lawless life.
2 So upon that, the whole crowd, amazed at the bravery of the
godly and pious race of Christians, shouted, "Kill the atheists!
Have Polycarp looked for!"

4   But one man named Quintus, a Phrygian who had recently
come from Phrygia, when he saw the wild beasts, was frightened.
He was the man who had forced himself and some others to come
forward of their own accord. The governor after much earnest
entreaty prevailed upon this man to take the oath and offer the
sacrifice. That, brethren, is why we do not approve those who
give themselves up, for the gospel does not teach us to do so.
5   But the most admirable Polycarp, when he first heard of this,

was not alarmed but wanted to stay in the city, but the majority
persuaded him to leave quietly. So he left quietly for a farm not
far from the city, and stayed there with a few others, doing
nothing night or day but pray for all men, and the churches all
over the world, as he was accustomed to do. And while he was 2
praying, three days before he was arrested he had a vision, and
saw his pillow ablaze with fire. And he turned and said to those
who were with him, "I must be burned alive."

As those who were looking for him persisted in their search, 6
he went over to another farm, and those who were looking for
him came up immediately, and when they failed to find him, they
seized two slave boys, and one of them when he was tortured
confessed. For it was impossible for him to hide, when those who 2
betrayed him belonged to his household. And the chief of police,
who happened to have the same name, being called Herod, was
in a hurry to get him to the arena to fulfill his own destiny and
become a sharer with Christ, while those who betrayed him
should incur the punishment of Judas himself.

So taking the slave along, on Friday, about suppertime, the 7
police and horsemen set out with their usual arms, as though
after a robber. And late in the evening they came up with him,
and found him in a cottage, in bed in an upstairs room. He could
have got away from there to another place, but he would not,
saying, "God's will be done."

So when he heard that they had come, he went down and 2
talked with them, while the onlookers wondered at his age and
vigor, and why there was such great haste to arrest such an old
man. So he immediately ordered food and drink, as much as they
wanted, set before them, at that hour, and he asked them to give
him an hour to pray without interruption. When they agreed, he
stood up and prayed, so filled with the grace of God that for two 3
hours he could not stop, and those who heard him were astonished, and many regretted that they had come out after such a
venerable old man.

8   When at length he concluded his prayer, after remembering all the people he had ever met, great and small, famous and obscure, and the whole catholic church all over the world, when the time came to leave they mounted him upon an ass and took

2 him into the city: it was a festival Sabbath day. The chief of police Herod and his father Nicetes met him, and took him into their carriage and sitting beside him tried to persuade him saying, "Why, what harm is there in saying 'Caesar is Lord,' and burning the incense, and so on, and saving yourself?" At first he made them no answer, but when they persisted, he said, "I am not going

3 to do what you advise me." When they failed to persuade him, they spoke threateningly to him, and put him out of the carriage so hastily that as he got out of it he hurt his shin. Without turning around, he went eagerly on without noticing it, and was taken to the arena, when the uproar in the arena was so great that nobody could be heard.

9   As Polycarp entered the arena, there came to him a voice from heaven,

"Be strong, Polycarp, and act like a man."

Nobody saw the one who spoke, but those of our people who were there heard the voice. When at length he was brought forward there was a great uproar when they heard that Polycarp

2 had been taken. So when he was brought forward the governor asked him if he was Polycarp and when he admitted that he was, he tried to persuade him to deny the faith, saying to him,

"Have some regard for your age," and so on, as they usually say. "Swear by the fortune of Caesar; change your mind, and say, 'Kill the atheists.'"

But Polycarp looked with an earnest face at all the throng of lawless heathen in the arena, waved his hand at them and groaned, and looking up to heaven said,

3   "Kill the atheists!" And when the governor insisted, saying,

"Take the oath, and I will let you go; revile Christ," Polycarp said,

"For eighty-six years I have been his slave, and he has done me no wrong; how can I blaspheme my king who has saved me?"

When he still insisted, and said,   **10**

"Swear by the fortune of Caesar," he answered,

"If you imagine that I will swear by the fortune of Caesar, as you say, and pretend not to know who I am, let me tell you plainly, I am a Christian. And if you want to learn the doctrine of Christianity, set a day and hear me."

The governor said,   **2**

"Convince the people."

Polycarp said,

"I thought you worth reasoning with; for we have been taught to pay suitable honor to governments and authorities, appointed by God, if it does us no harm; but as for these others, I do not think they are worth my defending myself before them."

The governor said,   **11**

"I have wild animals; I will throw you to them, unless you change your mind."

He said,

"Call them, for to change from the better to the worse is impossible for us, but it is right to change from violence to uprightness."

He said to him again,   **2**

"Since you despise wild animals, I will have you consumed with fire, if you do not change your mind."

Polycarp said,

"You threaten me with the fire that burns for an hour and in a little while goes out, for you do not know about the fire of the coming judgment and everlasting punishment, which is reserved for the wicked. But why do you wait? Bring on whatever you please."

Saying this and much more he was filled with courage and joy,   **12** and his face was filled with graciousness, so that not only did he not collapse at what was said to him, but on the contrary the governor was amazed and sent his own herald to the middle of the arena to announce three times.

2   "Polycarp has acknowledged that he is a Christian." When the herald said this, the whole throng of heathen and Jews living in Smyrna, in uncontrollable anger and with great roar, shouted back,

"This fellow is the teacher of Asia, the father of the Christians, the destroyer of our gods, who teaches many people not to sacrifice or worship."

They shouted these words at the Asiarch Philip, and asked him to let loose a lion upon Polycarp. But he said it was not lawful
3   for him to do so, since he had closed the wild-animal sports. Then they decided to shout to him in concert to have Polycarp burned alive. For the matter of the vision he had had about his pillow had to be fulfilled, when he saw it on fire as he was praying, and turned and said to the faithful about him,

"I must be burned alive."

13   This then happened with such speed, more quickly than words could say it, for the mob immediately collected sticks and firewood from the shops and baths, Jews as usual being especially
2   eager to help in this. When the pyre was ready, he himself took off all his clothes and unfastened his belt, and tried also to take off his shoes, though he was not in the habit of doing this before, because each of the faithful was always eager to be the first to touch his flesh. For because of his manner of life he had been treated even before his martyrdom with the utmost consideration.
3   So the appliances attached to the pyre were immediately put on him, but when they started to nail him too, he said,

"Leave me as I am, for he who enables me to endure the fire will also enable me to stay on the pyre without moving, without your fastening me with nails."

14   So they did not nail him, but tied him. And he put his hands behind him and was tied in place, like a splendid ram out of a great flock, to be sacrificed, a burnt offering acceptable to God made ready, and he looked up to heaven and said,

"Lord God Almighty, Father of thy beloved and blessed child Jesus Christ, through whom we have received the knowledge of thee, God of angels and hosts and all creation, and of the whole race of the upright who live in thy presence, I bless thee that 2 thou hast thought me worthy of this day and hour, to be numbered among the martyrs and share in the cup of thy Christ, for resurrection to eternal life, for soul and body in the incorruptibility of the holy Spirit. Among them may I be accepted before thee today, as a rich and acceptable sacrifice, just as thou, the faithful and true God, hast prepared and foreshown and brought about. For this reason and for all things I praise thee, I bless 3 thee, I glorify thee, through the eternal heavenly high priest Jesus Christ, thy beloved child, through whom be glory to thee with him and the holy Spirit now and for the ages to come. Amen."

When he had uttered the Amen and finished his prayer, the 15 men in charge of the fire lighted the fire. And as a great flame blazed we who were permitted to see it saw a wonder, and have been preserved to tell the rest what happened. For the fire as- 2 sumed an overarching shape, like the sail of a ship filled by the wind, and made a wall around the martyr's body, and it was there in the center not like flesh burning but like bread baking, or like gold and silver being refined in a furnace. For we perceived such a fragrance as a breath of incense or some other precious spice.

At last the wicked men, when they saw that his body could not 16 be consumed by the fire, ordered an executioner to go up and stab him with a dagger. And when he did so, a dove and a quantity of blood came out, so that it put out the fire, and all the people wondered if there was such a difference between the unbelievers and God's chosen, of whom this most wonderful Poly- 2 carp had been one, and shown himself an apostolic and prophetic teacher in our times, and bishop of the catholic church at Smyrna. For every word that he uttered with his mouth has been fulfilled and will be fulfilled.

17 But the jealous, envious Evil One, the adversary of the race of the upright, when he saw the greatness of his martyrdom, and his irreproachable life from the beginning, and that he was now crowned with the wreath of immortality and had won an incontestable prize, took care that not even his corpse should be taken away by us, though many desired to take it and to touch his holy

2 remains. So he instigated Nicetes, the father of Herod and the brother of Alce, to petition the governor not to give up his body,

"For fear," he said, "they may leave the one who was crucified and begin to worship this man."

He said this at the instigation and insistence of the Jews who also watched us when we were going to take him out of the fire —unaware that we will never be able to desert Christ who suffered for the salvation of the whole world of those who are saved,

3 the blameless for the sinners, or to worship anyone else. For we worship him as the Son of God, but we love the martyrs as disciples and imitators of the Lord, and rightly so, for their unsurpassable devotion to their king and teacher. May we too prove to be their partners and fellow disciples.

18 Then the captain, when he saw the dispute occasioned by the Jews, put the body in the middle of the fire, as they are accus-

2 tomed to do, and burned it. So we afterward picked up his bones, which are more valuable than precious stones and better than

3 gold, and laid them in a suitable place. As we gather there as often as we can with joy and exultation the Lord will permit us to observe the day of his martyrdom as a birthday, in memory of those who have already competed, and the preparation and training of those who are to do so.

19 Such is the story of the blessed Polycarp who though he was the twelfth, including those from Philadelphia, to suffer martyrdom at Smyrna, is the only one particularly remembered by everybody, so that he is talked of even by the heathen everywhere. He was not only a distinguished teacher, but a notable martyr, whose martyrdom all desire to imitate, for it followed

the pattern of the gospel of Christ. By his endurance he defeated 2
the unjust governor and thus won the wreath of immortality, and
rejoices with the apostles and all the upright, glorifying the Almighty God and Father and blessing our Lord Jesus Christ, the
savior of our souls and the pilot of our bodies and the shepherd
of the catholic church which is all over the world.

You asked to have what has happened explained to you in full, **20**
but for the present we have reported them in brief through our
brother Marcion. So when you have received this information,
send the letter to the brethren beyond you, so that they too may
glorify the Lord who makes selections from his slaves.

Now to him who is able to bring us all by his favor and bounty 2
into his eternal kingdom through his only child Jesus Christ be
glory, power, honor, and majesty forever! Greet all God's people.
Those who are with us greet you, and so does Euarestus, who
writes the letter, and his whole household.

Now the blessed Polycarp was martyred on the second, early **21**
in the month of Xanthicus, on the seventh day before the kalends
of March, a high sabbath, at two o'clock. He was arrested by
Herod, when Philip of Tralles was high priest, and Statius Quadratus was governor, but our Lord Jesus Christ was reigning forever. To him be glory, honor, majesty and eternal dominion from
generation to generation. Amen.

We bid you farewell, brethren, as you live by the teaching of **22**
Jesus Christ in the gospel; with him be glory to our God and
Father and the holy Spirit for the salvation of his chosen saints
just as the blessed Polycarp suffered martyrdom. May we too be
found in his footsteps in the kingdom of Jesus Christ!

This account Gaius copied from that of Irenaeus, a disciple of 2
Polycarp; he lived with Irenaeus. I, Socrates, wrote it out in
Corinth from the copy of Gaius. Grace be with you all.

Again, I, Pionius, searched it out and wrote it out from the 3
earlier copy, when the blessed Polycarp disclosed it to me in a

vision, as I will explain later. I gathered it together, when it was almost worn out by age; the Lord Jesus Christ gather me also with his chosen into his heavenly kingdom! To him be glory with the Father and the holy Spirit forever and ever. Amen.

Another form of conclusion in place of verses 2 and 3,
from the Moscow manuscript

2　This account Gaius copied from the papers of Irenaeus, and he had also lived with Irenaeus, who had been a disciple of the
3　holy Polycarp. For this Irenaeus was in Rome at the time of the martyrdom of the bishop Polycarp, and taught many. Many most excellent and sound writings of his are current, in which he mentions Polycarp, saying that he had been his pupil. He ably refuted every heresy and handed down the generally accepted rule of
4　the church, just as he had received it from the saint. And he says this also, that once when Marcion, after whom the Marcionites were named, met the holy Polycarp, and said,
5　"Recognize me, Polycarp," he said to Marcion,
　　"I recognize you! I recognize Satan's first-born." And this also is recorded in the writings of Irenaeus, that on the day and at the hour that Polycarp was martyred at Smyrna, Irenaeus, who was in the city of Rome, heard a voice like a trumpet say, "Polycarp has been martyred."
6　So from these papers of Irenaeus, as already stated, Gaius made a copy, and from the copy of Gaius Isocrates made another at Corinth. And again I, Pionius, wrote it out from the copy of Isocrates, after searching for it in obedience to a revelation of the holy Polycarp, gathering it together when it was almost worn out by age; the Lord Jesus Christ gather me also with his chosen into his heavenly kingdom! To him be glory with the Father and the Son and the holy Spirit forever and ever. Amen.

The Apology of Quadratus

To their heathen contemporaries the early Christians seemed to be following a degraded superstition, and scandalous stories of their religious proceedings were in general circulation. As the new faith came to self-consciousness, it sought to correct these misapprehensions, and defend itself against such calumnies. Christians also sought protection from unjust persecution. So arose the apologies, or defenses of Christianity. The first such literary effort was the so-called Preaching of Peter, which has almost entirely disappeared, except in so far as it was reproduced in the Apology of Aristides, A.D. 138-147. But the first substantial piece of this literature that has come down to us is from the Apology of Quadratus.

Hadrian visited Athens in A.D. 125 and it was probably then, or possibly on his next visit there, four years later, that Quadratus, a Christian philosopher of that city, presented to him a defense of the Christians. All that we know of this we learn from Eusebius, for what Jerome says about it, he evidently learned from him. Eusebius tells the story, and quotes a sentence or two from the Apology.

The Apology of Quadratus

A FRAGMENT

After Trajan had reigned for twenty whole years lacking six months, Aelius Hadrian succeeded to the imperial authority. To him Quadratus addressed and presented a discourse, having composed a defense of our religion because some wicked men were trying to annoy our people. The work is still current among most of the brethren, and is in my hands, and from it it is possible to recognize clear proofs of the man's intelligence and of his apostolic orthodoxy. He himself reveals his own early date in his own words when he says,

"But the works of our Savior were always present, for they were real—those who had been cured, those who had been raised from the dead, who were seen not only when they were cured and raised, but always when they were present, and not only while the Savior was on earth, but after he was gone, they survived for a long time, so that some of them lived even to our day."

Eusebius, *Church History*, 4.3.1-2.

259

The Fragments of Papias

In the second quarter of the second century there lived in the Phrygian city of Hierapolis, in Asia, a Christian named Papias who whenever he met an elderly believer who might have known people who had ever seen or heard any of the original apostles, eagerly questioned him and wrote down what he had to tell. These reports about A.D. *140, or perhaps a little later, he put into a book of his own, the* Interpretations of the Sayings of the Lord.

While this book has disappeared, Irenaeus and Eusebius read it and quoted it, and though Eusebius thought little of Papias's judgment, what they took from it shows that it contained some material of importance and value. Many later Christian writers reflect it—Jerome (†420), Philip of Side (about A.D.*430), Andreas of Caesarea (late sixth century), Maximus the Confessor (†662), Anastasius of Sinai († about* A.D.*700), Georgius Hamartolus (about* A.D.*842), and Photius (*A.D.*890). It is clear that his book was still read at the end of the ninth century, and old library catalogues at Nismes and Stams show that it still existed in* A.D. *1218 and* A.D. *1341.*

The Fragments of Papias

When creation, renewed and liberated, shall yield an abundance 1
of all kinds of food, from the dew of heaven and the fertility
of the earth, just as the elders, who saw John, the disciple of the
Lord, related that they had heard how the Lord would teach
about those times and say,

"The days will come when vines will grow each with ten thou- 2
sand shoots, and ten thousand branches on each shoot, and ten
thousand twigs on each branch, and ten thousand clusters on
each twig, and ten thousand grapes in each cluster, and each
grape, when crushed will yield twenty-five jars of wine. And 3
when one of the saints takes hold of a cluster, another cluster
will cry out, 'I am better, take me, bless the Lord through me.'
In the same way a grain of wheat will produce ten thousand
heads, and every head will have ten thousand grains, and every
grain will produce ten pounds of fine flour, bright and clean.
And other fruits, seeds and grass will produce in corresponding
proportions. And all the animals will use those foods that are the
products of the soil and become in turn peaceable and in harmony
with one another, and in complete subjection to man."

This is also attested in writing by Papias, who was a hearer of 4
John and a comrade of Polycarp, in his fourth book, for there are
five books that were composed by him. And he goes on to say,

"But to believers these things are credible. And," he says, 5
"when Judas, the betrayer, refused to believe and asked, 'How

will such production be effected by the Lord?' the Lord said,
'Those who reach those times will see.'"

Irenaeus, Against Heresies, 5.33.3-4.

II

1 There are five books of Papias extant, and they are entitled
Interpretations of the Sayings of the Lord. Irenaeus also mentions
these as the only works written by him, saying something like
2 this: "This also" etc. [compare Irenaeus, 5.33.4 above]. These
are the words of Irenaeus. But Papias himself, in the preface to
his discourses, does not at all assert that he was himself a hearer
and eyewitness of the holy apostles, but shows by the language
he uses that he received the matters of the faith from those who
were acquainted with them:

3   "But I will not hesitate to put down along with my interpretations whatever I carefully learned at any time from the elders,
and carefuly remembered, assuring you of their truth. For I did
not, like most people, enjoy those who have much to say, but
those who taught what was true; nor those who relate commands
of others, but those who report the ones given by the Lord to
4 the faith and proceeding from the truth itself. And if anyone
should come my way who had been a follower of the elders, I
would ask for the accounts given by the elders—what Andrew
or what Peter said, or what Philip or what Thomas or James, or
what John or Matthew said, or any other of the disciples of the
Lord, and what Aristion and the elder John, the disciples of the
Lord, say. For I did not think that the contents of books would
profit me as much as what came from the living and surviving
voice."

5   Here it is worth noting that he twice lists the name of John.
The first one he mentions along with Peter and James and Matthew and the rest of the apostles, clearly meaning the evangelist,
but the other John, after an interval, he classes with others outside the number of the apostles, putting Aristion before him, and

distinctly calls him an elder; so that by this he shows that the 6
statement of those is true who say that two men in Asia had the
same name, and that there are two tombs in Ephesus, and each
is still called John's. It is necessary to take note of this, for it is
probable that it was the second, if one is not willing to accept
the first, that saw the Revelation that is current under the name
of John. And Papias, of whom I am now speaking, acknowledges 7
that he received the sayings of the apostles from those that had
followed them, but says that he was himself a hearer of Aristion
and John the Elder. Anyway he mentions them frequently by
name and includes traditions of theirs in his writings. These matters I hope have been not unprofitably related by me.

It is worth while to add to the utterances of Papias that have 8
been given, some others of his, in which he relates other wonderful things as having been handed down to him by tradition. That 9
Philip the apostle lived in Hierapolis with his daughters has
already been stated, but it must here be pointed out that Papias,
who was their contemporary, mentions that he heard a marvelous
story from the daughters of Philip. For he relates that in his time
a man rose from the dead. And again he tells another wonderful
story about Justus, who was called Barsabbas, that he drank a
deadly poison, and yet, by the Lord's favor, experienced nothing
unpleasant. This Justus the Book of Acts records that the holy 10
apostles after the ascension of the Savior put forward with Matthias, and prayed that one might be chosen in place of the betrayer Judas, to fill out their number. This is its account: "Then
they proposed two men, Joseph called Barsabbas who was known
as Justus, and Matthias, and they prayed, saying." The same 11
writer has recorded other matters also as coming to him from un-
written tradition, strange parables and teachings of the Savior,
and some other more mythical statements. Among others he says 12
that there will be about a thousand years after the resurrection
from the dead, and then Christ's kingdom will be set up in bodily
form right on this earth. I suppose he got these ideas through
misconstruing the accounts of the apostles, without perceiving

13 that the things they said were uttered in figures, mystically. For he appears to have been a man of very limited understanding, as one can say judging from his own statements. Yet he was to blame that so many ecclesiastical writers after him adopted a like opinion, urging the antiquity of the man in its support, as for instance Irenaeus and anyone else who has held and maintained such

14 views. And in his own writing he hands down other accounts, given by Aristion, who has already been mentioned, of the Lord's sayings, and traditions of John the Elder, to which we refer the inquiring, but I must add to his utterances already quoted a tradition about Mark who wrote the gospel, which he sets forth in the following words:

15 "The Elder said this also: Mark had been the interpreter of Peter, and wrote down accurately, though not in order, everything that he remembered that had been said or done by the Lord. For he neither heard the Lord nor followed him, but afterward, as I said, attended Peter, who adapted his instructions to the needs of his hearers, but had no design of giving a connected account of the Lord's oracles. So then Mark made no mistake in thus writing some things as he remembered them; for he made it his one concern not to omit anything that he had heard, or to make any false statement in them."

16 This, then, is what Papias relates about Mark. But about Matthew he says this: "So Matthew composed the Sayings in the Aramaic language, and everyone translated them as well as he could."

17 The same man uses proofs from the first epistle of John and likewise from the epistle of Peter. And he relates another story about a woman who was accused of many sins before the Lord, which the Gospel according to the Hebrews contains. And this also we must certainly take account of, in addition to what has been stated.

Eusebius, *Church History*, 3.39

III

Apollinarius: "Judas did not die by hanging, but lived on, hav- 1
ing been taken down before he choked to death. And the Acts of
the Apostles show this, saying that he swelled up, and burst open
in the middle, and his vitals poured out. Papias, the disciple of
John, records this more plainly in the fourth book of the *Interpretation of the Sayings of the Lord*:

"Judas went about this world a terrible example of impiety, 2
with his flesh swollen to such size that he could not get through,
not even the bulk of his head, where a wagon could easily pass.
They say that his eyelids swelled so that he could not see the
light at all, and his eyes could not be seen even by a physician
with an instrument, they had sunk so far from the outer surface.
. . . He died, they say, after much torment and punishment, in 3
a place of his own. . . . (The further account of Judas is altogether repugnant to modern taste.)

Compiled from fragments and catenas edited by Wolf,
Cramer, and others.

IV

Papias says this, word for word: "To some of them (evidently
the angels, who at first were holy), he gave dominion over the
regulation of the earth, and he ordered them to rule well." He
goes on to say, "But it turned out that their administration came
to naught."

Andreas of Caesarea, *On the Apocalypse*, ch. 34, Serm. 12

V

As to the inspiration of the book (that is, the Revelation of
John) I think it is unnecessary to speak at length, since the
blessed Gregory (I mean the Theologian) and Cyril bear witness

to its genuineness, as well as those of earlier times, Papias, Irenaeus, Methodius, and Hippolytus.

Andreas of Caesarea, Preface to the Revelation.

VI

Starting from Papias the great, of Hierapolis, who was intimate
with him who leaned on Christ's bosom, and Clement and Pan-
taenus the priest of Alexandria, and the most wise Ammonius,
the ancient interpreters before the councils, who understood the
whole work of the six days of Christ and the church.

Anastasius of Sinai
Considerations on the Hexaemeron, i.

VII

So the more ancient interpreters of the church, I mean Philo, the
philosopher and contemporary of the apostles, and the famous
Papias of Hierapolis, the pupil of John the evangelist . . . and
their associates viewed the references to paradise spiritually, and
applied them to the church of Christ.

Anastasius of Sinai
Considerations on the Hexaemeron, vii.

VIII

Those who practiced guilelessness toward God they called children, as Papias also shows in the first book of the Lord's *Interpretations* and Clement of Alexandria in the *Tutor.*

Maximus the Confessor, Scholia
On Dionysius the Areopagite,
On the Ecclesiastical Hierarchy, ch. 2.

IX

He says this hinting, I suppose, at Papias, who was then bishop of Hierapolis in Asia, and flourished in the days of the holy evangelist John. For this Papias in the fourth book of his *Interpretations of the Sayings of the Lord* mentioned the enjoyment of food in the resurrection. . . . And Irenaeus of Lyons says the same thing in the fifth book of his work *Against Heresies*, and cites the Papias already mentioned in support of his statements.

Maximus the Confessor, Scholia
On Dionysius the Areopagite, ch. 7.

X

Nor again does Stephen follow Papias, the bishop and martyr of Hierapolis, nor Irenaeus, the holy bishop of Lyons, when they say that the kingdom of heaven will be enjoyment of certain material foods.

Photius, *Bibliotheca*, 232, on Stephen Gobar.

XI   1

Papias, bishop of Hierapolis, who had been a hearer of John the Theologian, and a companion of Polycarp, wrote five books of *Sayings of the Lord*. In them, in giving a list of the apostles, after Peter and John, Philip and Thomas and Matthew, he included among disciples of the Lord Aristion and another John, whom he also called the Elder. (He says) that some think that the two short general letters which bear the name of John are the work of this John, because the ancients accept only the first epistle. Some have mistakenly considered the Revelation also to be by him. Papias is also wrong about the Millennium, and Irenaeus also, after him. Papias says in his second book that John the 2 Theologian and James his brother were killed by Jews. The above-mentioned Papias related, stating that he had it from the daughters of Philip, that Barsabbas, also called Justus, when he was put to the test by the unbelievers, drank viper's poison in the name of Christ and was preserved unharmed. He records other marvels also, and particularly the one about Menahem's mother, who rose from the dead. As for those raised from the dead by Christ, he says that they lived until the times of Hadrian.

Philip of Side, *Church History*

XII

1 After Domitian, Nerva reigned for one year. He recalled John from the island to live in Ephesus. He was at that time the sole survivor of the twelve apostles, and after writing the gospel that 2 bears his name he was thought worthy of martyrdom. For Papias, bishop of Hierapolis, who was an eyewitness of him, says in the second book of the *Sayings of the Lord,* that he was killed by Jews, manifestly fulfilling with his brother Christ's prophecy about them, and their own confession and agreement about this. For when the Lord said to them, "Can you drink the cup that I am drinking?" and they eagerly assented and agreed, he said, "You shall drink my cup, and undergo the baptism that I am undergoing." And this was natural, for it is impossible that God should 3 speak falsely. So the learned Origen too in his interpretation of Matthew asserts that John suffered martyrdom, indicating that he had learned this from the successors of the apostles. In fact the very learned Eusebius says in his *Church History,* "Parthia was allotted to Thomas, and Asia to John. There he lived for some time, and died in Ephesus."

Georgius Hamartolus, *Chronicle.*

XIII

1 Here begins the summary of the Gospel according to John.

The Gospel of John was made known and given to the churches by John while he was still in the body, as one Papias by name,

of Hierapolis, a beloved disciple of John, has related in his *Interpretations*, that is, in the last five books. [But he wrote the gospel 2
down correctly at John's dictation. But the heretic Marcion, since
he had been disapproved by him, because he disagreed with him,
was disowned by John. But he had brought him writings or
letters from the brethren who were in Pontus.]

A Vatican manuscript, Alex. 14, of the ninth century.

The Address to Diognetus

Eighty years ago there was in the city library of Strasbourg a Greek manuscript of the thirteenth or fourteenth century containing works mistakenly ascribed to Justin. Among these was a fragment of ten or twelve pages in defense of the Christians, addressed or dedicated to Diognetus, probably meaning Aurelius' tutor of that name. The manuscript was destroyed in the burning of the library during the siege of the city in 1870, and the fragment has never been found in any other manuscript, nor has any mention of the work or quotation from it ever been found in any work of early Christian literature. In form it is not a letter, though it is usually called one, but is more like an address or apology.

The text is broken at 7.7 and 10.1, and chapters 11 and 12 are from another work and author, perhaps a homily by Methodius, Hippolytus, or even Melito.

Chapters 1-10 are very rhetorical in style; the writer revels in antitheses, and seems more concerned with his style than with his theme. The work has none of the sense of stern reality that pervades genuine Christian apologies. It even suggests that it may not be a work of antiquity at all, but a composition of some humanist of the Renaissance, though its apparent acquaintance with the Apology of Aristides *is against this. The writer declares that Christians are in the world what the soul is in the body. He*

273

denounces idolatry and the animal sacrifices of the Jews. If the piece is an ancient work, as most scholars hold, it probably belongs to the third century.

The Address to Diognetus

Since I see, your Excellency Diognetus, that you are more than 1
eager to learn the religion of the Christians, and to raise very
clear and careful questions about them, what God they believe
in, and how they worship him, so that they all disdain the world
itself, and despise death, and disregard those whom the Greeks
consider gods, and do not observe the superstition of the Jews;
and what strong affection they have for one another, and what
this new race or way of life that has come into life now and not
before can be, I welcome this eagerness of yours, and I ask God,
who empowers us both to speak and to listen, to enable me to
speak in such a way that you may be made better by hearing,
and that you may hear in such a way that the speaker may not
be sorry.

Come, then, free yourself from all the prejudices that occupy 2
your mind, and lay aside the habit of mind that deceives you, and
become as it were a new man, from the beginning, as if you were
about to hear a new doctrine, as you yourself admit, and see not
only with your eyes but with your intelligence, of what substance
or what shape those whom you call gods and regard as such happen to be. Is not one of them stone, like what you tread on, and 2
another bronze, no better than vessels made of bronze for our use,
and another wood, already rotten, and another silver, which needs
a man to keep it from being stolen, and another iron, ruined by
rust, and another pottery, no handsomer than what is produced

3 for the lowest use? Are not all of them made of perishable material? Were they not forged with iron and fire? Did not a sculptor make one, a coppersmith another, a silversmith another, and a potter another? Before they were shaped by their skill into the forms they have, was it not possible—is it not even now—for each of them to have been shaped into something else? Might not dishes which are now of the same material, if they should fall into the hands of the same craftsmen, be made like these?
4 Could not these again which are now worshiped by you be made by men into dishes like the rest? Are they not all dumb? Are they not blind? Are they not lifeless? Are they not insensible? Are they not motionless? Do they not all decay? Do they not all perish?
5 You call these things gods, you serve them, you worship them,
6 and finally you become like them. This is why you hate the
7 Christians—because they do not think these are gods. For, though you think and suppose you are praising them, are you not despising them much more yourselves? Are you not mocking and insulting them much more when you worship the stone and pottery ones without guarding them, but lock up the silver and gold ones at night and set guards over them by day, to keep them
8 from being stolen? With the honors you think you are offering them, if they have any perception, you are punishing them instead; but if they have not, you convict them of it when you
9 worship them with blood and steaming fat. Let one of you undergo this sort of thing! Let him endure having these things done to him! Why, there is not a single human being who would consent to endure this punishment, for he can feel and think. But the stone endures it, for it cannot feel. Do you not, then, prove that it
10 has no sense perception? So as to the fact that Christians are not enslaved to such gods, I could have much else to say, but if what I have said should seem to anyone insufficient, I think it is superfluous to say any more.
3   And next I suppose you are especially longing to hear about
2 their not worshiping in the same way as Jews. Jews indeed, in re-

fraining from this service already described, are right in claiming to worship one God and Master of all, but in so far as they offer him this worship in the same way as those already described they are wrong. For while the Greeks in making these offerings to 3 things that cannot feel or hear, show their folly, these others supposing they make offerings to God as though he needed them, should consider it folly, not worship. For he who made heaven 4 and earth and all that is in them, and provides all of us with what we need, would not himself need any of the things which he provides for those who think they are giving them. But those 5 who think they can offer sacrifices to him with blood and steaming fat and burnt offerings, and distinguish him with these honors, seem to me not to differ at all from those who show the same consideration to dumb objects; the former offer it to things that cannot enjoy the honor, while the latter think they offer it to the one who is in need of nothing.

But surely that their timidity about food and superstition about 4 the Sabbath and pride in circumcision and pretense of fasting and New Moon are ridiculous and unworthy of discussion, I do not think you need to have me tell you. For why is it not godless 2 to accept some of the things created by God for man's use as well created, and to reject others as useless and superfluous? And why is it not impious to lie against God as forbidding us to do 3 any good thing on the sabbath day? And why is it not ridiculous 4 to boast of the mutilation of the flesh as proof of divine selection, as if they were especially beloved by God on account of it? And 5 as for their watching the stars and the moon to ensure the observance of the months and days, and their making differences among the arrangements of God and the changes of the seasons according to their own inclinations, making some into feasts and some into times of mourning, who would think it an example of piety and not much more of folly? Therefore, that Christians are 6 right in abstaining from the general silliness and error and from the fussiness and arrogance of the Jews I suppose you are sufficiently informed. But you must not expect that you can learn from any man the mystery of their own religion.

5 For Christians are not distinguished from the rest of mankind
2 in country or speech or customs. For they do not live somewhere in cities of their own or use some distinctive language or practice
3 a peculiar manner of life. They have no learning discovered by the thought and reflection of inquisitive men, nor are they the
4 authors of any human doctrine, like some men. Though they live in Greek and barbarian cities, as each man's lot is cast, and follow the local customs in dress and food and the rest of their living, their own way of life which they display is wonderful and
5 admittedly strange. They live in their native lands, but like foreigners. They take part in everything like citizens, and endure everything like aliens. Every foreign country is their native land,
6 and every native land a foreign country. Like everyone else they marry, they have children, but they do not expose their infants.
7,8 They set a common table, but not a common bed. They find
9 themselves in the flesh, but they do not live after the flesh. They
10 remain on earth, but they are citizens of heaven. They obey the established laws, and in their own lives they surpass the laws.
11, 12 They love all men, and are persecuted by all men. They are unknown, and they are condemned; they are put to death, and they
13 are made alive. They are poor, and they make many rich. They
14 are in need of all things, and they abound in all things. They are dishonored, and in their dishonor they are glorified. They are
15 abused, and they are vindicated. They are reviled, and they
16 bless. They are insulted, and they do honor. When they do good, they are punished as evildoers; when they are punished, they re-
17 joice as though they were being made alive. By the Jews they are warred upon as aliens, and by the Greeks they are persecuted, and those who hate them cannot give a reason for their hostility.

6 To put it briefly, what the soul is to the body, Christians are
2 to the world. The soul is scattered through all the parts of the
3 body, and Christians are, through all the cities of the world. The soul lives in the body, but it is not of the body; Christians also

live in the world, but they are not of the world. The soul which is 4
invisible is imprisoned in the body which is visible, and Christians
are known to be in the world, but their religion remains invisible.
The flesh hates the soul and wars against it, though it is done no 5
wrong, because it is hindered from enjoying its pleasures; the
world hates Christians too, though it is done no wrong, because
they oppose its pleasures. The soul loves the flesh which hates it, 6
and loves its members, and Christians love those who hate them.
The soul is shut up in the body, but itself holds the body together; 7
and Christians are kept in the world as in a prison, but themselves
hold the world together. The soul, though it is immortal, lives in 8
a mortal tent, and Christians live as strangers in perishable ones,
waiting for immortality in heaven. When the soul is badly treated 9
in food and drink it is made better; and Christians when they are
punished increase the more in number every day. To so high a 10
station God has appointed them, and it is not right for them to
refuse it.

For as I said it is no mere earthly discovery that was com- 7
mitted to them, nor is it a mortal idea that they think fit to guard
so carefully, nor have they been entrusted with merely human
secrets. But in reality the omnipotent, all-creating, invisible God 2
from heaven introduced among men the truth and the holy and
incomprehensible word and has established it in their hearts, not
as one might imagine, sending men some servant or angel or ruler,
or one of those who manage things on earth, or one of those who
have been entrusted with the administration of affairs in heaven,
but the designer and creator of the universe himself, by whom he
created the heavens, by whom he enclosed the sea in its own
limits, whose secrets all the elements faithfully keep, from whom
the sun has received the measures of the courses of the day to
keep, whom the moon obeys when he commands her to shine at
night, whom the stars obey, as they follow the course of the moon;
by whom all things have been constituted and had their limits set
and made subject, the heavens and the things in the heavens, the
earth and the things on the earth, the sea and the things in the

sea, fire, air, abyss, the things in the heights, the things in the
3 deeps, the things between—him he sent to them. Did he though
do it as a man might suppose, like a tyrant with fear and terror?
4 Not at all. But with gentleness and meekness, like a king sending
his son, he sent him as king, he sent him as God, he sent him as
man to men; he sent as seeking to save, as persuading, not
5 compelling, for compulsion is not the way of God. He sent as one
6 calling, not pursuing; he sent as one loving, not judging. For he
7 will send him as judge, and who will endure his coming? . . . Can
you not see them thrown to wild beasts, to make them deny their
8 Lord, and yet not overcome? Do you not see that the more of
9 them are punished, the more numerous the others become? These
do not seem to be the works of man, they are the power of God,
they are signs of his coming.

8,2   For what man knew at all what God was, before he came? Or
do you accept the empty, silly accounts of the recognized philos-
ophers, some of whom said that God was fire (they call that God
to which they will go!), and others, water, and others some other
3 one of the elements created by God? And yet if any of these statements is worth accepting, every other created thing could be pro-
4 nounced God. But this is marvel-talk and imposture of tricksters.
5 No man has ever seen him or discovered him, but he has revealed
6 himself. And he has revealed himself through faith, through which
7 alone it is granted to see God. For God, the master and creator
of the universe, who made all things and put them in order, was
8 not only kind, but long-suffering as well. Why, he always was,
and is and will be so—kindly, good, free from anger, true, and he
9 alone is good. He formed a great, marvelous plan and communi-
10 cated it to his child alone. So as long as he kept it secret and kept
11 his own wise counsel, he seemed to neglect and disregard us, but
when through his beloved child he revealed and displayed what
he had prepared from the beginning, he gave us everything at
once, both to share his benefits and to see and understand things
that none of us would ever have expected.

So having now arranged everything in his own mind with his **9**
child, in the former time he allowed us to be borne along as we
pleased, by irregular impulses, being carried away by pleasures
and passions, not of course delighting in our sins, but putting up
with them, and not approving that period of iniquity, but creating this present period of uprightness, in order that we who in
that former period were convicted by our own doings as unworthy of life might now by the goodness of God be made worthy
of it, and though we had shown that it was impossible for us by
ourselves to enter the kingdom of God, we might by the power
of God be made able. And when our iniquity had reached its **2**
fullness and it had been made perfectly clear that punishment
and death were to be expected as its recompense, and the time
came which God had fixed henceforth to display his goodness
and power (oh the surpassing kindness and love of God!) he
did not hate us or reject us or lay it up against us, but he was
long-suffering, forbearing, in his pity he took upon himself our
sins, he himself gave his own Son as a ransom for us, the holy for
the lawless, the upright for the unrighteous, the incorruptible for
the corruptible, the immortal for the mortal. For what else but **3**
his uprightness could have covered our sins? Through whom was **4**
it possible for us sinful and ungodly men to be made upright
except through the Son of God alone? What a sweet exchange! **5**
What an unsearchable operation! What unexpected beneficence!
that through one upright being the iniquity of many should be
concealed, and the uprightness of one should make many sinful
men upright. So having in the former time proved the inability **6**
of our nature to obtain life, and now having revealed the Savior
able to save even what was incapable of being saved, for both
these reasons he wished us to believe in his goodness, to regard
him as nourisher, father, teacher, counselor, physician, mind,
light, honor, glory, strength, life, and not to be anxious about food
and clothing.

If you also desire this faith, receive first full knowledge of the **10**

2 Father. For God loved men, for whose sake he had made the world, and to whom he had subjected everything on earth, to whom he had given reason and mind, whom alone he had permitted to look up to him, whom he had formed from his own image, to whom he sent his only Son, to whom he promised the kingdom
3 in heaven, and will give it to those who have loved him. And when you get this knowledge, with what joy do you think you will be filled? Or how will you love him who has thus first loved
4 you? And having loved him you will be an imitator of his goodness. And do not wonder if a man can be an imitator of God.
5 He can, if he will. For true happiness is not oppressing one's neighbors, or wishing to have more than weaker men, or being rich, or using compulsion on one's inferiors, nor can a man in these ways imitate God, but these things are no part of his great-
6 ness. But whoever assumes his neighbor's burden, who wishes to benefit another who is worse off in that in which he is stronger, who supplies to those in need what he has received from God, and becomes a god to those who receive it—he is an imitator of
7 God. Then, though you find yourself on earth, you will see that God lives in heaven, then you will begin to utter divine mysteries, then you will both love and admire those who are punished for not being willing to deny God; then you will condemn the deceit and error of the world when you realize what true life in heaven is; when you despise what here seems to be death, when you fear the real death, which is reserved for those who will be condemned to the eternal fire which will punish unto the end those
8 delivered to it. Then you will admire those who for uprightness endure the transitory fire, and think them blessed when you understand that other fire.

A Fragment of an Ancient Homily

11   I have nothing strange to say, nor any surprising questions to raise, but having been a disciple of apostles I am becoming a teacher of heathen. It is what has been handed down that I offer

to those who are becoming disciples of truth. For who that has 2 been rightly taught and has become devoted to the word does not seek to learn definitely the things that were clearly shown by word to disciples, to whom the Word appeared and revealed them, speaking plainly, unperceived by unbelievers, but relating them to disciples, who being deemed faithful by him learned the Father's secrets? That is why he sent the Word to appear to the 3 world, who was dishonored by the people, preached through apostles, and believed by heathen. It is he who was from the begin- 4 ning, who appeared new and proved to be old, and is ever born young in the hearts of saints. He is the eternal, today counted a 5 son, through whom the church is enriched and grace unfolding is multiplied in the saints, affording understanding, revealing secrets, announcing dates, rejoicing over the faithful, given to those who seek for it, that is, to those whose pledges of faith are not broken and the boundaries set by the fathers have not been passed over. Then the fear of the law is praised in song, and the grace of the 6 prophets is learned, and the faith of the gospels is established, and what has been handed down from the apostles is guarded, and the grace of the church exults. If you do not offend this grace, 7 you will learn what the Word talks about through those through whom he wishes to talk, when he pleases. For whatever we have been moved painstakingly to utter by the will of the word that commands us, it is out of love of the things revealed to us that we come to share them with you.

When you have faced these things and listened earnestly to 12 them, you will know what God bestows on those who love him as they should, who become a paradise of delight, causing to grow in themselves a thriving tree bearing all kinds of fruit, and being themselves adorned with various fruits. For in this place are 2 planted the tree of knowledge and the tree of life. But the tree of knowledge does not kill, it is disobedience that kills. For the 3 things that are written leave no doubt that God from the beginning planted a tree of knowledge and a tree of life in the midst

of paradise, pointing to life through knowledge, and when those first created failed through the serpent's deceit to use it purely,
4 they were made naked. For there is neither life without knowledge, nor sound knowledge without true life; therefore they were
5 planted near each other. Seeing the force of this, and censuring the knowledge which is employed apart from the truth of the command that leads to life, the apostle said, "Knowledge gives
6 people airs, but love is what builds up character." For whoever thinks he knows anything apart from knowledge that is true and supported by life knows nothing, he is deceived by the serpent, because he did not love life. But he who recognizes and with
7 fear pursues life plants in hope, expecting fruit. Let your mind be knowledge, and your life the true message, fully compre-
8 hended. If you carry its tree and pick its fruit, you will always gather the vintage of the things desired by God, which the serpent cannot touch nor deceit defile by contact. Eve is not corrupted
9 but trusted as a virgin, Salvation is set forth, and apostles are given understanding, and the Passover of the Lord proceeds, and the seasons are brought together and are harmonized with the world, and the Word rejoices in teaching the saints; through him the Father is glorified. To him be glory forever. Amen.

Appendix

The Place of the Doctrina in Early Christian Literature

The Didache and the Doctrina are the Jacob and Esau of early
Christian literature; the younger has stolen the elder's birthright.
It is now some seventy years since Bryennius discovered the long-lost
Greek Didache (1873) and announced it (1875), and more than
sixty years since he published its text (1883). Its primitive instructions as to baptism, fasting, prayer, the Lord's Supper, and the
treatment of visiting missionaries and prophets seemed to reflect a
very early stage in church development, while the identity of much of
its material, 1.1-3a, 2.2-5.2, with that in the latter part of Barnabas,
chapters 18-20, suggested that the writer of one document must have
made use of the other, unless both were indebted to a third. And
more recently it has become clear that this last solution is indeed the
fact. The discovery of the Latin form of the primitive Didache, the
Doctrina, has shown that the Didache derived the so-called "Two
Ways" material from a more primitive Didache, preserved for us only
in a Latin version.

The Didache is a manual of Christian morals and of church pro-
cedure. It retains the name and reproduces more than seven-eighths
of the contents of the Doctrina, which has steadily been dismissed
as a very imperfect translation of the Didache into Latin. But a close
comparison, phrase by phrase, of the relevant parts of Doctrina,
Didache, Barnabas, and the Life of Schnudi shows plainly that the
indebtedness is to the Doctrina, of course in its original Greek; and
that it once existed in Greek can hardly be doubted in view of its
influence on Schnudi, which was composed in Coptic, a literature
far more indebted to Greek than to Latin models.

The history of the four texts would thus appear to be that a short

Greek Didache was composed about the year 100 (now lost but represented by translation in the Doctrina); that a Greek Barnabas was written about A.D. 130, and appears reflected in the Latin version of chapters 1–17; that with the aid of this short form of Barnabas, the primitive Didache was expanded soon after A.D. 150 into the Greek Didache published by Bryennius; and that Barnabas itself in turn was later with the aid of the primitive Didache expanded into the present Greek Barnabas.

It must not be forgotten that the Latin documents, Doctrina and the short Barnabas, are just as truly documents of early Christian literature as the Greek Barnabas and the Greek Didache, and just as much entitled to consideration and treatment. To one familiar with the development of Christian writings in the first, second, and third centuries, the idea that Doctrina and the short Barnabas were produced, the latter by lopping off the closing chapters 18-21, and the other by first making these closing chapters of Barnabas the basis and beginning of the Didache, and then excerpting them from the Didache directly into Latin, seems about as improbable as the ancient idea that the Gospel of Mark was made by condensing Matthew. It hardly needs to be observed that early Christian literature usually grew not by partition and reduction, but by combination and expansion.

Even before the publication of the Didache, Krawutzcky in 1882 had very skillfully reconstructed the primitive source of Barnabas, the Apostolic Church Ordinances and the Apostolic Constitutions, as the "Two Ways." The scholars who first examined the Didache and compared it with Barnabas were quick to see that some common source about the Two Ways, supposedly Jewish, lay back of these two documents. Schlecht's discovery of the De Doctrina Apostolorum, in 1899, gave learning the very document it had conjectured, and very much as it had reconstructed it. Yet because it was Latin, not Greek, and Christian, not Jewish, and did not fit with perfect nicety the picture that had been made of it, scholars passed it by, and made no place for it in the second century, or in the third, in Greek or Latin Christian literature. But such neglect does not dispose of it; it must be dealt with, and fitted into one's reconstruction of early Christian literature at some point and to some purpose.

Nor is there any real difficulty in doing this. For a close comparison of it with Didache and Barnabas shows there is really no objection to identifying it with precisely the lost Two Ways document long desiderated. Doctrina is not indeed that identical document, but a Latin translation of it, and we may well remember that one of the most important documents of second-century Greek Christianity, Irenaeus' *Refutation of Gnosticism*, has come down to us, as a whole, only in a Latin translation.

That the Latin translator left out a few lines of his Greek original, even a paragraph or two, is nothing to boggle at. The ease with which such omissions may be made, by ancient scribes and modern scholars, is strikingly shown by the list of Biblical books written into the sixth-century Codex Claromontanus, which (clearly by mistake) omitted from its list of Pauline letters Philippians, I and II Thessalonians, and perhaps Hebrews also, between Ephesians and I Timothy; while Harnack in printing its list has further omitted from it I, II, and III John and Jude, between James and Barnabas.[1] Out of a probable thirty-one items the List originally contained, the Clermont scribe, or his exemplar, omitted four, and Harnack, four more. The scribe omitted about one-eighth of the List, and Harnack about one-seventh of what was left of it. This is recited here only to show how easy it is even for a modern scholar to omit a string of short items, especially where what is being copied is not continuous discourse.

Even in a translation, the great bulk of the document is here. Naturally enough, in Didache, which took over the name of the old tract which formed its basis, Doctrina's order is more closely followed, and its substance is more fully reproduced. In the Greek Barnabas, of which it formed only a later appendix and afterthought, less of Doctrina is reproduced, and its order is less regarded.

It must not be forgotten that, aside from all external evidence, the internal evidence in both the Greek Barnabas and the Greek Didache strongly suggests disunity. In the middle of chapter 6, Didache bids farewell to "this Way of the Teaching" and turns from moral injunction to prescribing definite church observances—what food to eat, how to

[1] *Die Entstehung des Neuen Testaments*, p. 76, n. 1; English translation, *The Origin of the New Testament*, p. 114. M. Omont of the Bibliothèque Nationale was kind enough years ago to provide me with a photograph of the pages of Claromontanus containing the list, so that I might determine with certainty its actual contents.

baptize, when to fast, how to pray and how often. These the writer introduces with the same artless abruptness with which he has let go of the "Two Ways" tract. "Concerning food," he begins, "bear what you can." This is a favorite way with him for introducing new subjects: "Concerning baptism . . . Concerning the Thanksgiving . . . Concerning apostles and prophets. . . ."

In the Greek Barnabas the break is less abrupt, but not less noticeable, for it is marked by the crudest of transitions: "Now let us pass to a different Gnosis and Didache. There are Two Ways of Didache and authority. . . ." This practically notifies the reader that he is now going to read the Didache, in some form or other; but clearly not in the form exhibited by the Greek Didache found by Bryennius.

Both these Greek documents thus encourage the reader to look further for the elements they so clumsily put together, and behold! the Latin Barnabas, lacking the whole Didache section; and the Latin Doctrina, which substantially supplies it.

It would seem to me immediately apparent that the indubitable composition of Didache 1.3–2. wholly out of materials from Matthew, Luke, I Peter, Hermas (Command ii.4–6), and an unknown work (vs. 6), marks Didache as a secondary, not a primary work. It would at once suggest that what preceded and what followed (1.1, 2; 2.2 f.) might also be appropriated from some other work, and the Doctrina proves to reflect just such a work, though in a Latin translation. Didache 1–6 is in fact simply a mosaic made up from very early sources, the chief of which was the Greek original of the Doctrina. To suppose that original to have been produced by cutting away from the Bryennius Didache all the materials from Matthew, Luke, I Peter, Hermas, etc., would seem an unnatural proceeding, almost unprecedented in early Christian literature.

The Doctrina certainly influenced and in part shaped the Life of Schnudi and the Apostolic Church Ordinances, as well as the Greek Didache and the long form of Barnabas, and it also passed into a Latin version. In these circumstances it seems strange that students of this literature either neglect it altogether or go so far as to deny its very existence. In view of the great indebtedness of Coptic literature to Greek, from which it was largely translated, the use of the Doctrina materials in Schnudi would seem to establish the existence of Doctrina in Greek, as its reproduction in Didache, Barnabas, and the Apostolic Church Ordinances plainly suggests. In these circumstances I should think the existence of a primitive Greek Didache corresponding to the Latin Doctrina firmly established.

The presence of much of the Two Ways material in the Apostolic Church Ordinances, about A.D. 300, has long been recognized. Indeed, the parallels were conveniently set forth side by side with those in the Apostolic Constitutions, in Hitchcock and Brown's revised edition of *The Teaching of the Twelve Apostles*, in 1885, pp. xlvi-lxiv, though the Church Ordinances were somewhat confusingly designated as the Apostolic Canons. The opening sentence of the Church Ordinances is so much like that of Barnabas that it must be derived from it: "Greeting, sons and daughters, in the name of the Lord Jesus Christ." Barnabas begins, "Greeting, sons and daughters, in the name of the Lord who has loved us, in peace." But it is plainly not from Barnabas but a form of the Doctrina that the Church Ordinances obtained 83 of the moral injunctions and warnings that it contains. For these include that entire series, nos. 39–56, so strikingly absent from Barnabas. So, while the Church Ordinances probably got its opening greeting from Barnabas, it must have derived these 83 items from some form of the Doctrina, presumably its Greek original. These are of course enriched with some later material, but they appear for the most part in just the order that Doctrina has them in. It is only fair to add that at two points (after Doctrina's 1.37 and 1.44) the Church Ordinances has additional elements not found in Doctrina but present in Didache (after 37, "some reprove, and for some pray," and after 44, "Be not lustful, for lust leads to fornication; nor foul-spoken nor one who lifts up his eyes; for all these things breed adulteries"). It would seem that at these points the Greek Doctrina has sustained slight losses, either in the course of its Greek transmission or in the course of translation, or of its Latin transmission. But these five items combined are slight compared with the loss of Didache 1.3b–2.1, a body of thirty-eight items, unreflected in Doctrina, Barnabas, Church Ordinances, the Summary of Doctrine, the Fides Nicaena, and the Life of Schnudi.

For this is not all. The (Pseudo?) Athanasian Syntagma, or Summary, of Doctrine, which Harnack dated between 350 and 370, and the Fides Nicaena, which he dated 375–381, he regarded as resting on a form of the Teaching which lacked 1.3b–2.1, but was not confined to the Two Ways material alone.[2] These documents may be consulted in Migne, *Patrologia Graeca*, 28, col. 835 f. and 1637 f. It is true the form of the Teaching which they reflect lacked 1.3b–2.1, but I find no trace of Didache 7–16 in either of them, except the casual reference to Wednesday and Friday as the regular Christian fast days. But it did not require the Didache to tell the writer this; he and all his readers must have been familiar with the church practice about fast days; and his neglect of all the rest that Didache 7–16 had to offer is clear evidence that he did not have it. The Fides seems to be largely based upon the Summary, much of which it repeats, often with modifications.

Of the 161 items we have listed in the Doctrina, about twenty-six can be easily identified in the Syntagma and the same twenty-six reappear in the Fides. There is here hardly a detail that could be credited to Didache 1–6 that is not also found in Doctrina, and this trifling variation may be due to the fourth-century writers' familiarity with the New Testament, the language of which both occasionally appropriate. Certainly it is the Greek form of the Doctrina, not the Greek Didache, that is reflected in both Syntagma and Fides, and probably the compiler of the Fides got his Doctrina materials from the Syntagma. Yet this is not certain, for sometimes Fides' form is the more original.

The Doctrina items that are identifiable in Syntagma are 10, 11, 16, 15, 19, 18, 20, 29, 28, 31, (49), 55, 127, 20, 21, 46, 32, 38, 77, 90, 59, 60, 34, 95, 96, 153, 154. Fides has these in the same order, with few deviations.

The evidence of Syntagma and Fides then points to the use, direct or indirect, of the Greek Doctrina, not the Greek Didache, in their composition, and they may be added to the four documents already listed, as showing its unmistakable use. Indeed, it has now become clear that, while the considerable use of Didache's materials in other Christian writings seems to be confined to the Didascalia, late in the third century, and the Apostolic Constitutions, late in the fourth, that of Doctrina can be traced in Didache, Barnabas, the Apostolic Church Ordinances, the Summary of Doctrine, the Fides Nicaena, and the Life

[2] *Geschichte der Altchristlichen Litteratur*, I. p. 87.

of Schnudi. The evidence for its literary influence is much greater than is that for the influence of Didache.

If we now look back to the theory of the origin of Didache given by some scholars—that Barnabas as a source supplied the Two Ways material to Didache, and that the Doctrina played no part in the development of the subsequent kindred literature, Schnudi, Church Ordinances, Summary of Doctrine, Fides Nicaena, Didascalia, Apostolic Constitutions—their theory seems to be shattered by the fact that the Life of Schnudi, the Apostolic Church Ordinances and the Summary of Doctrine agree in neglecting two-thirds of Didache, and the same two-thirds: that is, they make no use of 1.3b–2.1 and 6.3–16.8. The natural explanation of this is that they made use not of Didache but of a Greek document lacking just these parts; and just such a document the Greek text lying back of Doctrina would provide.

Neither Didache, Barnabas, nor Schnudi contains all the 161 phrases, clauses, or words into which Doctrina (omitting the trinitarian formula at the close) may be divided.

Eight scattered items are present in both Didache and Barnabas but are not recognizable in Doctrina:

You shall not show partiality in reproving for transgressions.

You must not forsake the commands of the Lord.

Duplicity.

Fraud.

You shall confess your sins.

Advocates of the rich (though Doctrina 151 may be a corruption of this and the following).

Unjust judges of the poor.

Utterly sinful.

The last three are especially striking as they form a sequence in both Didache and Barnabas.

On the other hand, 94 items are common to all three writings, Didache, Barnabas, and Doctrina; 145 appear in both Didache and Doctrina, and 104 in both Barnabas and Doctrina. Even in the abbreviated form of it in the Life of Schnudi, 77 parallels can be found. These are almost exactly the proportions in which Mark was reproduced in Matthew (90 to 95 per cent) and in Luke (about 60 per cent). Just 90 per cent of Doctrina appears in Didache, and about 60 per cent of it can be recognized in Barnabas. This only shows that there is nothing strange in Didache's using more of Doctrina and Barnabas less. Such were the literary habits of the early church.

A few items are present in Barnabas and Doctrina, but not in Didache: (the ways) of Light and Darkness; angel guards set over them; and a larger number in Didache and Doctrina but not in Barnabas: Life and Death; and most strikingly items 39–56 in one block.

The common material appears in Didache in very much the same order as in Doctrina, but in Barnabas it is very differently arranged, being naturally and properly recast and reduced, since it is to form just an appendix—a cauda—to a larger work in a more ambitious key.

But is Doctrina the source of the other two, and did Didache take over about 90 per cent of its material, interpolating it with material from Matthew 5 and Luke 6, as well as I Peter and Hermas, while Barnabas took over almost 60 per cent of it, rearranging it and adding to it here and there? There is much to encourage this view, but the presence of eight substantial items in both Didache and Barnabas which are not in Doctrina is almost fatal to it.

But Doctrina is not an original Greek text but a Latin translation of one, made of course long after the Greek document which it translated was written. Can that Greek document have been the original source of the long artless string of moral injunctions that appear in all three? We should then have to suppose that the eight items (5 per cent of the whole) were lost either from the Greek original before it was translated, or lost in making the translation. The generally detached character of the style may be said to favor this, and the tendency toward omission on the part of ancient scribes is well known. Clark claimed that the transmission of an ancient Greek or Latin text is like the experience of a traveler who leaves a piece of luggage behind every time he changes cars.

This is the probable solution of the problem, and it does not call for the postulating of any imaginary source, for of course Doctrina is a translation of a (lost) Greek document; it is that lost Greek document, certified by the existence of the Latin version of it, the Doctrina, on which first the writer of Didache and then the editor of the second edition of Barnabas drew; Didache was a second edition of it.

Both the Teaching of the Apostles and the Letter of Barnabas, in short, underwent expansion. The Teaching was originally simply the original Greek form of Doctrina. After a generation of usefulness it was expanded into the church manual we know as the Didache. Much of it was also embodied in the second edition of Barnabas, soon after A.D. 150, in the Apostolic Church Ordinances, ca. 300, in the Summary of Doctrine, 350–370, the Fides Nicaena, 375–381, and the Coptic Life of Schnudi. The fuller Greek Didache itself was in time worked into the Didascalia, 250–300, and the Apostolic Constitutions, about 380.

Barnabas, chapters 1–17, was written about A.D. 130, and a generation later was enlarged by the addition of about 60 per cent of the Greek original of the Doctrina. But the first edition of Barnabas continued to circulate, for it was later translated into Latin, without any such additions.

A closer examination of Barnabas' great omission, Doctrina, clauses 39–56, shows that much of it—murder, lust, enchantment, magic, lying, avarice, grumbling—are covered elsewhere in Barnabas, Chapters 18–21, mostly in *positive* command, adjusted to a loftier plane of Christian living: Be simple (straightforward) in heart and rich in spirit; As far as you can, you shall be pure. Anger, murder, enchantment, magic, and grumbling are covered either generally or specifically in Barnabas 19.3–11. It is a mistake to suppose Didache superior to Barnabas in its presentation of the Two Ways material; Didache is in fact inferior, for it contains some repetitions which Barnabas strips off. That is, Didache *copies* the Greek original of Doctrina, Barnabas *rewrites* it. Moreover, Barnabas presents not so much vices to be shunned as virtues to be cultivated, a far superior method, of course. The average Christian then as now does not so much need to be told not to murder, rob, lust, or lie as to be kind, generous, pure and true. The editor who added the Two Ways material to Barnabas perceived this. He was not writing to "the heathen" but to a public so familiar with the Jewish scriptures that they would enjoy the allegories of Barnabas 1–17, and naturally so advanced in the Christian life that some rudimentary morals might be taken for granted.

The way of life and the way of death as moral alternatives go back at least as far as Jer. 21:8, "I set before you the way of life and the way of death," with which we may compare Deut. 30:15, Ps. 1:6 and 16:11, Testament of Asher 1:3–5, and Enoch, ch. 91; but Matt. 7:13 was probably better known to the writer of the original Didache. In fact, first-century Christian literature is constantly echoed in it, a point lost sight of by those who would explain it as a work of Jewish origin.

The most difficult resemblance between Didache and Doctrina to explain is Doctrina 1.94, "For the Lord wishes to give of his gifts to all." Didache 1.4 reads, "For the Father wishes that it be given of his own gifts (Gr. *charismatôn*) to all." But in Didache this occurs in the midst of what is clearly an appropriation from Hermas, Commandment ii.4–6, where it reads, "For God wishes that it be given of his own gifts (Gr. *dôrêmatôn*) to all." The solution probably is that the compiler of Didache in making up his mosaic from Matt. 5, Luke 6, I Peter, and Hermas, Command ii.4–6, took this line over with its context from Hermas, and then when he came to the same line in his Two Ways source, 1.94, naturally omitted it. Perhaps its occurrence in his Two Ways source recalled its fuller expression in Hermas. As between Hermas and the Greek lying back of Doctrina, the Greek Doctrina probably derived the saying from Hermas, unless both obtained it from some source unknown to us.

To recapitulate: of the 161 items in Doctrina 77 can be recognized in the Life of Schnudi; 94 in both Didache and Barnabas; 104 in Barnabas; 145 in Didache; and 149 in Didache and Barnabas taken together. The bearing of these figures is unmistakable; Doctrina closely approximates the source of all three of the other documents. It is reasonable to suppose that the original Greek of Doctrina was the source of all the others, as well as of the Summary of Doctrine and the Fides Nicaena. Doctrina is not a Latin version of Didache 1–6, as modern patristic writers carelessly assume. Nor can these relationships be reversed, so as to make Barnabas the source of Didache and Doctrina, or Didache the source of Barnabas and Doctrina.

The prevalent confusion as to the relations of Doctrina, Didache, and Barnabas can probably be somewhat relieved by a conspectus of their parallel portions, with some line numbers to guide the reader to actual parallels. I have made the Latin Doctrina our base, numbering its lines in fives, in the old textbook manner; putting after each line of the others the number of the parallel line in Doctrina.

It is here reprinted, with much of the preceding argument, with the editor's permission from the *Anglican Theological Review*, XXVIII (1945), pp. 228-247. So much of the text reappears in the Life of Schnudi that I have included the pertinent parts of it, but not its continuous text. Opinions may differ as to the closeness of some of these parallels, but not so much, I think, as to affect the general conclusion, that the Greek document of which Doctrina is a translation is the basic Two Ways underlying all six—Didache, Barnabas, Church Ordinances, Summary of Doctrine, Fides Nicaena, and Life of Schnudi; and, through the Didache, influencing also the Didascalia and the Apostolic Constitutions.

De Doctrina Apostolorum

I. Viae duae sunt in saeculo
vitae et mortis,
lucis et tenebrarum.
5 In his constituti sunt angeli duo,
unus aequitatis,
alter iniquitatis.
Distantia autem magna est du-
arum viarum.
Via ergo vitae haec est.
10 Primo diliges deum aeternum qui
te fecit;
secundo proximum tuum ut te
ipsum.
Omne autem quod tibi fieri non
vis
alio (corr. alii) non feceris.
Interpretatio autem horum ver-
borum haec est.

Didache

[*Continuation of col. 2*]
Blessed is he who gives according
to the Commandment;
for he is innocent.
Woe to him who receives;
for if a man receives because he is
in need,
he will be innocent;
but he who receives when he is not
in need
shall stand trial,
as to why he received and for what,
and being put in prison
he will be examined about what he
has done,
and he will not come out of it
until he pays the last penny.
6. But of this it was also said,
Let your charity sweat in your hands
until you know to whom to give.

The Teaching (Didache) of the Lord to the Heathen by the Twelve Apostles (1)

i. 1. There are two ways, (2)
one of life and one of death, (3)
and there is a great difference between the two ways. (8)
2. The way of life is this: (9)
first, you shall love God, who made
you, (10)
second, your neighbor as yourself;
(11)
and everything that you would not
have done to you, (12)
do not do to another.(13)
3. Now the teaching of these words
is this: (14)
Bless those that curse you,
and pray for your enemies,
and fast for those that persecute you;
for what merit is there
if you love those that love you?
Do not even the heathen do the
same?
But love those that hate you,
and you will have no enemy.
4. Abstain from physical [and bodily]
cravings.
If someone strikes you on the right
cheek,
turn the other to him too,
and you will be perfect.
If anyone forces you to go one mile,
go two miles with him.
If anyone takes away your coat,
give him your shirt too.
If anyone takes from you what is
yours, do not demand it back,
for you cannot.
5. Give to everyone that asks of you,
and do not demand it back.
For the Father wishes that from his
own gifts it should be given to
all. (94) [*Continued in col. 1*]

The Letter of Barnabas

xviii. 1. But let us pass to another gnosis and Didache. (1)

There are two ways (2)
of teaching (Didache) and power,
that of light and that of darkness; (4)
and there is a great difference between the two ways. (8)

For on one are stationed light-giving angels (5)
of God, (6)
but on the other, angels of Satan. (7)

2. And the one is Lord from eternity to eternity, while the other is ruler of the present time of iniquity.

xix. 1. This then is the way of light, if anyone wishing to make his way (9)
to his appointed place would be zealous in all his works. (60)

The knowledge then that is given us so that we may walk in it is as follows: (14)

2. You shall love your maker, (10)
you shall fear your Creator,
you shall glorify him who redeemed you from death;
you shall be simple in heart and rich in spirit.

You shall not join those who walk in the way of death. (65, 3)

You shall hate everything that is not pleasing to God, (105)

you shall hate all hypocrisy. (104)

You must not forsake the commands of the Lord.

The Life of Schnudi

i. 1. The way consists of Two Ways (2)
one to Life, and the other to Death, (3)
and there is an important difference between these two ways. (8)

2. And this is the way of life: (9)

Above all things you shall love the Lord your God from your whole heart, from your whole soul, with all your thoughts, (10)
and you shall love your neighbor as yourself; (11)

And what you do not wish for yourself (12)
do not do to another. (13)

Doctrina

Didache

ii. 1. The second Commandment of the Teaching is:

15   II. Non mechaberis,
non homicidium facies,
non falsum testimonium dices,
non puerum violaberis,
non fornicaberis,

2. You shall not murder, (16)
you shall not commit adultery, (15)
you shall not corrupt boys, (18)
you shall not commit fornication, (19)
you shall not steal,

20 non magica facies,
non medicamenta mala facies,
non occides filium in avortum
nec natum succides,
non concupisces quicquam de re proximi tui,

you shall not practise magic, (20)
you shall not use enchantments, (21)
you shall not murder a child by abortion, (22)
nor kill one when born. (23)
3. You shall not desire your neighbor's goods, (24)

25 non perjurabis,
non male loqueris,
non eris memor malorum factorum
nec eris duplex in consilium dandum
neque bilinguis,

you shall not commit perjury, (25)
you shall not bear false witness, (17)
you shall not speak evil, (26)
you shall not hold a grudge. (27)
4. You shall not be double-minded, (28)

30 tendiculum enim mortis est lingua.
Non erit verbum tuum vacuum nec mendax.
Non eris cupidus nec avarus nec rapax nec adolator
nec contentiosus nec malemoris (corr.).

or double-tongued, (29)
for the double tongue is a deadly snare. (30)
5. Your speech shall not be false or vain, (31) but fulfilled in action.
6. You shall not be covetous (32)
nor rapacious, nor a hypocrite (33)
nor malicious, nor proud. (43)
You shall not entertain an evil design (35)

35 Non accipies consilium malum adversus proximum tuum.
Neminem h o m i n e m oderis (corr.);

against your neighbor. (36)
7. You shall not hate any man, (37)
but some you shall reprove,
and for some you shall pray,
and some you shall love more than your life. (38)

quosdam amabis super animam tuam.
III. Fili fuge ab homine (omni?) malo
40 et homine (omni?) sim(ili illi?)

iii. 1. My child flee from everyone evil, (39)
and from everyone like him. (40)

Barnabas

3. You shall not exalt yourself, (62) but shall be humble-minded in all things.
You shall not take glory to yourself. (63?)
You shall not form an evil design (35) against your neighbor. (36)
You shall not admit arrogance to your soul. (64)
4. You shall not commit fornication, (19)
you shall not commit adultery, (15)
you shall not corrupt boys. (18)
The word of God shall not go forth from you among the impurity of any.
You shall not show favoritism in reproving anyone for transgression. (80? 100?)
You shall be meek, (57)
you shall be quiet, (59)
you shall stand in awe of the words that you have heard. (61)
You shall not hold a grudge against your brother. (27)
5. You must not doubt whether a thing shall be or not. (81)
You must not take the name of the Lord in vain.
You shall love your neighbor more than your life. (11, 38)
You shall not murder a child by abortion, (22)
nor kill it when it is born. (23)
You must not withhold your hand from your son or from your daughter, (95)
but from their youth up you shall teach them the fear of God. (96)

Schnudi

3. You shall perform the following acts, one after another.
ii. 1. The first of them is:
2. You shall not kill, (16)
you shall not commit adultery, (15)
you shall not defile yourself through love of what is unclean; (18?)
you shall not commit fornication, (19)
you shall not steal,
you shall not practise magic, (20)
you shall not cause abortion (22) through any potions, (21)
you shall not kill a new-born child, (23)
you shall not desire any of the property of your comrade and your neighbor. (24)
3. You shall not commit perjury, (25)
you shall not bear false witness, (17)
you shall not speak evil of any man, that the Lord may not be angry with you. (26)
4. Of having a divided heart [beware] in all your concerns. (28)
5. You shall not speak falsely or with idle talk. (31)
You shall not diminish the pay of the day-laborer, lest he call upon the Lord for help, and be heard, for the Lord Jesus Christ is not far from us. (80?)
6. My son, do not be a robber, or a thief, (33)
or a usurer,
or a denier of evil.
My son, do not be proud, for the proud is rejected by God. (64)
Make no evil design (35)

Doctrina	*Didache*
Noli fieri iracundus	2. Do not be irascible, (41)
quia iracundia ducit ad homicidium.	for anger leads to murder, (42)
Nec appetens eris malitiae nec animosus.	nor jealous nor contentious nor passionate; (34, 43)
De his enim omnibus irae nascuntur.	for all these things breed murders. (44)
	3. My child, do not be lustful,
	for lust leads to fornication,
	nor foul-spoken nor one who lifts up his eyes; (127)
	for all these things breed adulteries.

45 Noli esse mathematicus, neque delustrator (3d hd.delusor)	4. My child, do not be a dealer in omens, (45)
quae res ducunt ad variam superstitionem,	since it leads to idolatry, (47)
	nor an enchanter, nor an astrologer, (46)
	nor a magician, (21)
nec velis ea videre nec audire.	and do not wish to see or hear them, (48)
Noli fieri mendax,	for all these things breed idolatry, (47)
50 quia mendatium ducit ad furtum,	

Barnabas

6. You must not desire your neighbor's goods; (24)
you must not be covetous. (32)

You shall not join heartily with haughty people, (65)
but shall associate with humble and upright men. (66)
You shall accept the experiences that befall you as good, (67)
knowing that nothing happens without God. (68)
7. You shall not be double-minded (28)

Schnudi

against your comrade, your neighbor and your debtor; if you have done so, God will love him more than you. (36)
7. My son, hate no man, for they are the image of God and like him. (37)
If a man slips, and through his stumbling falls into sin,
reprove him between you and him alone, as is proper in view of your conduct to one another, and love him as yourself. (38)
iii. 1. Flee from everyone evil (39) and have nothing to do with an evil-doer that your life may not be cut short and you die before your time.
2. My son, do not be jealous, or quarrelsome, or deceitful, (34)
for these things lead men to murder. (42)
3. My son, your care shall not direct itself to lusts,
for lust leads to fornication.
My son, do not use foul language, (26)
nor have a greedy eye (35)
for these things breed false witness.
4. My son, do not ask "Who is he?" or "Why is he?" (45)
for these things lead to idolatry, (47)
and do not be an astrologer, for woe, lamentation, fear and terror lodge with such. (46)
My son, do not go to the magicians, do not resort to the exorcists, nor their discourses;

Doctrina

neque amator pecuniae nec va-
nus.
De his enim omnibus furta
nascuntur.
Noli fieri murmuriosus
quia ducit ad maledictionem.
55 Noli fieri audax, nec male
sapiens.
De his enim omnibus maledic-
tiones nascuntur.
Esto autem mansuetus,
quia mansueti possidebunt sanc-
tam terram.
Esto patiens
60 et tui negotii bonus
et tremens omnia verba quae
audis.
Non altabis (corr.) te
nec honorabis te apud homines,
nec dabis animae tuae super-
biam.
65 Non junges te animo cum altio-
ribus
sed cum justis humilibusque
conversaberis.
Quae tibi contraria contingunt
pro bonis excipies
sciens nihil sine deo fieri.

IV. Qui loquitur tibi verbum
domini dei,
70 memineris die ac nocte,

revereberis eum quasi dominum.
Unde enim dominica procedunt,
ibi et dominus est.

Require autem facies sanctorum

Didache

5. My child, do not be a liar, (49)
since lying leads to theft, (50)
nor avaricious nor vainglorious, (51)
for all these things breed thefts, (52)
6. My child, do not be a grumbler,
(53)
since it leads to blasphemy, (54)
nor self-willed nor evil-minded, (55)
for all these things breed blasphe-
mies; (56)
7. but be meek, (57)
since the meek will inherit the earth.
(58)
8. Be long-suffering and merciful and
guileless, (59)
and quiet and good, (60)
and always revere the words that
you have heard. (61)
9. You shall not exalt yourself, (62)
nor admit arrogance to your soul.
(64)
Your soul shall not associate with
lofty men, (65)
but you shall live with upright and
humble men. (66)
10. You shall accept the experiences
that befall you as good, (67)
knowing that nothing happens without God. (68)
iv. 1. My child, night and day you
shall remember him (70)
who speaks the word of God to you,
(69)
and you shall honor him as the Lord,
(71)
for where the Lord's nature is talked
of (72)
there the Lord is. (73)
2. And you shall seek daily the faces
of the saints, (74)

Barnabas

or double-tongued (29)
for a double tongue is a deadly snare. (30)
You shall obey your masters with modesty and fear, (102)
as a symbol of God. (103)
You must not give orders in bitterness (98)
to your man or woman slave, who hope in the same God, (97)
lest they cease to fear the God who is over you both, (99)
for he came not to call men with partiality, (100)
but those whom the Spirit had prepared. (101)
8. You shall share everything with your neighbor, (90)
and shall not call things your own. (91)
For if you share what is imperishable, (92)
how much more the things that are perishable? (93)
You shall not be quick to speak,
for the mouth is a deadly snare. (30)
As far as you can you shall be pure for your soul's sake.
9. Do not be stretching out your hands to take, (82)
and closing them when it comes to giving. (83)
You shall love as the apple of your eye (71)
everyone who speaks the word of the Lord to you. (69)
10. Night and day you shall remember the Day of Judgment, (70)
and every day you shall seek the company of the saints, (74)

Schnudi

through such man does not come near to God.
5. My son, do not be a liar, (49)
for lying leads to theft. (50)
My son, do not love money, nor exalt yourself (51)
for from these things comes murder, (42, 52)
6. My son, do not be a grumbler, (53)
for grumbling leads to blasphemy. (54)
My son, do not be faint-hearted, and cherish no evil design. (55)
7. But be meek, (57)
for the meek shall inherit the earth. (58)
8. My son, be patient, long-suffering, merciful, of an honest heart, (59)
upright in all your doings, (60)
always fearful and trembling before the word of God and his commands. (61)
9. Do not be proud in your soul, (64)
but always be humble.
My son, do not cling to the rich, to be near them, (65)
but associate with the pious and humble, for through humility the prophet David was often saved. (66)
10. Whenever good fortune or ill fortune overtakes you, accept it with thanksgiving, (67)
for you know nothing happens to you without the command of God, your God. (68)
iv. 1. My son, night and day remember in your heart (70)

Doctrina

75 ut te reficias verbis illorum.
Non facies dissensiones.
Pacifica litigantes.
Judica juste
sciens quod tu judicaberis.

80 Non deprimes quemquam in
casu suo,
Nec dubitabis verum erit an non
erit.

Noli esse ad accipiendum ex-
tendens manum,
et ad reddendum subtrahens.

Si habes per manus tuas
85 redemptionem peccatorum,

non dubitabis dare,
nec dans murmuraveris (corr.)
sciens quia (quis?) sit hujus
mercedis bonus redditor.
Non avertes (2d. hd.-tas) te ab
egente
90 communicabis autem omnia cum
fratribus tuis.
Nec dices tua esse.
Si enim [in im] mortalibus socii
sumus,
quanto magis hinc initiantes esse
debemus?
Omnibus enim Dominus dare
vult de donis suis.

95 Non tolles manum tuam a filiis

sed a juventute docebis eos ti-
morem domini.

Didache

to find rest in their words. (75)
3. You shall not cause division, (76)
but you shall reconcile fighters. (77)
You shall judge uprightly, (78)

you shall not show partiality (100?)
in reproving for transgressions. (80?)
4. You shall not doubt whether it
will be or not. (81)

5. Do not be stretching out your
hands to take, (82)
and closing them when it comes to
giving. (83)
6. If you have it through your hands
(84)
you shall give a ransom for your
sins. (85)
7. You shall not hesitate to give,
(86)
nor grumble when you give, (87)
for you shall know who is the good
payer of wages. (88)
8. You shall not turn the needy
away, (89)
but you shall share everything with
your brother, (90)
and you shall not say it is your own.
(91)
For if you share in what is immortal,
(92)
how much more in mortal things!
(93)

9. You shall not withhold your hand
from your son or from your daughter, (95)
but from their youth up you shall
teach them the fear of God. (96)

Barnabas

either laboring by word of mouth
and going out to exhort,
and busying yourself in saving souls
by the word,
or you shall work with your hands
(84)
for the ransom of your sins. (85)

11. You shall not hesitate to give
(86)
nor grumble when you give, (87)
but you shall know who is the good
payer of wages. (88)
You shall keep the teachings you
have received, (106)
neither adding to them nor taking
from them. (107)
You shall absolutely hate evil. (104?)
You shall judge uprightly. (78)
12. You shall not cause division,
(76)
but shall bring fighters together and
reconcile them. (77)

Schnudi

the word of God, (99)
for the Lord is in the place (193)
where his name is remembered.
(192)
He is worthy of homage, and his
praise endures for ever,
2. My son, walk always in the way
of purity, (74)
then you will be strong and mighty,
you will enjoy the goodness of their
talk, (75)
and their profitable discourse.
3. My son, do not mix in the quarrels
and contentions of brothers (76)
but strive to make peace among
quarrellers. (77)
4. Then judge uprightly, (78)
and do not be ashamed
to reprove the wicked for his wickedness, and the sinner for his transgression.
5. My son, do not open your hand
to take (82)
and close it when it comes to giving
(83)
Beware of doing this.
6. As long as you can, (84)
give to the poor, (86)
that your many sins may be out-
weighed. (85)
7. But when you give, do not be of
a divided heart, (87)
so if you have given, do not be sorry,
and do not regret it, if you have
practised charity;
you must know that it is the true,
the just, the Lord Jesus, the for-
giver of sin, who repays. (88)

306   APPENDIX

Doctrina

Servo tuo vel ancillae qui in
eundem sperant dominum
in ira tua non imperabis;

timeat utrumque dominum et te.

100 Non enim venit ut personas in-
vitaret
sed in quibus spiritum invenit.

Vos autem servi subjecti dominis
vestris estote,
tanquam formae dei cum pudore
et tremore.
Oderis omnem affectationem,

105 et quod deo non placet non
facies.

Custodi ergo, fili, quae audisti,

neque appones illis contraria
neque diminues.

Non accedas ad orationem cum
conscientia mala.
Haec (corr.) est via vitae.
110 V. Mortis autem via est illi contraria.
Primum nequam et maledictis
plena.
Mechationes.
homicidia.
falsa testimonia.
115 fornicationes.
desideria mala.

magicae.

Didache

10. You shall not give orders in your
bitterness, (98)
to your man or woman slave who
hope in the same God, (97)
lest they cease to fear the God who
is over you both; (99)
for he came not to call men with
partiality, (100)
but those whom the Spirit prepared.
(101)
11. And you slaves shall obey your
masters, (102)
as a symbol of God, with modesty
and fear. (103)
12. You shall hate all hypocrisy,
(104)
and everything that is not pleasing to
the Lord. (105)
13. You must not forsake the commandments of the Lord,
but you shall keep the teachings you
have received, (106)
neither adding to them nor taking
from them. (107)
14. In church you shall confess your
transgressions,
and you shall not approach prayer
with an evil conscience. (108)
This is the way of life. (109)
v. 1. But the way of death is this:
(110)
First of all it is wicked and full of
cursing; (111)
murders, (113)
adulteries, (112)
lusts, (116)
fornications, (115)
thefts, (119)
idolatries, (120)
magic arts, (117)

Barnabas	*Schnudi*
	8. My son, do not turn your face from the poor, (89)
	but give to him according to your ability, (90)
	and *associate with everyone who is afflicted and everyone who needs you.*
	And if we share in temporal things with those who must be in want, (93)
	we will share with them in the enduring, eternal things. (92)
You shall confess your sins. You shall not approach prayer with an evil conscience. (108)	If we keep these commands we will walk in the way of life (109)
This is the way of light. (109)	and in the blessed path to eternity, which belongs to the only King, the Ruler Jesus Christ, who is gracious to those who desire him.
xx. 1. But the way of the Black One (110)	v. 1. And as concerning the Way of Death, (110)
is crooked and full of cursing. (111)	he who follows its track and walks in its paths,
For it is a way of eternal death with punishment, (3)	truly, he will die the death of destruction for all his evil deeds,
and in it are the things that destroy men's souls,	which are:
idolatry, (120)	
arrogance, (129)	
the exaltation of power, (131)	
hypocrisy, (122)	
duplicity,	
adultery, (112)	blasphemy,
murder, (113)	murder, (113)
robbery, (121)	
pride, (130)	
transgression,	
fraud,	
malice, (124)	
wilfulness, (125)	

Doctrina	*Didache*
medicamenta iniqua.	enchantments, (118)
furta.	robberies, (121)
120 vanae superstitiones.	false witnessings, (114)
rapinae.	hypocrisies, (122)
affectationes.	duplicity, (132)
fastidia.	fraud,
malitia.	pride, (123)
125 petulantia.	malice, (124)
cupiditas.	wilfulness, (125)
impudica loquela.	covetousness, (126)
zelus.	foul speech, (127)
audatia.	jealousy, (128)
130 superbia.	arrogance, (129)
altitudo.	exaltation, (131)
vanitas.	boastfulness. (130)
non timentes (deum corr.).	
persequentes bonos.	2. Persecutors of good men, (134)
135 odio habentes veritatem.	hating truth, (135)
amantes mendatium.	loving falsehood, (136)
Non scientes mercedem veritatis.	ignorant of the wages of uprightness, (137)
non applicantes se bonis.	not adhering to what is good, (138)
non habentes judicium justum.	nor to upright judgment, (139)
140 pervigilantes non in bono sed in malo.	lying awake not for what is good but for what is evil, (140)
quorum longe est mansuetudo. et superbia proxima.	from whom gentleness and patience are far away; (141)
	loving vanity,
persequentes remuneratores.	seeking reward, (143)
Non miserantes pauperum.	without pity for the poor, (144)
145 non dolentes pro dolente.	not toiling for the oppressed, (145?)
non scientes genitorem suum.	ignoring their Maker, (146)
peremptores filiorum suorum.	murderers of children, (147)
avortuantes.	corrupters of God's creatures, (148)
avertentes se a bonis operibus.	turning away the needy, (149?)
150 deprimentes laborantem.	oppressing the afflicted, (150)
	advocates of the rich,
advocationes justorum devitantes.	unjust judges of the poor, (151?) utterly sinful.

<table>
<tr><th>Barnabas</th><th>Schnudi</th></tr>
</table>

Barnabas

enchantment, (118)
magic, (117)
covetousness, (126)
disregard of God, (133)

Schnudi

robbery, (121)
abduction,
hypocrisy, (122)
every pernicious act.
vi. 1. And what we have stated is
to serve the end
that no one go wrong,
fall into the Way of Death, (2, 110)
and walk its paths,
in consequence of his pernicious acts,
and that what is pernicious shall not
prevail,
even without anyone's misleading one
to it. . . .

2. persecutors of good men, (134)
hating truth, (135)
loving falsehood, (136)
ignorant of the wages of uprightness,
(137)
not adhering to what is good, (138)
nor to upright judgment, (139)
paying no heed to the widow and
orphan,
lying awake not in fear of God, but
for what is evil, (140)
from whom gentleness and patience
are far, far away; (141)
loving vanity (142)
seeking reward, (143)
without pity for the poor, (144)
not toiling for the oppressed, (145)
ready with slander,
ignoring their Maker, (146)
murderers of children, (147)
corrupters of God's creatures, (148)
turning away the needy, (149?)
oppressing the afflicted, (150)
advocates of the rich,
unjust judges of the poor, (151?)
utterly sinful.

(Ch. 21 shows no close resemblance to the Teaching material.)

Doctrina	*Didache*
VI. Abstine te fili ab istis omnibus	May you be delivered, my children, from all these. (152)
et vide ne quis te ab hac doctrina avocet.	vi. 1. See that no one leads you astray from this way of the Teaching, (153)
	for he teaches you without God. (154)
et si minus extra disciplinam doceberis.	
155 haec in consulendo si cottidie feceris	2. For if you can bear the whole yoke of the Lord, (155)
prope eris vivo deo.	you will be perfect; (156)
Quod si non feceris	but if you cannot, do what you can. (157)
longe eris a veritate.	
Haec omnia tibi in animo pone.	
160 et non deceperis (-cip- corr.) de spe tua	(The rest of Didache, 6:3–16:8, seems to show no relation to the Teaching material.)
sed per haec sancta certamina pervenies ad coronam.	
Per dominum ih(esu)m xp(istu)m	
regnantem et dominantem cum deo patre	
et spiritu sancto in saecula saeculorum. Amen.	

Quotations and References

DOCTRINA

1.1 Mt. 7:13
1.1 Herm. Com. 6.2.1
1.2 Mt. 22:37,39; Mk. 12:30,31;
1.2 Lev. 19:18; Tobit 4:15; Mt.
 7:12
2.1,2 Ex. 20:14
2.2 Ex. 20:13
2.2 Ex. 20:17
2.3 Ex. 20:16; Mt. 5:33
2.3 Lev. 19:18
2.4 Cf. Jas. 3:8
2.6 Ex. 20:17
3.1 Cf. Jas. 4:7
3.2 Mt. 5:22
3.7 Mt. 5:5; Ps. 37:11
3.9 Rom. 12:16
3.10 Jas. 1:2,3
4.1 Cf. Heb. 13:7; Mt. 10:40
4.3 Cf. Mt. 7:1
4.5 Ecclus. 4:31
4.6,7 Tobit 4:10,11
4.8 Acts 4:32; Rom. 15:27; Jas. 1:5
4.9 Prov. 13:24
4:11 Eph. 6:5; Col. 3:22
4.13 Cf. Rev. 22:18,19
4.14 Mt. 5:23,24; cf. 7:14
5.1 Mt. 7:13
5.1,2 Cf. Rom. 1:29-31

DIDACHE

1.1 Jer. 21:8; Mt. 7:13,14

1.2 Mt. 22:37-39; Mk. 12:30,31;
 Lev. 19:18
1.2 Tob. 4:15; cf. Mt. 7:12; Lk.
 6:31
1.3 Mt. 5.44,46,47; Lk. 6:32,33
1.4 I Pet. 2:11; cf. Tit. 2:12
1.4 Mt. 5:39, 48
1.4 Mt. 5:41,40
1.4 Lk. 6:29,30
1.5 Lk. 6:30
1.5 Herm. Com. 2:4
1.5 Herm. Com. 2:5,6
1.5 Mt. 5:26
2.2 Mt. 19:18
2.2 Ex. 20:17
2.3 Mt. 5:33; 19:18
3.7 Mt. 5:5; Ps. 37:11
4.2 Deut. 1:16; Prov. 31:9; cf.
 John 7:24
4.7 Cf. Acts 4:32
4.13 Deut. 4:2; 12:32
5.1 Mt. 15:19
5.1 Rom. 1:29,30
5.2 Rom. 12:9
5.2 Ps. 4:2
5.2 Is. 1:23
5.2 Wisd. 12:6
6.1 Mt. 24:4
6.2 Mt. 11:29
6.3 Acts 15:29
7.1 Mt. 28:19
7.3 Mt. 28:19
8.1 Mt. 6:16
8.2 Mt. 6:5
8.2 Mt. 6:9-13

8.2	I Chron. 29:11
9.2	Heb. 13:21
9.4	Cf. Ps. 72:16
9.5	Mt. 7:6
10.3	Wisd. 1:14; Ecclus. 18:1; 24:8; Rev. 4:11
10.6	Cf. Mt. 24:31
10.6	I Cor. 16:22
11.3	Mt. 10:40,41
11.6	Cf. Mt. 10:9,10
11.7	Mt. 12:31
12.1	Mt. 21:9; Ps. 118:26; cf. John 5:43
13.1	Mt. 10:10; cf. Lk. 10:7; I Cor. 9:13,14; I Tim. 5:18
14.1	Rev. 1:10
14.1,2	Cf. Mt. 5:23,24
14.3	Mal. 1:11,14
15.1	Cf. Phil. 1:1
15.3	Mt. 5.22-26; 18:15-35
15.4	Mt. 6:1-15
16.1	Mt. 24:42, Lk. 12:35
16.1	Mt. 24:44
16.1	Mt. 25:13
16.2	Bar. 4:9
16.4	Mt. 24:24; cf. II Thes. 2:8,9; Rev. 13:2,13
16.5	Mt. 24:10
16.5	Mt. 10:22; 24:13
16.6	Mt. 24:30
16.6	Mt. 24:31; cf. I Cor. 15:52; I Thes. 4:16
16.7	Zech. 14:5
16.8	Mt. 24:30; 26:64

BARNABAS

1.4	Tit. 1:2; 3:7
1.6	Tit. 1:2; 3:7
2.5	Is. 1:11-13
2.7	Jer. 7:22,23
2.8	Zech. 8.17
2.10	Ps. 51:17
3.1	Is. 58:4,5

3.3	Is. 58:6-10
4.3	Enoch 89:61-64; 90:17
4.4	Dan. 7:24
4.5	Dan. 7:7,8
4.7	Ex. 34:28
4.7	Ex. 32:16
4.8	Ex. 32:7; Deut. 9:12
4.11	Is. 5:21
4.11	Is. 33:18
4.12	I Pet. 1:17; Rom. 2:11; Gal. 2:6
4.12	II Cor. 5:10
4.14	Mt. 22:14
5.2	Is. 53:5,7
5.4	Prov. 1:17
5.5	Gen. 1:26
5.6	II Tim. 1:10
5.6	I Tim. 3:16
5.9	Mt. 9:13; Mk. 2:17
5.12	Zech. 13:6,7; cf. Mt. 26:31
5.13	Ps. 22:20
5.13	Ps. 119:120
5.14	Is. 50:6,7
6.1	Is. 50:8,9
6.2	Is. 28:16; cf. Rom. 9:33; I Pet. 2:6
6.3	Is. 28:16; Gen. 3:22
6.3	Is. 50:7
6.4	Ps. 118:22,24
6.5	I Cor. 4:13
6.6	Ps. 22:16,18; 118:12
6.7	Is. 3:9; Wisd. 2:12
6.8	Ex. 33:1,3; Lev. 20:24
6.10	Ex. 33:1,3
6.11	Eph. 2:10; 4:22-24
6.12	Gen. 1:26
6.12	Gen. 1:28
6.13	Mt. 19:30; 20:16
6.13	Ex. 33.3
6.14	Ezek. 11:19; 36:26
6.16	Ps. 22:22
6.18	Gen. 1:26,28
7.2	II Tim. 4:1; I Pet. 4:5
7.3	Mt. 27:34,48

7.3	Lev. 23:29
7.5	Mt. 27:34,48
7.6	Lev. 16:7,9
7.7	Lev. 16:8,10
7.9	Lev. 16:8
7.9	Rev. 1:7,13
7.10	Lev. 16:7
8.1	Num. 19
9.1	Ps. 18:44
9.1	Is. 33:13
9.1	Jer. 4:4
9.2	Jer. 7:2,3
9.2	Ps. 34:12; Ex. 15:26
9.3	Is. 1:2
9.3	Is. 1:10
9.3	Is. 40:3
9.5	Jer. 4:3,4
9.5	Deut. 10:16
9.5	Jer. 9:25,26
9.8	Gen. 17:23,27; 14:14
10.1	Lev. 11; Deut. 14
10.2	Deut. 4:1,5
10.4	Lev. 11:13-16
10.5	Lev. 11:10
10.6	Lev. 11:5
10.8	Lev. 11:29
10.10	Ps. 1:1
10.11	Lev. 11:3; Deut. 14:6
11.2	Jer. 2:12,13
11.3	Is. 16:1,2
11.4	Is. 45:2,3
11.5	Is. 33:16-18
11.6,7	Ps. 1:3-6
11.8	Ps. 1:3
11.9	Ezek. 20:6
11.10	Ezek. 47:1-12
11.11	Ezek. 47:9
12.1	II Esdr. 4:33; 5:5
12.2	Ex. 17:8 ff.
12.4	Is. 65:2
12.5	Num. 21:6 ff.
12.6	Deut. 27:15
12.7	Num. 21:8,9
12.8	Num. 13:16
12.9	Ex. 17:14
12.10	Mt. 22:42-44
12.10	Ps. 110:1
12.11	Is. 45:1
12.11	Mk. 12:37; cf. Mt. 22:45; Lk. 20:44
13.2	Gen. 25:21
13.2	Gen. 25:22,23; cf. Rom. 9:10-12
13.4	Gen. 48:11
13.5	Gen. 48:9,14
13.5	Gen. 48:13-19
13.7	Gen. 15:6
13.7	Gen. 17:4,5; cf. Rom. 4:13, 12
14.2	Ex. 24:18
14.2	Ex. 31:18
14.3	Ex. 32:7-19; Deut. 9:12-17
14.5	Tit. 2:14
14.7	Is. 42:6,7
14.8	Is. 49:6,7
14.9	Is. 61:1,2; cf. Lk. 4:17,19; Mt. 11:5
15.1	Ex. 20:8; Deut. 5:12; cf. Ps. 24:4
15.2	Jer. 17:24,25; cf. Ex. 31:13-17
15.3	Gen. 2:2
15.4	Gen. 2:2
15.4	Ps. 90:4; II Pet. 3:8
15.5	Gen. 2:2
15.5	Ex. 20:11
15.8	Is. 1:13
16.2	Is. 40:2
16.2	Is. 66:1
16.3	Is. 49:17
16.5	Enoch 89:56,66,67
16.6	Dan. 9:24-27?
16.8	Dan. 9:24-27; cf. Enoch 91:13; Tobit 14:5; II Sam. 7:13
18.1	Cf. Hermas, Com. 6.2.1
19.4	Is. 66:2
19.5	Ex. 20:7; Deut. 5:1

19.9   Deut. 32:10; Ps. 17:8; Prov. 7:2
19.11   Deut. 12:32
19.11   Deut. 1:16; Prov. 31:9
20.2   Rom. 12:9
20.2   Ps. 4:2
20.2   Is. 1:23
20.2   Wisd. 12:5
21.3   Is. 40:10

I CLEMENT

1.3   I Pet. 1:17
2.1   Acts 20:35
2.2   I Pet. 4:19
2.4   I Pet. 2:17; 5:9
2.7   Tit. 3:1
2.8   Prov. 7:3 (II Cor. 3:3)
3.1   Deut. 32:15.
3.3   Is. 3:5
3.3   Is. 59:14
3.4   Wisd. 2:24
4.1-5   Gen. 4:3-8
4.8   Gen. 27:41 ff.
4.9   Gen. 37.
4.10   Ex. 2:14,15
4.11   Num. 12
4.12   Num. 16
4.13   I Sam. 18 ff.
5.2   Gal. 2:9
5.6   II Cor. 11:23 ff.
6.3   Gen. 2:23
7.3   Ps. 132:1 (I Tim. 2:3)
7.4   I Pet. 1:19
7.5   Wisd. 12:10
7.6   Gen. 7.
7.7   Jon. 3; Mt. 12:41
8.2,3   Ezek. 33:11-27
8.4   Is. 1:16-20
9.3   Gen. 5:24; Heb. 11:5
9.4   Gen. 6:8 ff.; Heb. 11:7
10.1   Is. 41:8; II Chron. 20:7
10.1   Jas. 2:23
10.2   Heb. 11:8

10.3   Gen. 12:1-3
10.4,5   Gen. 13:14-16
10.6   Gen. 15:5,6; Rom. 4:3
10.7   Gen. 18; 21; 22; Heb. 11:17
11.1   Gen. 19
12.1   Josh. 2; Jas. 2:25; Heb. 11:31
12.2   Josh. 2:1-3
12.3   Josh. 2:6
12.4   Josh. 2:3-5
12.5   Josh. 2:9-13
12.6   Josh. 2:14
12.7   Josh. 2:18
13.1   Jer. 9:23,24; I Sam. 2:10 (1 Cor. 1:31); II Cor. 10:17; Acts 20:35
13.2   Mt. 5:7; 6:14,15; 7:1,2,12; Lk. 6:31, 36-38
13.4   Is. 66:2
14.4   Prov. 2:21,22; Ps. 37:9,38
14.5   Ps. 37:35-37
15.2   Is. 29:13; Mk. 7:6
15.3   Ps. 62:4
15.4   Ps. 78:36,37
15.5   Ps. 31:18
15.5-7   Ps. 12:3-5
16.3-14   Is. 53:1-12
16.15,16   Ps. 22:6-8
17.1   Heb. 11:37
17.2   Is. 41:8; II Chron. 20:7; Jas. 2:23
17.2   Gen. 18:27
17.3   Job. 1:1
17.4   Job. 14:4,5
17.5   Num. 12:7; Heb. 3:2
17.5   Ex. 3:11; 4:10
17.6   ?
18.1   Ps. 89:20; Acts 13:22
18.2-17   Ps. 51:1-17
19.2   Heb. 12:1
20.7   Job 38:11
21.2   Prov. 20:27
21.9   Heb. 4:12
22.1-8   Ps. 34:11-17
22.8   Ps. 32:10

23.3,4   ?
23.5   Is. 13:32; Mal. 3:1
24.1   I Cor. 15:20,23
24.4   I Cor. 15:35 f.
24.5   Mt. 13:3 f.; Mk. 4:3 f.; Lk. 8:5 f.
26.2   Ps. 28:7?
26.2   Ps. 3:5; 23:4
26.3   Job. 19:26LXX.
27.2   Heb. 6:18
27.4   Wisd. 9:1; Heb. 1:3
27.5   Wisd. 12:12
27.7   Ps. 19:1-3
28.3   Ps. 139:7,8
29.2   Deut. 32:8,9
29.3   Deut. 4:34; 14:2; Num. 18:27
30.2   Prov. 3:32; I Pet. 5:5; Jas. 4:6
30.4,5,   Job. 11:2,3
30.6   Rom. 2:29
31.2   Gen. 12:2,3
31.3   Gen. 22
31.4   Gen. 28 f.
32.2   Rom. 9:4,5
32.2   Gen. 15:5; 22:17; 26:4
33.1   Rom. 6:1
33.1   Tit. 3:1
33:5   Gen. 1:26,27
33.6   Gen. 1:28
34.3   Is. 40:10; 62:11; Prov. 24:12; Ps. 62:12; Rev. 22:12
34.4   Tit. 3:1
34.6   Dan. 7:10; Is. 6:3
34.8   I Cor. 2:9
35.5   Rom. 1:29-32
35.6   Rom. 1:32
35.7-12   Ps. 50:16-23
36.1   Heb. 2:18; 3:1
36.2   Eph. 1:18; 4:18
36.2   Heb. 1:3,4,7
36.3   Ps. 104:4
36.4   Heb. 1:5; Ps. 2:7,8
36.5   Heb. 1:13; Ps. 110:1

37:3   I Cor. 15:23
37.5   I Cor. 12:21
39.3-9   Job 4:16-18; 15:15; 4:19-5:5
41:1   I Cor. 15:23
42.5   Is. 60:17
43.1   Num. 12:7; Heb. 3:5
43.2   Num. 17
43.6   John 17:3
45.6   Dan. 6:16
45.7   Dan. 3:10 ff.
46.2?
46.3   Ps. 18:26,27
46.6   Eph. 4:4-6
46.7   Eph. 4:25
46.7   Acts 20:35
46.8   Mk. 14:21; Mt. 26:24; Lk. 22:22; 17:2; (Mt. 18:6; Mk. 9:42)
47.2   Phil. 4:15
47.3   I Cor. 1:10 ff.
48.2,3   Ps. 118:19,20
48.4   Lk. 1:75
48.5   I Cor. 12:8,9
49.1   John 14:15; I John 5:1-3
49.5   Prov. 10:12
49.5   I Cor. 13:4-7
50.4   Is. 26:20; Ezek. 37:12
50.6   Ps. 32:1,2; Rom. 4:7-9
51.3   Num. 16
51.4   Num. 16:32,33; Ps. 49:14
51.5   Ex. 14:23
52.2   Ps. 69:30-32
52.3   Ps. 50:14,15
52.4   Ps. 51:17
53.2   Deut. 9:9,12; Ex. 32:7,8
53.3   Deut. 9:13,14; Ex. 32:9,10
53.4   Ex. 32:31,32
54.3   Ps. 24:1
55.2   I Cor. 13:3
55.4   Judith 8 ff.
55.6   Esther 7; 4:11,16
56.3   Ps. 118:18
56.4   Prov. 3:12; Heb. 12:6

56.5   Ps. 141:5
56.6-15   Job 5:17-26
57.3-7   Prov. 1:23-33
59.2   I Pet. 2:9 (Acts 26:18)
59.3   Eph. 1:18
59.3   Is. 57:15; 13:11; cf. Ps. 32:10
59.3   Job 5:11; I Sam. 2:7; cf. Lk. 1:53
59.3   Deut. 32:39; I Sam. 2:6; cf. II Kgs. 5:7; Num. 27:16
59.4   Judith 9:11; Ps. 119:114
59.4   I Kgs. 8:60; II Kgs. 19:19; Ezek. 36:23
59.4   Ps. 79:13; 95:7; 100:3
60.1   Joel 2:13; Ecclus. 2:11; II Chron. 30:9
60.2   Ps. 40:2; I Kgs. 9:4; Deut. 12:25,28; 13:18; 21:9
60.3   Ps. 67:1; 80:3,7,19; Num. 6:25; Gen. 50:20; Jer. 21:10; 24:6; Am. 9:4; Ex. 6:1; Deut. 4:34; 5:15; Jer. 32:21; Ezek. 20:33,34
61.2   I Tim. 1:17; Tob. 13:6,10
61.3   Cf. Heb. 2:17; 3:1; Deut. 12:28
64.1   Eph. 1:4,5; Num. 16:22; 27:16; cf. Heb. 12:10; Deut. 14:2

6.8   Ezek. 14:14,20
6.9   Cf. Mt. 22:11 ff.?
7.6   Is. 66:24; Mk. 9:48
8.5   Lk. 16:10-12
9.5   John 1:14
9.11   Mt. 12:50; Mk. 3:35; Lk. 8:21
11.2-4?   Cf. I Clem. 23:3,4
11.6   Heb. 10:23
11.7   I Cor. 2:9
12.2   Gospel of the Egyptians?
13.2   Is. 52:5
13.2?
13.4   Lk. 6:32,35
14.1   Jer. 7:11; Mt. 21:13
14.2   Eph. 1:22
14.2   Gen. 1:27
14.2   I Pet. 1:20
14.5   I Cor. 2:9
16.3   Mal. 4:1; Is. 34:4
16.4   I Pet. 4:8
17.3   Rom. 12:16; cf. Phil. 2:2
17.4   Is. 66:18
17.5   Is. 66:24
17.7   Rev. 11:13
19.2   Eph. 4:18
19.3   I Pet. 5:10
20.5   Cf. I Tim. 1:17

THE SHEPHERD OF HERMAS

II CLEMENT

VISIONS

1.1   Acts 10:42
1.8   Cf. Rom. 4:17
2.1-3   Is. 54:1; Gal. 4:27
2.4   Mt. 9:13; Mk. 2:17; Lk. 5:32
2.7   Lk. 19:10
3.2   Mt. 10:32; Lk. 12:8
3.5   Is. 29:13; Mt. 15:8; Mk. 7:6
4.2   Mt. 7:21
4.5   Gospel of the Egyptians?
5.2-4   Gospel of the Egyptians?
6.1   Lk. 16:13; Mt. 6:24
6.2   Mt. 16:26; Mk. 8:36; Lk. 9:25

i.1.6   Ps. 2:4; 123:1
i.1.7   Gen. 1:28; 8:17; 9:1; 28:3 etc.
i.1.9   Jer. 3:22
i.3.4   Ps. 58:16; etc.
i.3.4   Ps. 136:6
ii.1.2   Ps. 86:9,12
ii.2.7   Ps. 15:2; Acts 10:35; Heb. 11:33
ii.3.2   Heb. 3:12
ii.3.3   Ps. 106:3; 15:2
ii.3.4   Eldad and Modat

iii.3.5 I Pet. 3:20

iii.4.3 Ps. 86:9,12

iii.6.3 I Thes. 5:13; cf. Mk. 9:50

iii.7.2 Heb. 3:12

iii.7.2 I Cor. 2:9; cf. Mk. 4:18; Mt. 13:20,22

iii.7.3 Acts 19:5 (10:48;2:38)

iii.7.3 Cf. Ecclus. 18:30

iii.9.2 I Thes. 5:13

iii.9.2 Cf. Acts 20:35

iii.9.6 Jas. 5:4

iii.9.7 Mt. 23:6; Mk. 12:39; Lk. 11:43; 20:46

iii.9.8 Ps. 47:2 etc.; Mt. 5:35

iii.9.10 I Thes. 5:13

iii.11.3 Ps. 55:22; I Pet. 5:7

iv.1.3 Ps. 86:9,12; 99:3

iv.2.1 Rev. 21:2; cf. Ps. 19:5

iv.2.4 Ps. 55:22

iv.2.4 Acts 4:12

iv.2.4 Dan. 6:22; cf. Heb. 11:33

iv.2.5 Ps. 55:22

iv.2.6 Mt. 26:24; Mk. 14:21

iv.3.4 II Pet. 2:20

iv.3.4 I Pet. 1:7; cf. Ecclus. 2:5; Prov. 17:3; Job 23:10

COMMANDS

i.1 Eph. 3:9

i.1 II Macc. 7:28; Wisd. 1:14

ii.2 Jas. 4:11

ii.4 Did. 1:5

ii.7 Jas. 1:27

iii.1 I John 2:27

iii.2 II Tim. 1:14

iii.2 Eph. 4:30

iv.1.6 Mk. 10:11; Mt. 19:9; cf. I Cor. 7:11

iv.2.1 Mk. 6:52

iv.2.2 Judg. 2:11; 3:12; 4:1; 10:6; 13:1; I Sam. 15:19 etc.

iv.4.1 I Cor. 7:38-40

v.2.3 Tobit 4:19

vi.1.5 Jer. 24:7; Joel 2:12

vi.2.4 Mt. 7:16

vii.1 Eccles. 12:13

ix.2 Jer. 24:7; Joel 2:12

ix.6 Ps. 2:12 etc.

ix.6 Cf. Jas. 1:8

x.1.6 Ps. 111:10; Prov. 1:7 etc.

x.1.6 Ecclus. 2:3

x.2.2 Eph. 4:30

x.2.4 Eph. 4:30

xi.5 Jas. 3:15

xii.2.4 Eph. 6:13 ff.

xii.2.4 Jas. 4:7

xii.3.1 Ps. 15:2

xii.3.4 Ps. 19:8; cf. 104:15

xii.5.2 Ps. 8:6

xii.5.2 Jas. 4:7

xii.6.2 Jer. 24:7; Joel 2:12

xii.6.2 Ps. 15:2

xii.6.3 Jas. 4:12

PARABLES

i.7 Ps. 103:18

i.8 Jas. 1:27

v.1.5 Mt. 19:17; cf. Lk. 1:6

v.3.8 Phil. 4:18; cf. Is. 56:7 etc.

v.5.2 Mt. 13:38

v.5.2 Eph. 3:9

v.5.2 Cf. Ps. 68:28

v.6.3 Ps. 15:11; Prov. 16:17

v.6.3 John 10:18; 12:49,50; 14:31; 15:10

v.7.3 Mt. 28:18

vi.1.1 Jas. 1:21

vi.1.1 Ps. 1:12; 119:1

vi.3.6 Ps. 51:10

vi.3.6 Ps. 7:11

vi.3.6 Ps. 62:12

vi.3.6 Mt. 21:22; I John 3:22

vii.4 Eph. 3:9; Ps. 68:28

viii.2.9 I Tim. 2:4

viii.6.4 Jas. 2:7; cf. Gen. 48:16 etc.

viii.7.2 I Thes. 5:13

viii.9.1	II Pet. 3:9	5.2	John 6:33
ix.12.2	Col. 1:15	5.3	Prov. 3:34; Jas. 4:6; I Pet. 5:5
ix.12.2	Prov. 8:27-30	7.1	Cf. Phil. 3:2
ix.12.4	John 3:5; cf. Mk. 9:47; 10:23-25; Mt. 5:20; 7:21; 18:3	7.2	Cf. Mt. 9:12
		8.2	Cf. Rom. 8:5,8
		9.1	I Pet. 2:5; cf. I Cor. 3:9
ix.12.5	John 3:5	10.1	I Thes. 5:17
ix.12.6	Cf. John 14:6	10.2	Col. 1:23; cf. Rom. 4:20; I Cor. 16:13
ix.13.5	Eph. 4:4		
ix.13.7	Eph. 4:4	14.1	I Tim. 1:5
ix.13.7	II Cor. 13:11; Phil. 2:2; 4:2; Rom. 12:16	14.2	Mt. 12:33
		15.1	Ps. 33:9; cf. 148:5, Judith 16:14
ix.13.7	Ps. 15:2; Acts 10:35; Heb. 11:33		
		15.3	I Cor. 3:16
ix.14.3	Is. 43:7	16.1	I Cor. 6:9,10;cf. Eph. 5:5
ix.15.2	John 3:5	16.2	Mk. 9:43
ix.15.3	Deut. 34:4	17.1	Mt. 26:7; John 12:3
ix.16.2	John 3:5	17.1	Cf. John 12:31;14:30;16:11
ix.16.3	John 3:5	18.1	I Cor. 4:13
ix.16.4	John 3:5	18.1	Gal. 5:11; I Cor. 1:23
ix.17.4	Eph. 4:3-6	18.2	John 7:42; Rom. 1:9; II Tim. 2:8
ix.18.5	Ps. 9:2; 86:9,12; 99:3		
ix.19.2	Phil. 1:11; Heb. 12:11; Jas. 3:18	19.3	Rom. 6:4
		20.2	Rom. 1:3
ix.20.1	Mt. 13:22; Mk. 4:18,19		
ix.20.2	Mt. 19:23; Lk. 18:24		
ix.20.3	Mk. 10:24		MAGNESIANS
ix.23.4	Jas. 4:12	5.1	Acts 1:25
ix.26.4	Mt. 10:39; Lk. 9:24; 17:33; John 12:25	7.1	John 5:19,30; 8:28
		7.1	Cf. Eph. 4:4
ix.28.2	Acts 15:26	9.2	Cf. Mt. 27:52
ix.28.5	I Pet. 4:13,15,16	10.2	I Cor. 5:7
ix.28.6	Mt. 5:11,12; Lk. 6:22; I Pet. 4:14	10.3	Is. 66:18
		11.1	Lk. 3:1
ix.29.3	Mt. 18:3	12.1	Prov. 18:17
ix.30.4	Eph. 4:29	13:1	Ps. 1:3
x.2.3	Acts 2:11	13.2	Eph. 5:21
x.4.1	Acts 2:11		
			TRALLIANS
	IGNATIUS: EPHESIANS	2.2	I Tim. 1:1
2.2	Philem. 20	2.3	I Cor. 4:1; 10:33
2.2	Cf. I Cor. 1:10	4.2	John 12:31; 14:30; 16:11
3.2	Cf. Philem. 9	5.1	I Cor. 3:1,2

5.2   Col. 1:16
8.2   Is. 52:5
9.2   I Cor. 15:12 ff.
11.1 Mt. 15:13
12.3 I Cor. 9:27
13.3 I Cor. 1:9; II Cor. 1:18

3.2   Cf. Lk. 24:39
3.2   Acts 10:41
4.2   Phil. 4:13
6.1   Mt. 19:12
10.2 II Tim. 1:16
11.3 Phil. 3:15

ROMANS

2.1   I Thes. 2:4; Gal. 1:10
4.3   Cf. I Cor. 7:22
5.1   I Cor. 4:4
5.3   Col. 1:16
6.1   Cf. Mt. 16:26
6.1   I Cor. 9:15
7.1   Cf. John 12:31; 14:30; 16:11
7.2   Cf. Gal. 6:14
7.2   John 4:10; 7:38
7.3   John 6:33
7.3   John 7:42; Rom. 1:3; II Tim. 2:8
9.2   I Cor. 15:8,9
10.3 II Thes. 3:5

PHILADELPHIANS

2.1,2 John 10:10-12
3.1   Mt. 15:13
3.3   I Cor. 6:9,10
4.1   I Cor. 10:16,17
6.1   Mt. 23:27
7.1   I John 3:8
7.1   I Cor. 2:10
8.1   Cf. Is. 58:6
9.1   John 10:7,9

SMYRNAEANS

1.1   I Cor. 1:7
1.1   Rom. 1:3
1.1   Mt. 3:15
1.2   Lk. 3:1
1.2   Is. 5:26; 11:12, etc.
1.2   Eph. 2:16

TO POLYCARP

1.2   Eph. 4:2
1.3   Mt. 8:17
2.2   Mt. 10:16
3.1   I Tim. 1:3; 6:3
4:3   I Tim. 6:2
5.1   Eph. 5:25,29
6.2   II Tim. 2:4
6.2   Cf. Eph. 6:11-17

POLYCARP TO THE PHILIPPIANS

1.2   Acts 2:24
1.3   I Pet. 1:8
1.3   Eph. 2:5,8,9
2.1   I Pet. 1:13; cf. Eph. 6:14; Ps. 2:11
2.1   I Pet. 1:21
2.1   Cf. Phil. 3:21; 2:10
2.1   Acts 10:42 (II Tim. 4:1; I Pet. 4:5)
2.2   II Cor. 4:14 (I Cor. 6:14; Rom. 8:11)
2.2   I Pet. 3:9
2.3   Mt. 7:1,2; Lk. 6:36-38
2.3   Lk. 6:20; Mt. 5:3, 10
3.2   Acts 16:12,13
3.3   Gal. 4:26; I Cor. 13:13
4.1   I Tim. 6:10
4.1   I Tim. 6:7; cf. Job 1:21
4.1   II Cor. 6:7
4.3   I Tim. 5:5
4.3   I Cor. 14:25
5.1   Gal. 6:7
5.2   I Tim. 3:8
5.2   John 5:21

5.2 II Tim. 2:12; cf. Rom. 8:7
5.3 I Pet. 2:11; cf. Gal. 5:17
5.3 I Cor. 6:9,10
6.1 Prov. 3:4 (II Cor. 8:21; Rom. 12:17)
6.2 Mt. 6:12,14,15
6.2 Cf. II Cor. 5:10
6.3 Ps. 2:11; Heb. 12:28
7.1 John 4:2,3; II John 7
7.2 I Pet. 4:7
7.2 Mt. 6:31
7.2 Mt. 6:41; Mk. 14:38
8.1 I Tim. 1:1
8.1 I Pet. 2:24
8.1 I Pet. 2:22
9.2 Phil. 2:16
9.2 Cf. I Clem. 5:4
9.2 II Tim. 4:10
10.1 Cf. Col. 1:28; I Cor. 15:58
10.1 I Pet. 3:8; 2:17; John 13:34; 15:12,17; Rom. 13:8, etc.
10.2 Tob. 4:10; 12:9
10.2 I Pet. 5:5; Eph. 5:21
10.2 I Pet. 2:12
10.3 Is. 52:5
11.2 Eph. 5:5; Col. 3:5
11.2 Jer. 5:4
11.2 I Cor. 6:2
11.3 Phil. 1:3-7; cf. 4:15
11.3 II Thes. 1:4
11.4 II Tim. 2:25
11.4 II Thes. 3:15
12.1 Ps. 4:5; Eph. 4:26
12.2 Heb. 6:20; 7:3
12.2 Gal. 1:1
12.3 I Tim. 2:1,2
12.3 Mt. 5:44; Lk. 6:27,28
12.3 Phil. 3:18
12.3 John 15:16; I Tim. 4:15
12.3 Jas. 1:4

MARTYRDOM OF POLYCARP

Prol. Jude 2

1.2 Phil. 2:4
2.3 I Cor. 2:9 (Is. 64:4)
4.1 Mt. 10:23
6.2 Mt. 10:36
7.1 Mt. 26:55
7.1 Acts 21:14; cf. Mt. 6:10
8:1 John 19:31
9.1 Josh. 1:6
9.1 Acts 9:7
10.2 Rom. 13:1
10.2 I Pet. 2:13
14.2 John 5.29

PAPIAS

ii.17 John 7:53-8:11
iii.1 Acts 1:18
xii.2 Mk. 10:38, 39; cf. Mt. 20:22, 23

DIOGNETUS

3.4 Ex. 20:11; Ps. 146:6; Acts 14:15
5.7 II Cor. 10:3; Rom. 8:12,13
5.9 Phil. 3:18-20
5.12 II Cor. 6:9
5.13 II Cor. 6:10
5:15 I Cor. 4:12
6.3 John 17:11,14,16
6.4 Gal. 5:17
6.5 John 15:18,19
6.6 Mt. 5:44; Lk. 6:27
7.1 I Cor. 9:17
7.4 Zech. 9:9
7.4 John 3:17
7.6 Mal. 3:2
9.1 Rom. 3:21-26
9:1 Tit. 3:3
9.1 John 3:5
9.2 Tit. 3:4,5
9.2 Rom. 8:32
9.2 Eph. 1:7; I Tim. 2:6
9.2 I Pet. 3:18

9.6   Mt. 6:25-31
10.2   John 3:16; I John 4:9
10.2   Gen. 1:26
10.2   I John 4:9
10.3   I John 4:19
10.6   Gal. 6:2
10.7   Eph. 6:9
10.7   Col. 4:1

11.3   John 1:9
11.3   I Tim. 3:16
11.4   I John 1:1
11.5   Ps. 2:7; Mt. 3:17
12.1   Gen. 2:15; 3:24
12.2   Gen. 2:9
12.5   I Cor. 8:1
12.6   I Cor. 9:10